D0586321

Vorlich
224

Dalcraghan

Doune

Ochills

Ben Cleuch
2363

Sherrifmuir

Dumyat
1576

Fife Hills

Dunblane

Bridge of Allan

Craig Forth

Stirling Castle

Wallace Monument

A panorama painted about 1930 from a sketch made by Duncan Buchanan.
It depicts the view from Redgate Hill looking north over Kippen,
with the greenhouses of the vineyard shown on the left.

THE KINGDOM OF KIPPEN

THE KINGDOM
OF
KIPPEN

Tom Begg

JOHN DONALD
EDINBURGH

Published in 2000 by John Donald,
an imprint of Birlinn Limited
8 Canongate Venture
5 New Street
Edinburgh
EH8 8BH

© Tom Begg 2000

The right of Tom Begg to be identified as the author
of this work has been asserted by him in accordance with
the Copyright, Designs and Patents Act 1988

All rights reserved. No part of this publication may be reproduced,
stored, or transmitted in any form, or by any means, electronic,
mechanical or photocopying, recording or otherwise, without
the express written permission of the publisher.

ISBN 0 85976 539 3

British Library Cataloguing-in-Publication Data
A catalogue record for this book is available from the British Library

Typeset by Textype, Cambridge
Printed and bound in Great Britain by
Creative Print and Design Wales, Ebbw Vale

To Sarah and Christopher
and to Kippenites everywhere

CONTENTS

LIST OF ILLUSTRATIONS

LIST OF MAPS

ACKNOWLEDGEMENTS

This book has been in mind for many years, but the push to do something about it – as with so many other ventures in and around Kippen over the years – originated in a suggestion by Winnie Dunlop. Winnie, following in the footsteps of her celebrated forbear, William Chrystal, loves Kippen and cherishes its history. Over the years she has gathered a huge assemblage of photographs and other memorabilia of the district and its people and she urged me to put some flesh on this collection by writing a book, preferably in time to mark the millennium.

First thoughts envisaged a fairly slim gazetteer type of publication capable of being written quite rapidly. However, once the research was commenced it quickly became clear that, set against the context of the wider history of Scotland, the history of Kippen was a fascinating subject that demanded full attention and effort. The consequence was a much longer project and the rather more substantial book as it now appears.

Thanks are due to many people who contributed various pictures. Where the right to reproduce has been granted by the owners of major collections, acknowledgement has been made within the relevant captions. However, private individuals have also donated photographs and I wish to thank in particular Terry Buchanan, G.L. Davidson, Mrs A. Dewar of Meikle Loan, Winnie Dunlop, Suzanne and Alec Edwards, Jane Laidlaw, Anne McLean, John More of the Quern, William More of Glendarroch, and William More formerly of Mains of Boquhan.

Members of staff of various libraries were helpful on many occasions and I am grateful to those of The National Library of Scotland, the Scottish Record Office, Edinburgh Central Library, Stirling Council Archives, Stirling Public Library, and the library of Queen Margaret University College, for their unfailing courtesy and support. In addition, thanks are due to Iona Marr for her assistance with some of the early library research and to Edward Younie for reading and commenting on the draft text.

I also wish to express my gratitude to Hugh and Hubert Andrew and their colleagues at John Donald / Birlinn for producing the book in its final form.

Finally, as ever, I am more grateful than I can say to my wife Mary for patiently tolerating my silent preoccupation over many months.

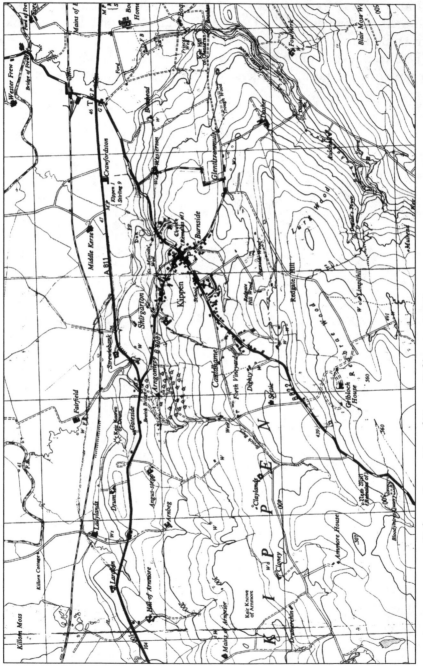

Ordnance Survey Map of Kippen (Fifth series, 1955)

1

'OOT O' THE WORLD'

To understand Kippen and much of its history it is necessary to consider the significance of its geographical situation and to keep in mind the fact that the physical appearance of the district has changed dramatically over the last 250 years.

A modern motor journey west from Stirling on the A811 towards Kippen takes the traveller through one of the richest landscapes Scotland has to offer. Leaving the roundabout at the foot of Stirling Castle rock, close to the site of the King's Knot, and crossing over the M9, the road runs through the almost perfectly flat prime farmland of the carse of Stirling. On either side sturdy thorn hedges mark out the fields and many trees, typically oaks, deepen the margins. Depending on the season, most of the fields will be heavy with grain crops, traditionally 'timothy' hay, or now increasingly oil seed rape or lush silage, or are grazed by sleek cattle or horses. To the north the stunning panorama of the southern Highlands unfolds with Ben Vorlich, Stuc a' Chroin, Ben Ledi and Ben Venue forming the skyline, the last two rising behind the screen of the braes of Menteith. Close at hand to the south, from about Touch the, at first, thickly wooded slopes of the Gargunnock Hills develop an imposing rampart; and in the distance ahead rises the familiar outline of Ben Lomond. The whole impression conveyed by the Vale of Menteith to the newcomer must be of a beautiful broad valley surrounded by hills and filled with fine farms.

About five miles into the journey, from a point just beyond the pretty village of Gargunnock, the landscape on the left begins to change as the line of the hills swings round to the south. Now appears a steadily widening shelf of rolling fields and woodland and soon the top of the church tower rising through the tree line announces the approach to the parish of Kippen.

Drive on past the farm of Boquhan, with its distinctive copper-domed octagonal clock tower; resist the temptation to turn imme-

diately up to the village, and instead carry on past the road junction
at the old railway station. Now, without the obstruction to the view
of trees, it will be clear that the lands of Kippen form a promontory
that rises abruptly from the flat carse land before shelving gently
towards the receding Gargunnock Hills.

A glance at a map will show that a triangle can be formed which
has as its northern base the line of the A811 extending from the Inch
of Leckie to Garden, a mile or so beyond Arnprior, and its southern
apex at the junction at the old Lernock Toll on the B822 road two
miles north of Fintry. The eastern side of the triangle is essentially
formed by the hills as they slope towards Fintry, but it is also marked
by the line of the old 'back road' that runs from the Inch to Lernock.
That triangle outlines a slightly enlarged Kippen parish, but it includes
most of the territory that is the location of the history set out in this
book. It will be seen that the northern side of the area continues the
theme of good arable farmland, but to the south and east this gives
way to rough pasture and moor.

The modern view of Kippen, therefore, is one of a village and
parish on the southern side of the beautiful, well cultivated upper
Forth valley. That impression, however, is very different from the
description that might have been given at any time up to the 19th
century.

Geological studies have shown that when the last ice-age came to
its relatively abrupt end it left a situation where the North Sea
penetrated almost as far west as the locations of the villages of
Gartmore and Aberfoyle. At that time the promontory on which
Kippen stands was on the coast and would have formed a cape or
headland. As anyone who has built a house in the village knows, a
shelf of red sandstone is close to the surface of the earth at this point,
and this explains its shape.

Heavy silting occurred in the valley and eventually forced the
shore line to the east, creating the familiar estuary of the Firth of
Forth.[1] As the sea retreated so it left behind a sodden landscape of
bog and extensive moss and marsh. Contemporary archaeological
and palaeontological investigations (including radiocarbon dating)
of some of the surviving remnants of the wetlands of the western
carse of Stirling suggest that the deeper parts of Flanders Moss began
to form about 11,000 years ago, while for the smaller mosses at
Ochtertyre, Collymoon, Killorn and Cardross, inception occurred
between 5000 and 2500 BC.[2] Presumably the eastern mosses of the
carse, now almost all cleared, would have originated more recently.
In any event as far as humans were concerned the bed of the Forth

valley west of Stirling was dangerous ground and for many centuries it was an area to be avoided.

One of the best-known mediaeval maps of Scotland was that of the 12th-century monk of St Albans, Matthew Paris. He depicted the country as being divided in two, with seas cutting in from the east and west to Stirling, thus emphasising the crucial strategic significance of the bridge at Stirling as the only north–south crossing point. Given the physical difficulties of travel in his day it is not surprising that he was wrong, but it is clear that to Paris and his contemporaries, the watery land which still stretched west of the castle was as effective a barrier to north–south troop movement as any sea.

One of the recurrent features of early Scottish history is that of repeated conflicts and migrations sweeping up and down the east of the country, either ending at Stirling, or advancing further, but almost always on the east side. Only rarely did such movements occur to the west of Stirling and that can only be explained by the difficulty for large numbers of people attempting to cross the terrain stretching to Loch Lomond and the sea lochs on the north side of the Clyde estuary. Moreover, the northern approaches to the western end of the upper Forth valley are a rugged wilderness of loch and mountain and would have been extremely daunting in an age before the construction of roads.

No doubt much depended on whether the season was wet or dry, but flooding would presumably often have added to the dangers posed to people by the mosses of the Vale of Menteith. Perhaps it gives some notion of the problem when it is recalled that as late as the 19th century some of the buildings on the edge of the carse still had iron rings built into the stonework for tying up shallow marsh boats.

The narrowest crossing point of the Forth valley was at Stirling, for there only a mile separates the foot of the castle rock from the rising ground to the north at Airthrey. By contrast, further west the huge peat mosses of Lecropt, Drip, Blairdrummond and Flanders created a barrier, widening to three or more miles. For centuries, therefore, the garrison at Stirling controlled the main gateway between Highland and Lowland Scotland, and that explains the settlement there and the significance of the construction of the castle. Indeed, almost certainly, long before the castle was built an ancient fort would have stood in its place to discharge the same function. Stirling's dominance of the main crossing place also explains why the town was in proximity to many of the bloodiest battles in Scottish history, with

Stirling Bridge (1297), Bannockburn (1314) and Sheriffmuir (1715) merely being the most famous.

In fact, however – certainly in more recent times – there was also what might be termed a side entrance. It is impossible to say precisely when the valley dried sufficiently to permit men and horses to cross safely, but to the north of Kippen between the Blairdrummond and Flanders Mosses the gap separating the hard ground on either side narrows to only about two miles in breadth, and well before the Middle Ages the wet-lands there could be traversed under reasonable weather conditions. In addition, just east of the point where the Boquhan Burn enters the Forth both the river and its tributary, the Goodie Water, were often fordable. With a good local guide and favourable weather the fords there provided wanderers, mission-aries, adventurous travellers, raiders or invading armies with a means of crossing which avoided and bypassed Stirling. How important the 'famous Fords of Frew' were considered to be is indicated by the fact that they were noted among the Seven Wonders of ancient Scotland.[3] The line of the route over the Fords of Frew is today marked more or less by the road from Kippen north to Coldoch and Doune.

In the same way as the castle commanded Stirling Bridge, so Kippen dominated the fords, and this combination of bogs and mosses and a fording place were the features which for centuries gave the district its strategic significance and strangely remarkable history. However, it will be clear from the foregoing discussion that to understand much of that history it is necessary to put aside the mental picture of the modern fertile, luxuriant and well-manicured carse valley and to think rather of the Kippen promontory rising up from a marshy wilderness.

Approaching Kippen from the south-west on the back road from Cloney, a position a quarter of a mile or so from Claylands farm will afford an excellent view of one of the last remaining stretches of moss. As the view to the north opens out so the traveller will be able to look down onto Killorn Moss. It is probably much drier and darker in appearance than in earlier times, but it represents an important vestige of the past.

Whether or not the moss-lands were really quite so wet 2000 years ago raises an extremely interesting and important question. The ending of the ice age and the later withdrawal of the sea produced the conditions for the eventual creation of the ancient woodlands that once covered much of the landscape. The area to the east of Loch Lomond still contains some native woods which are typically made up of oak, ash, alder and elm and there is no doubt that these were the types of tree which predominated not only around Kippen but down on the floor of the valley. It is very probable that extensive woodlands would have helped to dry out the carse as the trees would have soaked up great quantities of water. However, a period in the distant past when many trees were felled or burnt may have contributed to preserving the wetlands as well as helping to turn marsh into deep peat moss.

The first detailed description of Kippen was provided by its distinguished late 18th-century minister, John Campbell, in his contribution to the first *Statistical Account of Scotland 1791–1799*. He was writing at precisely the time when the peat mosses (typically of from 10 to 13 feet in depth) were being cleared and subjected to the sustained improvement and drainage activities that eventually produced the modern flat farmland. He noted that workers removing the moss frequently uncovered the remains of a forest in the form of the trunks and stumps of great mature trees. In many cases the trunks were of 60 feet in length and four to six feet in diameter. The recovered timber under the moss blanket, while unsuitable for making furniture, often proved very useful for the production of fence posts or roof rafters and for other construction work. (In passing, some of the earliest clearance work occurred in the 16th century at Meiklewood near Gargunnock and no doubt – since 'meikle' is the Old Scots word for a great quantity – the estate received its name from the large number of tree-trunks being recovered.)

Mr Campbell speculated on the causes of the forest's destruction, pointing out that the trunks were lying in different directions, that few were torn up by the roots, that some had been burned, that most had been felled close to the ground and that axe marks were often visible. He therefore discounted natural disasters such as great storms and concluded that the destruction was the result of human activity.

There seems no reason to reject Mr Campbell's explanation of the essential process. There is no doubt that early humans destroyed many of the trees as they attempted to settle in and develop the area. But whereas this activity enabled the slopes around Kippen gradually to be cleared for farming, it may at times have increased the flooding in the valley and periodically retarded the drying-out process.

Mr Campbell, however, speculated that responsibility for hacking down the carse trees could be laid at the door of one specific group of arrivals – the Romans. He pointed out that the hostile tribes of

Scotland were rarely strong enough to confront the Legions in pitched battles and rather tended to form raiding parties to attack outposts or supply camps, before retreating to secret strongholds within the forests or among the remote hills. He suggests that to destroy such hiding places and to control the tribes the legionaries were ordered to clear the forests. He cites Tacitus's *Life of Agricola* where the Caledonian leader Calgacus is quoted as complaining at the extent to which the Romans had engaged in such work. Campbell implies that under Agricola such activity may at first have been intended as a preparation for long-term settlement and productive farming. Later, however, about 207 when the Emperor Septimus Severus responded to a series of attacks by bringing his army to suppress the troublesome northern tribes, the policy may have changed to a massive attempt to block the Forth Valley in order to create a kind of broad *cordon sanitaire* between Hadrian's Wall and the Scottish Highlands. Referring to the Greek recorders of this period of Roman history, Herodianus and Cassius Dio(n), Campbell claims that in this 'great undertaking', which cost some 50,000 casualties, the troops were assisted in the tree-felling by co-operative British tribes which were either local or brought to the area for the purpose.[4]

Campbell's attribution of entire responsibility for the destruction of the valley forest to the Romans is very understandable. The greatest historical literary event of the later years of the 18th century occurred over the period 1775–1788 with the publication of the six volumes of Edward Gibbon's *Decline and Fall of the Roman Empire*. The work aroused tremendous enthusiasm and stimulated the interest of educated people all over the country. Inevitably, in these circumstances, local antiquarians enthusiastically searched for archaeological evidence of Roman activity in their neighbourhoods and tended to ascribe to the Romans almost any indication of the activities of ancient man. Campbell's suggestions, therefore, have to be seen in the context of his time and treated with some caution.

It is, however, undoubtedly true that the Romans were in this part of the country. The most obvious example is the Antonine Wall that stretched across the waist of Scotland from Old Kilpatrick on the Clyde to Bridgeness on the Forth. This line of fortified encampments was created and employed in the period *c.* 145–165 as a means of dominating central Scotland, and then briefly partially re-occupied 40 years later by Severus. At these times and at other periods, campaigns, extended operations and reconnaissance patrols were conducted further north. For example, sites of early Roman encampments have been found forming a line from Drumquhassle, north of Drymen, through Menteith, Bochastle, near Callander and Dalginross in Strathearn, and on north-eastwards, blocking off the valleys leading into the Central Highlands. Camps dating from the Severan period have been found at Craigarnhall near Blair Drummond and at Ardoch near Braco.[5] It is inconceivable that the Romans would have failed to note the strategic importance of Stirling and it seems certain that they had a fortress approximately in the position on which the castle was later built.[6] Closer to Kippen what were believed to be Roman remains were found in the 19th century at the Parks of Garden, where a timbered road or causeway was uncovered – one of a number of such ancient roadways revealed under the cleared moss; at Cardross a fortified position was found complete with ditch and inner and outer ramparts, and a few artefacts including a copper kettle; and at Gargunnock the excavated remains of the keir hill revealed a few shards of glass and a bead.[7] In a lecture of 1873 the Kippen minister, William Wilson, writing specifically of the old roads found under the moss, concluded, 'these remains point undoubtedly to the fact that the growth of the moss in the valley is subsequent to the causeways. These roads or causeways are branches from the great Roman Via which penetrates the entire country.'[8]

Modern research sheds some additional light on this latter subject. As noted previously, investigations have recently been conducted into the western mosses and this included identification and radiocarbon-dating studies of samples of wood taken from the fragmentary remains of the structure in the Parks of Garden. These suggested alder from 3350–2920 BC, birch from 3340–2930 BC and oak from 3950–3700 BC. The conclusion offered was that either the structure dates from 3340–2930 BC and it contained oak recovered from the bog, or that there were two phases in its construction.[9]

If either of these propositions were accepted at face value, then clearly the timbered causeway would long predate the Roman period. However, this finding would seem to be far from conclusive. We know from Mr Campbell and others that as recently as the 18th century wood was indeed being retrieved from the mosses and used for construction work and there can be little doubt that the ancient builders of the road would have used this type of wood, particularly if it lay readily to hand. The age of the timber, therefore, does not tell us when it was used to form the causeway. What the dating does suggest, however, is that if the samples did not come from trees that succumbed to nature, tree felling must have commenced well before the Roman era.

It seems certain, therefore, that when the Romans arrived in central Scotland they encountered native tribes which had already carried out substantial tree clearance both on the surrounding slopes and on parts of the valley bed.

One of the oddities of the surviving traces of Roman activity is that no Roman fortification has yet been found in the immediate vicinity of the Frews. Given the obvious strategic importance of the one significant crossing-point west of Stirling Castle rock this seems very strange and suggests either that, at the time, the fords were impassable, or for one reason or another, unnecessary, or perhaps that the appropriate fort site remains to be identified.

It is worth here going back to one of the passages of Cassius Dio cited by Mr Campbell and describing Severus's campaign of 207–212. Dio is one of the more reliable of the Roman chroniclers of the period since not only was he a contemporary of the Emperor, Septimus Severus, he was himself a high-ranking officer in the imperial civil service, twice a consul and a member of the Councils of both Severus and his son Caracalla.[10] The relevant passage in his record may be translated as follows:

> When Severus struggled to bring everything under control he invaded Caledonia where he had the greatest difficulty. He occupied the high ground while he was felling trees and covering the marshes with water. There he also made bridges [causeways] linking the Roman habitations. He waged no war, nor did he see many of the enemy in battle array. Sheep and cattle were targets and after our people were successful in seizing these the enemy gave roads a wide berth and easily concealed themselves. At this stage of the campaign some of our people were completely isolated by the flooding and these scattered groups were sometimes ambushed. Because they could not withdraw they were sometimes slain by their own people to avoid being taken by the enemy. And so we lost up to fifty thousand. Even so, Severus did not stop until he came to the furthest limit of the island.[11]

According to Cassius Dio, therefore, Severus's army did carry out substantial tree-felling operations and this either caused or contributed to flooding with fairly disastrous consequences to some of the troops directly involved. It is true that there is no absolute confirmatory evidence that the operations in question were at least partly conducted in the upper Forth valley, but the account does seem to fit with our knowledge of the subsequent history of the area. However, it was based on both his observation of moss clearance and on his reading of Roman history that Mr Campbell attributed to Roman involvement the destruction of the carse forest.

A modern view might conclude that whereas substantial tree

clearance had been taking place in the valley for centuries, the Romans may well have both accelerated and systematised such activity and caused the wide-scale flooding that would have rendered the valley virtually impassable for many centuries (particularly to strangers and in periods of wet weather). This may have produced a barrier to significant human movement that was much more effective than the Antonine forts as, indeed, may well have been the intention, and created a situation where there was simply no longer a need to station troops in the area. If the residents to the south of the flooded valley were also friendly *foederati* tribes there would thereafter have been little need to maintain soldiers north of Hadrian's Wall.

How well does this adaptation of Mr Campbell's theory stand up to the test of modern scholarship on Roman history? Some supporting indirect confirmation does seem to be available from the work of present-day historians and archaeologists.

For example, Peter Salway in his *Roman Britain* (1981) also refers to Tacitus to show that Agricola did engage in major activities in the Forth–Clyde isthmus in 80 and 81, and this is confirmed by the leading scholar specifically on the Romans in Scotland, David J. Breeze.[12] Salway also draws attention to Cassius Dio's account of Severus's campaign of *c.* 207 to explain that the emperor brought his army to the Forth valley because the tribe known as the Maeatae which dwelled 'next to the cross-wall that divides the island in half' and which 'as far as we can ascertain, lived north of the Forth–Clyde isthmus', had been causing serious trouble through the previous few years.[13] About 200, taken by surprise and lacking the resources to suppress the Maeatae, the governor, Virius Lupus, had been forced to use a bribe to secure peace. Having received such a payment once, not surprisingly the Maeatae soon returned for more *c.* 205–206. The new governor Senecio complained that 'the barbarians there were in revolt, over-running the country, carrying off booty and destroying most things', and took the very unusual step of pleading with the emperor not just for reinforcements, but for 'an imperial expedition' to deal with the situation.[14]

On this occasion Severus was in a secure enough position in Rome to comply with the request and he collected an army which he brought to the Forth, probably mainly by sea, landing his troops in the vicinity of modern Cramond about 207. Salway suggests that the fighting campaign did not start in earnest until 'Severus was beyond the Forth–Clyde isthmus'. Like Mr Campbell, he cites Herodian, quoting the latter as claiming that 'skirmishes and battles occurred after the army had crossed 'the rivers and earthworks that formed the defence of the Roman empire'.[9] Nowhere does Peter Salway identify the upper Forth valley as the location of this defensive system, and he dismisses Herodian's account rather curiously as 'a vague description of the frontier region culled in conversation from those who had once been there or from some inaccurate or out-of-date written source'.[15] However, seen from the perspective of Mr Campbell's position as an observer of the moss clearance in the Vale of Menteith at the end of the 18th century, Herodian's words must have appeared to be entirely accurate.

On the other hand, Salway clearly recognises the emphasis the Roman writers gave to the 'engineering' activities that dominated the first year of Severus' operations in central Scotland. Only once these had been substantially progressed did the emperor move the main body of his troops further north-east in an attempt to provoke a decisive battle. Campaigning continued until *c.* 212 when Caracalla (who had succeeded his father Severus the previous year) felt able to conclude a treaty with the northern tribes and to withdraw the imperial army from Britain.[17]

Interestingly, Salway draws attention to the 'highly successful' results of Severus's campaign and the settlement made by Caracalla. The following century was very difficult for the empire, which was riven by many external and internal upheavals. However, 'the northern frontier remained unbreached for, at the least estimate, something like 85 years – in an age when other frontiers were being over-run, some never to hold again'. Moreover, this secure area was maintained despite garrisons in the north of England being largely withdrawn to help elsewhere.[18]

The next, and last, emperor to come north was Constantius Chlorus who engaged in a brief expedition in 305. His historian evidently also emphasises the problems experienced in 'the crossing of marshes . . . features that had given Severus considerable trouble before he overcame it with the loss of many men'.[19] Once again, this tends to confirm Mr Campbell's analysis.

Further evidence to support this theory may come from the Roman geographers who identified the locations of settlement of the various tribes of northern Britain. Scholars such as Ptolemy in the 2nd century and his successors must have had personal contact with officers who had campaigned in Scotland. It is interesting to note that on modern interpretations and reproductions of the early Roman maps, along the line of the Forth west of the position of Stirling, is included the word 'Bodotria'. Various suggestions have been offered as to the meaning of this word. For example, in Lewis and Short's version of *Freund's Latin Dictionary* it is curiously identified as the proper name of 'a bay in Scotland on which the present Edinburgh is situated, now the Firth of Forth'. It is difficult to accept this interpretation and the modern view places the word on a position clearly to the west of the Firth and along the upper Forth valley. More interestingly, while the author is no Latin scholar, it would seem to be possible to translate 'Bodotria' as 'the area or field of tree stumps'. Since it may be related accurately to a position where a great forest appears to have been felled under the supervision of the soldiers from whom the Roman geographers obtained their information, this explanation of the word seems much more probable.[20] We will shortly come back to the notion of an 'area of tree stumps'.

Returning to Salway's account for the moment, it is clear that during the Roman period many low-lying lands were subject to flooding, such as, for example, the fenland in England. It has been suggested by some commentators that the cause was a climatic change that resulted in rising sea levels. Others have argued that tree felling and inadequate attention to drainage were at least partly to blame, but it is not clear whether, or in what cases, Roman generals intended to cause flooding. In other words, when the Roman soldiers cut down the forests was it sometimes their intention that flooding would result? Alternatively, did unforeseen flooding occur, perhaps much later, during a particularly wet period? This subject was extensively investigated in both England and Italy by Dr Timothy Potter who concluded that there probably was some degree of significant climatic change.[21]

The activity in the Vale of Menteith in the period *c*. 80–306 would seem, therefore, to conform to a pattern evident elsewhere and may shed some additional light on Roman military engineering in the period. It may also provide some confirmation of a probable rise in sea levels due to some change in climatic conditions early in the third century.

Perhaps we shall never know the precise sequence, but in the light of the available information the conclusion might be as follows. Tree felling in the valley was commenced by tribes settling in the area up to 3000 years before the Roman period. (Modern scholars would tend perhaps to emphasise this earlier activity.) The valley floor would, however, have remained a dangerous place and its possibilities as a barrier would have been obvious to the Agricolan army which probably systematically extended the tree cutting in its operations *c*. 80–81. An investigation by Frank Noble of abandoned farmland near Monmouth showed that after about 50 years, 'as trees matured the undergrowth died back – the sodden ground was naturally dried out by the trees and the whole area became easily penetrable again'.[22] Conditions in the valley to the north of Kippen were likely to have been somewhat more severe than in Monmouth, not least because they were partly the result of a series of deliberate military activities, but Noble's study does illustrate the natural tendency of a forest to recover and to dry out the ground in which the roots are embedded. In this case, therefore, by *c*. 140 the forest may in places have substantially recovered so that the northern tribes were able once more to cross over and harass the tribes and garrisons to the south. No doubt the main crossing place was close to the position of Stirling, but there may have been various other points to the west.

The Antonine period may have marked an alternative approach based on the line of forts, but during this time no doubt further engineering operations in the Forth valley would have been attempted and these may have allowed the forts to be abandoned *c*. 165. While they were garrisoned they would have required a substantial commitment of troops and there must have been a strong desire for a more efficient system.

By *c*. 200, however, the tribes from the north were once again able to cross the valley, and to create sufficient trouble as to stimulate Severus's expedition *c*. 207–211. This time a sustained effort appears to have been made to develop and extend the tree cutting and earthworks to produce more comprehensive flooding and a more substantial barrier.[23] This operation, which seems to have cost many lives – perhaps by accident and linked to a rise in sea levels effecting the Forth estuary – was largely successful and virtually prevented further serious invasion by the northern tribes for at least the next 85 years. Whether or not the effect of the engineering work was definitely enhanced by climatic change, it is difficult to say, but even from observations of the modern valley there seems little doubt that a few wet seasons and a small rise in tidal waters would have produced extensive flooding and created swamp-like conditions. It is difficult to believe that this was not recognised by the responsible generals.

The Constantius venture of 306 may have been mainly to check the state of the barrier and to carry out any additional work to ensure that it remained an effective obstacle. Interestingly, such activity may again have succeeded since when, later in the century, the northern tribes attacked the empire once more, sometimes in combination with German Saxon invaders, they avoided southern

Scotland and sailed down the North Sea to harass the coast of the north of England.

If indeed, as is here suggested, the Romans constructed a defensive system in the Vale of Menteith by demolishing the trees and deliberately blocking and flooding the valley, this would throw a considerable light not only on Roman Britain, but also on much of Scotland's history over subsequent centuries.

Who were the first settlers on the Kippen promontory? It is unlikely that we will ever know the precise answer to that question. However, among the first would have been the creators of a 'crannog' type of dwelling that seems to have been located in the middle of Loch Laggan on Kippen Muir. Crannogs are believed to have been dwellings favoured by some of the earliest Celtic tribes. Normally they were constructed of wood on a platform floated onto the water and supported by piles driven into the bed of a loch. Examples of the remains of such structures are to be found all over Europe and in Scotland at Milton Loch in Kirkcudbright and in a few other places. In the case of Loch Laggan the platform seems to have been of stone and reached by a causeway. Part of the structure was clearly visible in the 18th century and 80 years ago traces could still be seen by swimmers looking down into the loch on a sunny day. Gradually, however, the stonework has sunk out of sight into the soft bottom of the loch and can no longer be detected. (Earlier, the more accessible stones were removed by a farmer and used in the construction of a dyke.)[24]

As has been noted, during the Roman occupation the geographer Ptolemy suggested the location of the various tribes of northern Britain and his account was later supplemented by the collection known as the *Ravenna Cosmography*. To the north of Scotland there were many tribes but basically arranged into two main Pictish kingdoms, one in the North-Western Highlands and the other to the south extending north-east from Menteith through Strathearn to Tayside. As we have seen, this tribe were known as the Maeatae and they appear to have left their mark on place names such as Menteith, Menstrie, Methven and Muthill. The southern Pictish kingdom is identified as Fortriu and its southern flank was on the north side of the upper Forth valley. (The Dalriadic Scots from Ireland began to migrate into the west of the northern Pictish lands from about 500.)

To the south-west of the Forth the dominant tribal group was the Dumnonii. They were not Picts, and are normally described as Britons or Cumbrians. At different periods these Britons formed

alliances with the Romans and when the latter withdrew from this
country about 400 they established the kingdom of Strathclyde or
Dumnonnia, with a capital based at Dumbarton (Dumbriton), at
times controlling the territory as far to the south as Galloway.
Similarly from Stirling, stretching along the south shore of the Firth
of Forth through the Lothians and down the east of the country to
Hadrian's Wall, the main tribe was the Votadini.

It has been argued that the Romans regarded these peoples 'as
ethnically distinct from the tribes who lived north of the
Forth–Clyde line'. The dividing line between Dumnonii, Votadini
and Pict was, therefore, an 'ethnic as well as a political and military'
boundary. Again, however, this analysis tends to emphasise the
considerable nature of the barrier that appears to have existed within
the upper Forth valley. The southern Scottish tribal, river and
settlement names recorded by Ptolemy and others, confirm that the
predominant speech of the southern tribes was a language (or Celtic
dialect) variously known as British, Brythonic or Cumbric, and
somewhat related to Welsh or Cornish.[25]

Inevitably the evidence from the so-called 'Dark Ages' which
followed the Roman period is fragmentary and confusing. However,
in the south-east of Scotland at some point the Votadini were sup-
planted by the Gododdin who were in turn challenged by the invading Northumbrians or Angles. For a time a sub-tribe of the Gododdin,
the Manau, created a little province around the head of the Firth of
Forth and left their name to both Clackmannan and the village of
Slamannan near Falkirk. However, this group did not penetrate
west, being blocked off by the mosses and 'Mount Bannog' (Earls
Hill – the eastern spur of the Campsie Fells).[26]

For at least seven centuries, however, the northern boundary of
the British kingdom of Strathclyde was the southern flank of the
upper Forth valley and the Kippen promontory was literally on the
frontier.

One of the curiosities of early Scottish history is the prolonged
survival of Strathclyde. Despite the fact that it was not considered to
be a very powerful kingdom the fact is that it seems rarely to have
been severely challenged by the Picts, nor later by the aggressive and
acquisitive Scots of Dalriada, nor even by the Angles of Northumbria
from the east. Indeed the only serious attacks on the Britons came in
the south in the 7th and 8th centuries when they were for a time
driven from Galloway, and much later, in 870, when the Norsemen
(assisted by the Scots) laid siege to the fortress capital Al Cluith, on
Dumbarton Rock. On that occasion the Vikings apparently carried

off huge numbers of captives in as many as 200 longships.[27] That attack seems to have significantly weakened Strathclyde, the crown of which subsequently appears to have become closely allied to the dynasty of Scottish kings. However, the kingdom retained its semi-independent status up to the 11th century.

One of the reasons for the survival of the British kingdom can only have been the security afforded by the impenetrability of its northern frontier. If the sequence of events in the upper Forth valley was as suggested above, the Britons inherited from the Romans a shield that gave their kingdom a vital degree of effective protection from its potentially extremely dangerous northern neighbours. Indeed, intriguingly, we are told that about 970, Kenneth II, King of Scots, enraged by the independence of Strathclyde, launched a punitive assault on the Britons which failed because 'his army came to grief when it was caught on boggy ground.'[28] The site of this disaster is suggested as having been close to Abercorn to the south of the Firth of Forth, but unless the Britons had by then extended their territory far to the east, this seems unlikely. Perhaps we shall never know, but it seems rather more probable that King Kenneth's army would have floundered into a bog if he had attempted an invasion across the Forth to the west of Stirling.

There is evidence to suggest that at the Frews the moss close to the banks of the Forth and Goodie was only a few feet deep and that some was cleared at an early stage to reveal the hard clay soil beneath. Indeed, O.G.S. Crawford suggested that this original clearance work enabled the fords to form a gateway between Strathclyde and the kingdoms to the north. He says 'the passage of the Fords of Frew was primarily a route leading from Dumbarton, the old British stronghold, into northern Scotland by Strathallan and Strathmore'.[29] West of the ford the route may be followed still over Kippen Muir to Killearn, to Cameron Muir, Bonhill and Dumbarton.

Exactly which sub-tribe settled in the Kippen area is obscure. At one stage a group of Britons who lived in the approximate district for a period appear, at about the time of the Roman withdrawal, to have migrated south to Wales. The ancient *Welsh Laws* tell of an occasion when a Welsh raiding party heading north disputed who should take the lead in crossing the river Gweryd (Forth) and the Fords of Frew have been suggested as the site of that incident.[30] Perhaps the tribe concerned was one that was settled in the area at Roman behest, but which later chose to withdraw when life on the frontier became more dangerous.

Even if one tribe moved south to Wales others would have stayed, intermarried with other tribes and been joined by new arrivals. In any event the Britons left traces of their language on the area.

The study of the origins of place names is a difficult subject. Names may have been altered, adapted, corrupted and overlaid with words from a number of languages. New names can be introduced and old names borrowed and resurrected, but applied to a different location. In these circumstances, evidence from place names has always to be treated with caution. Not surprisingly Kippen has names which have their roots in most of the languages and dialects which have been present in central Scotland over the centuries.

However, a leading authority on the subject has confirmed the Brythonic nature of a significant number of the names in the district. For example, he has explained that the sound made by the letter combination 'tref' is clearly from that language, occurs frequently in Cumbria and Wales and almost never in former Pictish areas. (By contrast Pictish names beginning with 'Pit' are often found in Fife and north east Scotland but not in the south-west of the country.) *Tref* meant a town or home and was the original ending of Fintry. (Thirteenth-century documents identify the place as Fintrif or Fyntryf.)[31] Glentirran (originally Terinterran) is also almost certainly Brythonic and recurs in Gwynedd in Wales. 'Fell' as in Campsie Fells is obviously familiar in Cumbria, as is the place-name 'Skidaw', which in Stirlingshire is the name of a crag in the hills above Fintry.

But the two key sounds which are most typically Brythonic and confined to areas in which Britons formerly lived are *cair*, meaning a fort, manor house or stockaded farm, and *pen*, an end or a head. The first of these can often be obscured by the later word *keir* which may sometimes have come from the related Gaelic word *cathair*, a fort. As will be discussed shortly, Kippen has a number of ancient fortified positions that have traditionally been described as 'Keir hills' but the derivation of the word in these cases is not clear enough to be identified with certainty. However, *cair* is sometimes rendered as *car* as in Carlisle, or Carmarthen and Cardross and Carbeth seem to be good examples from the Kippen area.[32]

On this subject 'Pen' is much more interesting because of its presence in Kippen. In old records the name is spelt in different ways such as Kippene, Kippone, Kyppane and Kippan, but none of these spellings create real problems because the word would certainly have predated its use in writing. In Cumbria, Wales and Cornwall 'Pens' are very common, but usually in the first part of the name, as in Penzance or Penrith. There are few in Scotland and these are almost all located in the south-west, such as Penpont (end of the bridge) near Dumfries. However, it is not unknown for later words to be added on to a Brythonic syllable. In the first *Statistical Account*, John Campbell suggested that the origin of the name was from the Gaelic *caep* (English, cape) which would relate to the promontory or headland shape of Kippen. (Kippford, a headland by a ford on the Solway estuary would be a similar example). That explanation is appropriate because the two words – *caep* and *pen* – convey the same 'headland' meaning.[33]

Another suggestion offered later by William Wilson is that the name may derive from the Gaelic word *ciopan*, pronounced kippan, which means the stumps or roots of trees. Wilson could not decide which of the two possible explanations was more probable,[34] but it is interesting that the author of the modern *Dictionary of Scottish Place Names* offers the latter without hesitation.[35]

Deciding this question is not easy, but it may be that there is no contradiction and that both names are valid. Brythonic is a Celtic language that was in use long before the Gaelic of the Scots from Dalriada was introduced to the country (both then spoken rather than written languages). It is possible that Kippen did indeed originate as a combined word to mean a headland. But by the time the Scots appeared on the scene it might have been very easy to identify the place with tree stumps (just as the informers advising the Roman geographers may have done to produce the word 'Bodotria'). No doubt a valley filled with the debris of a great forest gradually disappearing under a mossy swamp would have been an awesome and memorable sight for several centuries. Perhaps, therefore, it is possible that the word Kippen (eventually written in Gaelic, 'Ciopan') entered the Gaelic language meaning a place of tree stumps. We will never be certain, but that seems at least a possible explanation.

An interesting point is, of course, that the Gaelic explanation reinforces the idea that when the Scots reached the area it was still notable for the remains of the forest and tends to confirm the view that the Romans were indeed responsible for some of its destruction. Mr Wilson points to local names such as Kep and Keppoch that also translate as the 'field of the stumps', and more distinctly still, Kep-darroch, 'the field of oak trees'.

Perhaps the most intriguing aspect of the early history of Kippen is that connected with the origins of its church. A starting point to this remarkable story may well be the name St Mauvais, which was the name given to the figure who for long was regarded as the patron saint of the village. From at least the late 17th century an annual fair was held in his honour on 26th October. Mr Wilson and other previous investigators could not identify this saint nor establish the origin of his connection to the district. Moreover, none of the formal collections of saints records an individual with such a name. However, there clearly was a strong local oral tradition in respect of such a person and his name was particularly associated with a well located to the north of the village close to what is known as 'Cuthbertson's Cottage', where the Gaywood family have lived in recent years.

'St Mauvais' Well' is noted in the *Inventory of Stirlingshire*. It was examined about 1960 and it was described in the following terms by the inspector acting for the Royal Commission on the Ancient and Historical Monuments of Scotland:

> There appears to be some stone work now covered up with turf. From here the water is carried some ten feet by an iron pipe, and this discharges into a large round stone basin; the overflow from the basin is in turn carried away underground by a stone-built drain. It is to be noted that the site is only about 100 yards distant from that on which a pre-Reformation church has been alleged to have stood.

Citing the ancient *Annals of Ulster* as the source of information it is then suggested that 'the saint to whom this is sacred is Mobhi, abbot of Glas Naoibhen (in Ireland), who died in 544'. It is also noted that other dedications to this saint may be found in Perthshire, Mull and Kintyre, where the name takes the form Dadhi (Davie).[36] (Today, the well is thoroughly overgrown and little is visible beyond the flow of water.)

An initial reaction to this was that, if indeed it was a correct identification and the name could be pronounced 'Davie', it seemed possible that this was the 'saint' who had given his name to the Kippendavie estate at Dunblane. However, Kippendavie has been identified with one Dabius, Davius, David or Davy, an Irish missionary who, it is said, was ordained by St Patrick and who came to Scotland to spread the Gospel. He is claimed to have 'established monastic cells at Weem, Aberfeldy and Killin before arriving in Dunblane about 450.[37] (In passing, in this case the origin of the 'Kippen' part of the name is given as *ceapan* – a hillock or promontory.)

What are we to make of all this? Does either Mobhi or perhaps Dabius have any connection with Kippen's Mauvais? As Professor Lynch has remarked, 'unpicking the story of Scottish Christianity is as much a task of stripping off the layers of camouflage put in place by hagiographers as it is a search for clues beyond the few hard facts that exist.'[38] As he correctly suggests, the history of the church in Scotland during the dark ages is a subject which the historian approaches with more than a degree of suspicion and caution.

The problem is that not only are pieces of reliable information rare, but they are often obscured by the 'camouflage' of what were essentially political tracts written by mediaeval and later writers. For example, at different times there were disputes and power struggles between monastic and Episcopalian church authorities and these often produced attempts by scholars to establish the pedigree and, therefore, superiority of one or another tradition. Similarly, after the consolidation of Scotland into a unified kingdom in the 11th century there was a perceived need to confirm the legitimacy of the Columban church which had spread from Ireland with the Dalriadic Scots and this resulted in many hagiographic 'lives' of long dead Irish saints. These accounts were often a mixture of legend, myth and straight-forward invention, and typically served to do little more than increase and perpetuate the confusion. Later still, after the Reformation and again in the 19th century, the Scottish leaders of the Kirk were often anxious to distinguish their faith from the English Christian tradition and again emphasised the connection with Columba and Irish rather than Roman origins. Despite their general distrust of the whole con-cept of saints, these Presbyterian writers also tended to want to draw on a Celtic background and returned to the propaganda of the mediaeval Scottish church.

Confronted with this type of situation the wise historian will set aside secondary sources and concentrate as far as possible on facts for which there is clear primary evidence. In this case the facts worthy of serious consideration are as follows:

> There is a well which exists and which figured repeatedly in the religious and social life of the village.

> Close by there are un-excavated remains of a building which dates from the dark ages and which might be the remains of an early church.

> There is a strong oral tradition of a local connection with a 'saint' named 'Mauvais' and this is reflected in several ways including annual fairs held in his name over many centuries.

> And there is 'real' evidence of a potentially suitable candidate.

Scholars of the early church have long believed that by the time of the Roman withdrawal from Britain the Christian faith had become to some degree established among the British tribes which occupied the territory south of the Forth and Clyde.[39] Whether this church derived from direct contact with Christians among the Roman troops and traders or from the work of missionaries is less clear. Moreover, no doubt in the centuries which followed the Roman retirement the fate of Christians would have depended very much on local conditions and personalities and the lives of Christian communites would have waxed and waned accordingly.

A great deal of debate has centred on the existence or otherwise of St Nynia (or Ninian). Bede, writing in 731, claimed that the latter was a British bishop who was buried 'together with many other saints' in a place 'the English nation has just now begun to govern'. This place is believed to be Whithorn in Galloway, where Nynia had built 'a church of stone in a manner to which the Britons were not accustomed'.[40]

Bede's account is the main documentary source for Nynia and it clearly implies that he was a bishop of a British church which had been in existence for a considerable period (and whose church buildings were not constructed of stone). One of the principal modern investigators of this subject has concluded that Nynia founded his church at Whithorn somewhere between 400 and 450, and goes on to state that 'whether or not this is so, his consecration was the means by which a Christian community already in existence beyond the Roman 'limes' was integrated into the universal Church'.[41] It is also suggested that Nynia probably conducted a mission in central Scotland and perhaps established a church in the location of St Ninians near Stirling. Others have argued that the specific evidence for Nynia is fairly flimsy, but agreed with the basic proposition of a 5th-century British church in south-west Scotland, probably founded on an older Christian community with its roots in the Roman period.[42]

Without wishing at this stage to enter the Nynia debate, it does seem clear that there was a British Christian church in south-west Scotland at least as early as the 5th century.

Turning now to primary evidence, in the last century a number of ancient stones were discovered in the Rhinns of Galloway. Among these were the three Kirkmadrine stones that were unearthed and rescued – one had been used as a gatepost. They are now beautifully displayed in a mausoleum designed in the shape of a mediaeval chapel. The stone that may be of particular interest includes on one side a Latin inscription below a distinctive circled 'chi-rho' motif, itself surmounted by a capital A (for Greek 'alpha'), ET ('and') and presumably once another letter for the Greek 'omega', which has now flaked off. On the reverse side there is another 'chi-rho' of the same design. This symbol, sometimes known as Constantinian, is a cross composed of the first two letters of 'Christos', and was adopted by many of the early Christian groups. It was designed in a variety of styles and these help to date any particular version. The shape of the Latin lettering also assists the task of placing it in time and the 'angle bar' 'A's in the inscriptions are particularly significant in this context.

The outstanding scholar on the early Celtic church, Charles Thomas, has translated the inscription as follows: 'Here lie the holy and outstanding *sacerdotes*, that is, Viventius and Mavorius.' The word *sacerdotes* has given rise to considerable speculation, but probably does not mean saints. Thomas interprets it as 'priests, holders of sacerdotal office' and points out that *sacerdos* can mean both 'presbyter', priest and *episcopus*, bishop. On the basis of the form of the symbols and the lettering, Thomas felt able to date these gravestones fairly precisely as belonging to about the year 500 and he also suggests that the design is Gaulish.[43]

On the basis of this stone and other similar evidence of the condition of the Church in Galloway at about the end of the 5th century, it is reasonable to claim that there was an established Christian tradition in the area by that time. The men named on the stone were not saints in the traditional sense of the word, but they were priests and/or bishops. If the latter, they would not have been missionaries, but would have been leaders of an existing church of episcopal·rather than monastic nature. It is possible that they were originally members or second generation followers of a Gaulish rather than Irish mission to the Britons. Since, however, the stone was found in the far west of Galloway, it is equally possible that one or both of the men named also took part in a mission to Ireland.

The question, of course, is could this Mavorius be the same individual whose name has come down to us in Kippen as Mauvais? The spelling of the name Mauvais means little because for hundreds of years it would have been handed down from generation to generation as part of an oral rather than a written tradition. Moreover, the Latin sounding name, Mavorius, also means little, since at the time Romanised names were held to convey prestige and were often adopted by leading local figures. In addition, Latin was then the language of writing. Hence, if the stones commemorated Gaulish, British or Irish figures they would still have had their names rendered in a Latinised form. However, that said, the similarity of the two names is intriguing and does suggest more than coincidence. It is worth repeating that in the conventional compilations of the names of saints neither the name Mavorius nor Mauvais is recorded, nor is there a name that is even similar. Moreover, it is very difficult to believe that hundreds of years ago anyone in Kippen would have known anything about the names carved on a 'lost' stone in Galloway, still less have suggested one of them for adoption as patron saint of the village.

Concentrating on the real evidence then, we cannot doubt that the man whose name is carved in stone as Mavorius did exist. It is, therefore, quite possible that he did indeed carry out a mission to, and work with, the Christian Britons of Strathclyde. Thomas dates the stone from about 500. Bearing in mind that it is a gravestone and that it would have been inscribed after the man's death, presumably this means that his active ministry took place in the second half of the 5th century.

If we assume for the moment that Mavorius, a Gaulish priest, did come to work among the Christian Britons of south-west Scotland, probably under the authority of a bishop with his see based at Whithorn, he might well have come north through Strathclyde. E.A. Thompson has argued that the letters of St Patrick to Coroticus, King of the Dumbarton Britons about 460, tend to confirm the view that Coroticus 'and his nominally Christian followers were part of the flock of the bishop of Whithorn'.[44] If Mavorius was active in Strathclyde at that time it is perfectly possible that he came to the northern frontier of the kingdom and established a Christian community or church at Kippen, which, as we have seen, stood at the north-eastern entrance to the kingdom.

Is there any evidence of such a church?

There are perhaps three characteristics that may be indicative of a British church of the immediate post-Roman period. First, Bede suggested in the passage about Nynia quoted earlier that the Britons did not normally build their churches of stone and, if that is true, a church of the period would presumably have been of timber, but perhaps surrounded by an earthen stockade for protection. The suggested site of the church at Kippen conforms to that pattern.[45]

Second, with churches of the period the baptistery (place where baptisms took place) was usually outside and at a short distance from the actual church building and was intended for baptising adults or adolescents by partial or perhaps complete immersion.[46] The description of Mauvais' well provided in *The Inventory of Stirlingshire* and quoted previously would conform to the probable requirements of just such a baptistery.

Third, perhaps the most important indication would be a consecrated burial site of the period. Some of the very earliest Christian communities do not appear to have regarded an actual church building as being a necessary first requirement. On the other hand, a burial ground in which the company of believers could be laid to rest does seem to have been considered essential. In practice, interment often took place within a church building, but it is not always clear which came first, the burial crypts or the church. Sometimes, of course, the two were separate, but usually in close proximity.[47] Without archaeological investigation at the site in Kippen it is impossible to determine whether or not it contains an early burial ground, but that should be an easy matter for appropriate experts to rectify. However, there is historical indication that there was indeed an important burial ground at Kippen from a very early date.

The relevant church records betray the fact that when Scotland was finally unified in the 11th century, the local church authorities had no idea as to the origins of Kippen church. The Bishopric of Dunblane was said to have been established in the 8th century and, according to the *Pictish Chronicle*, was allegedly destroyed by raiding Strathclyde Britons in the year 857.[48] Not until the 12th century (1141 is the date normally given for its foundation) was the cathedral restored, by which time the records of its original existence had long since been lost. In any event it remained in a state of near desolation until 1238 when the Bishop appealed to the Pope to order its support.[49] In 1147 King David I had also founded the Abbey of Cambuskenneth where the community was formed by Augustinian monks who came from Aroise in Flanders. For several centuries thereafter the two authorities disputed the ownership of the church in Kippen and the rights to its revenues.

With the unification of Scotland considerable power was assumed by or delegated to the local magnate, the Earl of Menteith, whose territory now included the whole of the upper Forth Valley. The Bishops of Dunblane assumed that the records establishing sovereignty over Kippen had been lost and, as with other properties, the church and its land had been appropriated by the local secular powers, in this case, the Menteiths. The first edition of the *Gazetteer of Scotland* evidently includes this claim, by stating that in 1238 Kippen was erected as a perpetual canonry in the Church of Dunblane by an ecclesiatical convention acting for the Pope. No authorities are given as the source for this statement, hence it was probably a convenient invention.[50] In any event successive Abbots of Cambuskenneth rejected the suggestion and argued that the church properly belonged to the abbey.

There is no doubt that by the 13th century the Earls of Menteith did

claim authority over the church. In 1286 Walter, the first Stewart
Earl of Menteith and his son Alexander and daughter-in-law, Matilda,
gifted the church in Kippen to the Abbot of Cambuskenneth in return
for the right to be buried in the abbey. At his death Walter was the first
earl to be buried in the choir of Inchmahome Priory on the lovely
island in the Lake of Menteith and this actually fulfilled the bargain
since the priory came under the jurisdiction of the monks of
Cambuskenneth. However, the really interesting point is that the
Cartulary of Cambuskenneth indicates that 'the Earls of Menteith
previous to the time of Earl Walter of the house of Stewart, had their
burial place in the church of Kippen'. This idea is also repeated by
the historian of Menteith, Sir William Fraser, who writes, 'the
ancient burial place of the Earls of Menteith was at Kippen'.[51]

It was on the gift by Walter Stewart that the Abbot based his claim
to Kippen in a statement of 1496 which was subsequently ratified by
James IV, but still disputed by the bishop. However, a revealing
comment in the claim, which is set out in the *Cartulary*, seems to
establish the real truth: 'We also bear in mind how the aforesaid
Church and its patronage have existed from long past and beyond the
memory of man outside the jurisdiction of our said monastery . . .'[52]
(The dispute was finally settled in 1510 by amicable agreement
between the bishop and Andrew, the 23rd Abbot. Kippen church was
recognised as a canonry and prebend of Dunblane, but
Cambuskenneth reserved some of the land and revenues, while
Abbot Andrew was installed as canon of Kippen church for his
lifetime. As a result, he received 'the book, cup, and other furniture
of the high alter' in Kippen church on 21st July of that year.[53])

The truth then seems to be that to the mediaeval Scottish church
authorities the origins of the church in Kippen were lost in the
distant past 'beyond the memory of man'.

The suggestion that 'the ancient' burial ground of the Earls of
Menteith was at Kippen raises a number of very significant matters.

What does the word 'ancient' mean in this context? The implication
is that the earls who ruled in Menteith before Walter Stewart had
traditionally been buried in the church at Kippen and that this
tradition was of long standing. In other words, for a long period,
probably for several centuries, the rulers of Menteith were interred
in Kippen. Whether or not they were technically earls or petty kings,
or what the Scots called 'mormaers', does not really matter. The real
point is that the leading chieftains of Menteith seem to have had
their place of sepulture at Kippen.

If that was in fact the case, then two conclusions follow. First, in the general district of the Vale of Menteith, the church in Kippen must have enjoyed a very high status and must have been considered a particularly holy location. It is worth recalling that at the time the journey from Menteith to Kippen would have been difficult and would have involved either a trek over the rough terrain around the western end of the mosses, or a route along the north side of the valley and a crossing by the Fords of Frew. In either case there would have had to be a very strong motive to engage in such an expedition and one can only conclude that Kippen church must have been regarded as a place of special spiritual significance.

If the line of earls buried in Kippen extended back for several centuries, then the matter takes on an additional intriguing dimension. As has been explained, the valley was not only the frontier between two ancient kingdoms, Strathclyde and Fortriu, but the boundary between Briton and Pict, and, not surprisingly, it was at times heavily guarded on both sides. On the Kippen side the sites of four fortified places exist, the 'keir brae of Drum', the 'keir knowe of Arnmore', the 'keir brae of Garden' and, most directly positioned to command the fords, the 'keir hill of Glentirran'.[54] In addition, a castle, that is now untraceable, was once located on a site close to the middle of the village; the similar Arnprior Castle was situated by the glen west of the Mains of Arnprior and to the east there were the towers of Boquhan and Gargunnock. Not all of these would necessarily have been to provide for defence of the frontier, but some certainly did have such a purpose. On the north side a line of forts extended from Menteith to Lecropt, and Hume Brown, the celebrated late-19th-century historian, claimed that some of these were constructed at the behest of Kenneth II following the defeat of his army at the hands of the Britons about 970.[55]

Clearly there would not always have been tension or hostility on the frontier. But for a tradition to have developed whereby the local Pictish chieftains were brought for burial into British territory does suggest something quite remarkable.

As was mentioned previously, the Northumbrian monk Bede, writing in 731, wrote a few lines that make up the principal source of information in respect of the mission of Nynia. Bede included the comment: 'For these southern Picts . . . had long before . . . forsaken the error of idolatry and received the faith of truth, when the word was preached to them by Nynia, a most reverent bishop and holy man of the nation of the Britons . . .'[56] Because there is no clear evidence, scholars have long argued about Nynia's mission and speculated about the 'southern Picts'. The present study makes no claims to resolve that debate. However, if indeed the Pictish chieftains of Menteith were for centuries being buried at a church in Kippen, then someone must have begun that tradition by converting one of the ruling families of Fortriu. Whether that person was in fact Nynia or Mavorius or some other priest, they must have succeeded in impressing on the Menteith dynasty the notion of Christian holy ground at Kippen.

The existence or otherwise of an important dark-age burial ground at Kippen should be capable of resolution by archaeologists, but the matter may not be entirely straightforward. The site of the location of Mauvais' church appears to be in good condition. However, at some stage the old church was replaced by a stone structure that is believed to have been positioned on what is now a grassy knoll about 60 metres or so to the west of the well. By the mid-17th century this church had fallen into decay and the then patron of the parish petitioned the diocesan synod of Dunblane in 1665 for the erection of another new building. The Bishop, Robert Leighton, found 'the Kirk is ruinous, both walls and roof' and after he 'and his brethren perambulated the bounds of the paroch' suggested another new building to be located further to the south.[57] This third church, the bellcote and gable of which still stand in the village churchyard, was commenced in 1691. Interestingly, however, the graveyard contains no stones which predate 1700.

It will be seen, therefore, that there may be two sites that could contain ancient burial grounds – and that the original may be of particular importance.

The name of the field in which Mauvais' well is located is significant. Today, two houses are at the top of the field and the older inter-war bungalow is called Mavis Park, a pleasant corruption of Mauvais. However, the old name for the field is Kiln Park.[58] The Gaelic version of this is 'Cill an'. But W.F.H. Nicolaisen has pointed out that the Gaelic term developed from the British 'kil' meaning a church or graveyard or at least a hermit's cell. He also concluded that 'kil' names have a more restricted distribution than the Gaelic version, that there are few in areas not close to the Clyde or Solway and that most are connected to Christian sites which are not younger than *c.* 800.[59]

For the name Mauvais to have survived in Kippen down through the centuries purely through an oral tradition, it was necessary for something to have impressed itself deeply into the consciousness of the community. One of the factors that produced that outcome seems to have been the well.

Shortly after the Reformation Kippen church was incorporated into the Presbytery of Stirling. The records for Stirling in the period 1581 to 1587 are 'the earliest surviving presbytery records in Scotland'. They relate to a period just two decades after the introduction of kirk sessions, synods and general assemblies and the extracts of the minutes that concern Kippen throw a fascinating light on the community at that time.

Before considering some of the matters discussed in the minutes it is worth emphasising that the leaders of the reformed church were anxious to address what they regarded as some of the traditional superstitious abuses of the old Roman Catholic tradition. For example, they essentially rejected the whole concept of saints, particularly if the latter were seen as intermediaries to whom the faithful might pray for intercession. The Protestant ministers also objected to the idea of miracles and they tried hard to use both the Church and the secular law to stamp out such practices. As James Kirk, the editor of a published selection of the minutes explains, to the presbytery the

> problem of Roman Catholic recusancy took many forms. At one level, there existed a simple piety, less overtly Catholic, but none the less associated with older beliefs and such traditional practices, steeped in folk lore, as the veneration of shrines and pilgrimages to Christ's well whose waters was reputed to heal diseases. In 1581 and again, in 1583, the presbytery investigated the 'great abuse usit be the rascall sort of pepill that passis in pilgrimage to Chrystis woll and usis gret idolatrie or supertitious thairat, expres againis God's law'.[60]

Nowhere in the minutes is there any reference to a 'saint's' name, which, in the circumstances is not strange. Always the repeated references are to 'Chrystis woll', but that is merely an indication that while the ministers wished to reject the notion of saints they continued to recognise a Christian tradition in respect of the well.

Many, but not all of the references to the well relate to people from Kippen and the immediate district, but there is also repeated identification of individuals from the Stirling and Clackmannan areas. There was a long tradition of a St Ninian's well at the Wellgreen of Stirling and it is probable that the references in the minutes mean that the presbytery was objecting to people making pilgrimages to more than one location.[61] However, the many comments about men and women specifically identified as being from around Kippen leave little doubt that these instances at least relate to Mauvais' well.

To give just one example, in July 1583 a long list of people including John Harvie, Janet Harvie, Janet Gardener, Margaret Bauchok, John Chapman, Elizabeth Galbraith, Euphame Morrison, Agnes Graham, William Kay, John Campbell, and Elizabeth Lennox, all of Kippen parish, were named in cases of discipline regarding pilgrimages to the well. Usually they did little enough to cause offence when they were there, perhaps admitting to walking round the well making prayers, throwing the water over themselves or leaving a token or offering by the well. Some of the reported incidents make sad reading with obviously sick people visiting the well to seek relief from their ailment or to plead for help for a loved one. William Kay, for instance, explained that his child, John Kay, was sick. He had taken his child's apron string and left it by the well, had prayed by the well and had taken some of the water home and given it to the child to drink. Agnes Blair also had a sick child and when she appeared before the presbytery in 1587 she said that she took it to the well to bathe him there, believing that 'be the waschein of the bairne with the water of the said woll he sould ather dee or leive'. A number of pilgrims obviously attempted to plunge into the well and it is evident that not only was the well strictly guarded by the church authorities, but some device was in place to make immersion difficult. Finally, many complained at being obstructed since they had gone to the well because their 'foirbearis' had done so. Almost invariably the punishment for this conduct was an order to make public repentance at the church on the following Sunday. However, in 1583 such was the concern at the number of pilgrimages that the presbytery decided to petition 'Lord Doun, Stewart of Mentayth' urging him to enforce the recently passed Act of Parliament by imposing beatings and levying financial penalties on those who continued to visit the well.[62]

Clearly, then, over the centuries Mauvais' well had retained a deep hold on the religious memory of the community as a place of important spiritual power and individuals were still willing to court public rebuke and punishment by continuing to use it as a place of intercession. Moreover, not the least interesting matter to emerge from these minutes is the familiarity of many of the names, many of which are either still represented in the area, or were in recent times. To the ones previously mentioned might be added others such as John Adam, Duncan Carrick, John Forrester, Andrew Smart, Hellein Scott, John Buchanan, John Dow, Christine Clark, Robert Leckie, Duncan Watson, Janet Martin, Donald Ure and so on. These surnames confirm exactly the kind of continuity where old customs and practices could indeed have survived through being handed on from generation to generation.

Before leaving these presbytery minutes one other matter may be mentioned briefly. In 1587 the preacher at Kippen, William Stirling, was removed from office because he had been carrying out his duties improperly. As a result, for a time the church had been without a minister and a delegation from the parish asked the presbytery to examine four of their members before choosing one who could take over the task. The application was accepted and Andro Murdo was accordingly ordained and given the power to preach and administer the sacraments.[63] This procedure seems to suggest that, when necessary, the congregation was quite happy to select a minister from their own number and this may have been the kind of practice which had enabled it to survive over the centuries. Indeed, probably one of the duties of an incumbent was to train successors to take on the day-to-day duties.

Reviewing the foregoing discussion, what conclusions can be reached about the early church in Kippen? In summary:

There seems little doubt that a British Christian community was established at Kippen from a very early date, probably in the period 450–500.

That church was probably originally episcopal rather than monastic in character and may have resulted from a Gaulish rather than Irish mission.

The original church was almost certainly located at what is sometimes known as keir hill of Dasher and the baptistery appears to have been at Mauvais' well in Kiln Park.

The site probably contains an ancient burial ground, which may have been the location of the place of interment of the Pictish chieftains of Menteith. If so, this implies an early pre-Columban conversion of some of the leaders of the Picts of Fortriu and may vindicate the essential case for Nynia's mission.

The traditions of this British church were clearly handed down from one generation to another in Kippen and the process could well have accurately preserved the name of the original founder as sounding something like Mauvais or, orally, Mo-vay.

Was the church founded by the man named on the Kirkmadrine stone as Mavorius? We may never know for an absolute certainty, but logic suggests that it may well have been.

In his book *Christianity in Roman Britain to* AD *500*, Charles Thomas speculated about the Kirkmadrine stone and assumed that the two named individuals were bishops. He wrote 'the death of one bishop (Viventius?) was perhaps shortly followed by that of a sick or elderly successor (Mavorius). Both bishops would be later than Nynia.'[64] No explanation for that suggestion was offered, but if one examines the writing on the stone the reasoning seems clear enough. The letters of the name Mavorius are smaller than those of the previous text and appear to have been added on, but they are in the same style, and have the same angle-bar A's. Presumably, therefore, the stone was intended to mark the grave of Viventius, but because Mavorius died soon after, he was buried in the same place and his name was added. (Where the graves are located is not known, because the stone was obviously moved at some time in its history.)

If we are prepared to enter the realm of speculation, then one has to agree that it could have happened in accordance with Thomas' basic proposition. If Mavorius started as a young priest following in the footsteps of Nynia, he could well have had most of his active ministry in Strathclyde about 450–500 and that could have included establishing and serving the church in Kippen during that period. Possibly he consolidated a position established a few years earlier by Nynia. The latter may have been followed as bishop at Whithorn by Viventius, and in later years Mavorius may in turn have been recalled to take over the leadership of the diocese. If that was the case, the long walk south might have contributed to his death. Equally, of course, it is possible that he was recalled from elsewhere.

Thomas also states explicitly that Christianity in Strathclyde 'does indeed go back to the late fifth century' and that some Christian communities were probably established in nearby 'Pictish enclaves'.[65]

It seems fairly clear that both individuals named on the Kirkmadrine stone (and probably also Nynia himself) were originally part of a mission which came from Gaul and the group were almost certainly followers of St Martin of Tours. In his reference to Nynia quoted previously, Bede also states that Nynia and others at Whithorn were buried in 'the church of St Martin'.[66] Martin of Tours died about 397, but even before his death his example had given rise to something of a missionary cult which was particularly influential over the next two centuries. He was a Roman soldier who left the army after his own conversion and he became a wandering priest and later bishop who specialised in periodic adventures into wild and remote places, converting rural Gallo-Roman communities, 'destroying their pagan shrines and replacing each one with a Christian church'.[67] His followers were similarly enthusiastic for the challenge of taking the Christian faith to the country people on and beyond the fringes of civilisation and it is entirely in keeping with the cult of Martin that some of the young men picking up his challenge would have found their way to central Scotland.

The real point, therefore, is that Mavorius was clearly in the right time and place to have founded and served the church at Kippen. The coincidence of names seems convincing. Moreover, for the church to have survived it seems certain that he did not just conduct a mission and move on. He must have stayed long enough to create a burial ground, establish its reputation as a place of high and holy status on both sides of the valley, and train successors to act as priests. To modern minds this latter task seems strange, but for the early church it was an essential step. Almost certainly, having created his base at Kippen he also conducted missions into Fortriu, one of which may have involved establishing at least a cell at Dunblane and leaving his name to Kippendavie. It is quite conceivable that a name sounding like Mo-vay became Do-vay in a Pictish or later Scottish accent, and that the Kippen connection is the obvious one.

To put this account in context, if true, it means that the church in Kippen is among the oldest churches in Scotland. It appears to predate Columba's landing on Iona by about a century. Most astonishing of all, it seems that Kippen church has survived with an apparent continuous, unbroken record as a functioning Christian community. It is, of course, impossible to say precisely what happened throughout all of the centuries of the dark ages, but the remains of the ancient British and mediaeval churches and the evident ongoing use of the well and the burial grounds certainly suggest continuity.

Finally, the site of the original church, although a beautiful tranquil grove, is now surrounded by oak trees and therefore has little outlook. However, if one walks a hundred yards west to the open ground close to the position of the mediaeval building, it is very easy to see why Mavorius might have chosen it as the position on which to locate his church. Not only does it stand above the Fords of Frew, but it commands a breathtaking view across the valley to the majestic skyline of the Highlands. It must have seemed the perfect position on which to locate his beacon of hope.

However, this raises another matter, because the very earliest British churches were often located within the sites of Roman army encampments. This was probably done partly for reasons of security, but presumably also because the earliest Christians would have been local people who had been at least in contact with the troops. If Mavorius followed the pattern, this would suggest that the general site of the keir hill of Dasher was indeed the Roman fortified position from which the southern end of the Frews was controlled. The general rectangular shape of the site and, in particular, the northern entrance approach cleary possess the characteristic features of a Roman camp.

Careful and expert archaeological investigation of the sites of the camp, church, burial ground and baptistery are obviously required and one hopes that this can be done at an early date.

The foregoing narrative sheds an interesting light on a phrase which has come to us from the past and which gave a title to the poem that is reproduced later in this book – 'Oot 'o the world and intae Kippen'. How the expression was first coined, no one can tell, but it does suggest the kind of remote, other-worldly isolation that probably did characterise the parish for much of its history. After all it was for centuries not only on the edge of a wilderness of moss, but on the edge of a kingdom. Indeed, that may be precisely why its church was able to survive through the Dark Ages.

2

THE KINGDOM OF KIPPEN

The story of the King of Kippen has various forms, but the oldest version is as follows.

During the reign of James IV a family named Menzies were major landowners in the parishes of Kippen and Killearn. The family had been in this position for several generations and at the time in question a Menzies was acknowledged as the laird of Arnprior. However, this man was elderly, had no children to succeed him, his relatives had died and his land and position were coveted by one 'Forrester of Garden, a very topping gentleman of Arnpryor's neighbourhood'. Forrester decided to bully the old man and sent him a note demanding that he should make out a deed passing on his property to Forrester, failing which the latter would seize the estate by force.

'Arnpryor not being of power to oppose Garden, and being loath to give his estate by compulsion to his enemy, judged it the more proper, as well as honourable method, to dispone his estate to some other gentleman who would counter-balance Garden, and would maintain the rightful owner in possession thereof during his life.'

Deciding on this course, Menzies approached the laird of Buchanan, and offered to make one of Buchanan's sons his heir, if the latter would protect him from any attack by Garden. Buchanan agreed to do so, but regarded Garden with such contempt that he sent to Menzies only his second son, then still a child and with no more than his 'dry nurse' to guard him. When Garden heard what Menzies had done he rushed to Arnprior with the intention either to kill him or at least to force him to give up his property and to send Buchanan's son home. As luck would have it Menzies was out when Garden arrived, but the latter, in a towering rage, ordered the nurse to leave and to take the child home or have the house burnt down around her.

The woman replied that 'she would not desert the house for anything he durst do', and that if he harmed the child in any way,

swift revenge would follow. 'This stout reply was somewhat damp-
ing to Garden, who at the same time reflecting that he would not
only be obnoxious to the laws for any violent measures he should
take', also realised that he would be unable to resist an attack from
the Buchanans. He stormed off, but gave no further trouble so that
in due time young John Buchanan of Auckmar grew up to inherit the
barony of Arnprior.

Some years later, James V, 'a very sociable, debonair prince',
succeeded to the throne of Scotland. The road from Stirling to
Dumbarton passed through Buchanan's lands at Arnprior and
naturally was frequently used by the king's messengers laden 'with
necessaries for the use of the King's family'. One day, Buchanan saw
one of the royal couriers passing by and coveted the contents of his
baggage which he thought might enhance the quality of a banquet
which he intended to throw for his friends. Kippen parish was not
the usual destination of rare foods and fine goods and Buchanan was
keenly tempted. He asked if he might buy the load, offering to pay a
generous price, but his offer was rejected, the bagman stating that he
was the King of Scotland's messenger and could not risk offending
his master. However, Buchanan would not give way. Eventually
losing patience, he ordered the goods to be seized, telling the carrier
that if 'James was King of Scotland, he was king of Kippen, so it was
reasonable he should share with his neighbour king in some of these
loads so frequently carried' on the road through his kingdom.

The messenger rushed to Stirling Castle where King James was in
residence. Afraid of being punished for losing his goods, he told the
king's butler what had happened, repeating Buchanan's remarks
word for word. The tale was then passed on to James who determined not to be deprived of the use of the cargo. He summoned his
horse and a number of friends and set out for Arnprior Castle.

At the castle gate King James's squire demanded entrance, 'but the
tall fellow with a battle axe who stood porter at the gate' would not
let them pass, saying dinner had commenced and his master could
not be disturbed. James brusquely repeated the request for admission, whereupon he was ordered 'by the porter to desist, otherwise
he would find cause to repent his rudeness'. Seeing that he was
making no progress James then 'desired the gate-man to tell his
master that the goodman of Ballageich desired to speak with the
King of Kippen'. This message was duly conveyed to Buchanan who,
knowing that Ballageich was the name of the rock on which Stirling
Castle stands, realised who was calling at his gate. He rushed 'in all
humble manner to receive the king, and having entertained him with

much sumptuousness and jollity, became so agreeable to King James', that he was granted authority to take from passing royal messengers as many provisions as he might require. He was invited to attend the court in Stirling to have his hospitality repaid and the two men became firm friends. For the rest of his life John Buchanan was known as the King of Kippen.[1]

Sir Walter Scott was so delighted with this tale that he included a version of it in his collection of Scottish legends, *The Tales of a Grandfather*.

Is there any truth in the story? Who can tell? Buchanan may or may not have been the first to be known as the King of Kippen. What is true is that behind such stories there was often at least an element of fact. In this case, the Forresters of Garden were notorious bullies of the first order, who were more than willing to use force to intimidate their neighbours. For example, in 1592 Alexander Forrester had called out 'ane thowsand men on horse and fute' forcibly to prevent members of the Privy Council from examining a disputed boundary.[2] More broadly, given the nature of Kippen, it is certainly likely that in the distant past as far as most of the people were concerned the most powerful local laird or chieftain would have been the ultimate authority on most occasions. For day-to-day purposes they could have been accurately described as petty kings and, in that sense, Kippen was a little kingdom long before John Buchanan's time.

King James IV actually visited Kippen on one occasion to give thanks at the church after his success in suppressing a revolt. In 1489 the Earl of Lennox, keeper of Dumbarton Castle, had mounted an insurrection against the king and raised an army of about 2000 retainers. The king had only a small force available to him at Stirling Castle. However, when he gained information that Lennox and his men were encamped near Aberfoyle the king quickly gathered his troops and rushed through the Vale of Menteith. He reached the enemy camp at Gartalunane before dawn and he was able to surround and completely defeat Earl Lennox and his men. Next day, on his way back to Stirling, James stopped to offer prayers of thanks at Kippen church where (according to the accounts of the Lord High Treasury) he gave 'ane angell' as a thanksgiving gift for his success. An 'angell' was an English gold coin of similar value to a crown.[3]

In the two centuries following the unification of Scotland into one kingdom, Norman feudal practices were increasingly adopted. In the first half of the 12th century various earldoms were created and, as has previously been indicated, Kippen was incorporated into the earldom or stewartry of Menteith. For most of the next 500 years the Grahams were the earls and for some of that period their castle was on the Island of Inchtalla on the Lake of Menteith.

At about the same time the country was arranged into parishes, one being Kippen. The parish itself was divided into eleven baronies. Senior baronies were sometimes direct creations of the Crown, but lesser baronies typically were established on the gift of the earl or other feudal superior such as, for example, an ecclesiastical dignitary. Responsibility for setting up some of the Kippen baronies is lost in the past, because, as far as is known, their original charters have not survived. However, they probably were created about the time of Robert the Bruce and existed as functioning entities until about 1730.[4] The barons had military obligations to serve and support both the king and the earl and they had rights in respect of the people who lived on their lands. In addition, they were responsible for the administration of both civil and criminal law.

The, in some ways, surprising thing about Kippen is the sheer number of baronies into which the parish was divided. Perhaps this simply demonstrates the scarcity in Scotland at the time of reasonable and viable farmland capable of supporting a significant population. Alternatively, it may be that concern over the loyalty of those who were in control of the area in the vicinity of the fords, persuaded the rulers of the wisdom of involving a number of barons. Additionally, however, in Kippen some of the land came under the feudal superiority of the Prior of Inchmahome and this may have encouraged a further subdivision of estates.

The baronies fell into a sequence from east to west and the territory of each one seems to have extended from the river (or at least the edge of the moss) in the north to Kippen Muir and the hills in the south or south-east. From east to west the baronies were arranged as follows.

Glentirran (originally Terinterran) was the most easterly and included some of the lands currently forming part of the Boquhan estate. It has been suggested that this was the province of the principal baron, but there is no real evidence to support such a view and it seems unlikely since the apparent area of the barony is small. The keir hill at the rear of Boquhan is probably the site of the ancient seat of the lairds of Glentirran. In 1584 Alexander Livingstone, Baron of Terinterran, his daughter-in-law (a Graham) and some of his servants fell foul of the Stirling presbytery for their reluctance to accept the reformed church. On pain of excommunication they were ordered to receive the sacrament in Kippen Parish Kirk, but it appears that the Livingstones remained loyal at least to an episcopalian tradition.

Dasher was the barony that extended west from Glentirran and included the land on which the central part of the modern village is located. There is a considerable earthwork about 600 metres east-north-east of the present Dasher farm and it is described as a 'broken castle' on old maps. This may have been the keep of the first baron. However, there was also a castle located close to the present position of the timber bungalows at the entrance to Castlehill Loan, and this may have been the Dasher Castle of the Middle Ages. It would not have been a great building, but would have been a mixture of wood and stone, and was probably a three-storey tower capable of giving a measure of security in an emergency. No doubt when it was eventually replaced in less dangerous times by something more comfortable the stones would have been used to construct local cottages.[5] The Leckie family provided lairds of Dasher for centuries.

What is currently known as the village common was originally Dasher common, the land on which all the residents of the barony were entitled to graze their own animals – usually sheep or cattle – and where they could gather stones for building and cut turf, both for fuel and for roofing. This common extended within the lands of Dasher 'as far back over the hill known as the Black Brae' as it was possible to travel while still keeping in sight the belfry of the church.[6] Presumably that really only became the tradition after the church was built in 1691. Certainly it might have provided a good reason for preserving the belfry gable which still stands in the old churchyard.

Next to Dasher came Shirgarton, which appears in various spelling forms in the old records. For example, in the Stirling Presbytery records of 1587 it is noted as Scheirgartane, and elsewhere it is written as Skergaden, Shergetoun or Shargarton.[7]

There are a variety of origins claimed for the name. In his 1878 lecture William Wilson suggested that the latter part of the word derived from *gart* or *gort* (old English, *garth*, modern English, 'garden') which originally meant corn, and then later an enclosed or tilled field. *Shir* (Gaelic, *siar*) is west, so that Shirgarton could have meant the west field or enclosure, being west in relation to Dasher. Another suggestion, however, is that the name comes from the Gaelic *searbh*, meaning sour, which would make it the 'field of sour soil'.[8] In either case, the lands of Shirgarton that are close to the modern village were amongst the earliest in the area to be cultivated.

The main boundary between Shirgarton and Dasher seems to have formed a straight line from the western edge of what is now Scott Brae, through the top entrance to Oakwood, over the Black Brae and across Wright Park to at least the Boquhan Burn. The northern boundary was more complicated, principally because, in a process that was common at the time of the Reformation, Shirgarton estate incorporated some church lands that previously belonged to Cambuskenneth Abbey. The northern boundary between the old baronies, therefore, curved round to the east, taking in the lower part of what is now Fore Road, ran up the line of the old Dumbarton (or Back) Road before turning sharply back north to the river.

In the 16th century a dispute between feudal superiors led to Shirgarton being included in the county of Perth while the neighbouring baronies of Dasher and Broich were in Stirlingshire. This explains the eccentric county boundaries that survived until 1900 when they were finally revised by a Parliamentary Commission. It was said that the old boundaries had enabled the 19th century ministers, residing in the manse at what is now known as Glebe House, to have their meals cooked in the kitchen in Perthshire before being eaten in the dining room in Stirlingshire.[9] More interestingly, the ministers apparently also had the ability completely to confuse county tax collectors.

In 1495, James III granted the life-rent of 'Easter Leckie and Shargarton' to Lord Evandale. Forty-six years later James V gave a charter to 'the lands of Shirgarton in the stewartry of Menteith, and shire of Perth' to Robert, Master of Mar, whose main property was at Cardross. In 1597, the Earl of Mar, while retaining the feudal superiority, disponed Shirgarton to Buchanan of Arnprior (probably a son of the King of Kippen); and in 1619 it was passed on to James Ure and his wife Christina Wryt. The charter granted to them by John, Earl of Mar transferred 'all and the whole lands of Sheirgarten, with the houses etc. . . . To be holden in feu by all the righteous and old measures and boundaries, for payment yearly of . . . thirteen merks and eighteen pennies Scots at the accustomed terms (*viz* Pentecostes et St Martini) by equal portions.'[10]

In 1644 and again in 1647 a James Ure of Shargarton was identified as a member of the committee of war for the Sheriffdom of Perth and this appears to have been the father of the Covenanter of the same name (whose story is recounted in the next chapter).[11]

The mansion house of the Ures was located close to the site of the steading of the former Shirgarton farm, perhaps approximately in the position of the traditional red sandstone building which has recently been reconverted into a dwelling and which commands a fine view over the valley. (The present Shirgarton House was appar-

ently built about 1750 for Dr Duncan Glasford whose wife was
Mary Ure, granddaughter of the Covenanter.[12])

Because of the strange boundaries, Shirgarton not only included
the land on which the Fore Road edge of the modern village is
located, but also the area of Cauldhame (cold home). This name
appears to predate the village, so no doubt some cottages were
located there from a very early period. The Shirgarton common was
the stretch of land running through Redgatehill and on up the brae.
Here too residents had the right to graze animals, quarry stones and
so on; they also had the right to go down onto the moss lands of the
estate at Strewiebank to cut peat turfs.[13]

The next barony to the west was Broich, which later became
known as Arngomery, but has now happily reverted to the original
name. *Broich* is the old Scots word for a brae or a slope and it
describes accurately the topography of this estate. Arngomery apparently derives from a Gaelic term meaning 'the enclosed portion' and
this may have followed a time when a wall was built along the north-
east boundary. The original house of Broich was located further up
the glen above the present mansion house and there seems to have
been a fosse or ditch in front of the building, indicating that, if not a
castle, it was intended to be defendable.

West of Broich came Arnmanuel. The boundaries of this estate are
now lost in the past, but it may well have extended from the keir
knowe of Drum south to about Powside on Kippen Muir.

The keir at Drum was thoroughly examined in June 1957 by an
archaeological inspector for the Royal Commission on the Ancient and
Historic Monuments of Scotland. He concluded that it was a motte –
the remains of a fortified structure probably dating from 'the early
Middle Ages'. The inspector declined to offer a more precise date of
origin, but somewhere around the 12th century – the beginning of the
feudal period – would be a reasonable surmise. In this case the central
structure had been a square wooden tower surrounded by stockades,
earthworks and, for a stretch of the north side, a stone wall.[14]

Towers of this kind were typically three storeys in height. When
danger threatened the livestock was driven into the ground floor
while the women and children were housed in the second and third
storeys. The men kept watch and defended the battlement or bar-
tisan and maintained a wood-filled iron cone called the bale or need-
fire which could be lit at a moment's notice as a warning beacon to
the neighbouring baronies.

It seems possible that this keir knowe is the location of the original
keep of the baron of Arnmanuel and the estate may, at that time have

been known as Drum. 'Drummys of Kippane' is mentioned in a document of 1501–1502 as being part of a gift to Johne Striveling of Craigbernard, and this may be a reference to the barony. By that time, of course, the early wooden building would have been replaced by something more pleasant in which to live. (In passing, the description of the keir knowe of Drum probably gives us a fair notion of the likely appearance of the castle mentioned earlier which was once located about the centre of the present village of Kippen.)

The word Arn comes from the Gaelic *earran*, and occurs often in the names of the area. It simply means a division of land. The feudal superiority of much of the land around this part of the parish was at one time in the hands of the Prior of Inchmahome, or indirectly, the Abbot of Cambuskenneth. This is not surprising since it has been calculated that at the height of its power and influence the mediaeval Church owned as much as one quarter of all the arable land then available in mainland Britain. There is no doubt that the priory monks would originally have been responsible for bringing parts of Kippen district under the plough for the first time. Indeed, the fact that many of the early Augustinians had come from Aroise in Flanders probably explains why the neighbouring stretch of moss in the area came to be called Flanders Moss. Later, as the Church became more wealthy and commercial, the lands that had been brought into cultivation were often parcelled out to the management or tenancy of certain individual vassals in return for services or for rent in kind. In this case Manuel was probably a person's name, hence Arnmanuel may refer to the land which he was granted to hold for the Prior.[15] This estate probably included the modern farms of Drum and Angus-Stepp.

Arnbeg was the next barony. The name here means the 'small portion' and, as it suggests, this may have been the smallest of the estates under the superiority of the Prior. The farm of Ladylands, which may well have been in this barony, betrays its ecclesiastical history since it was clearly dedicated to the Virgin Mary and probably originally known as 'Our Lady Lands'.

Arnmore means 'the large portion' and this was presumably a substantial barony relative to its small eastern neighbour. It extended from the edge of Killorn Moss to beyond Loch Laggan. On this estate there is another keir knowe containing the remains of a motte.

Arnprior was obviously the barony originally retained under the direct control of the Prior, but it, of course, eventually passed into secular hands and became the seat of the Buchanan Kings of Kippen. Arnprior Castle was located on the edge of Arnprior Glen, west of the present Mains of Arnprior farm. As with Kippen Castle, few traces of the mediaeval structure remain, but it incorporated the natural defences of a promontory, the flanks of which fall steeply on either side. In its original form it would certainly have been a formidable stronghold.[16]

West of Arnprior the estate was Arnfinlay. Arngibbon appears to have been in the barony of Arnfinlay and both names are probably connected to the individuals who were initially made responsible for the relevant portions of land. The family names Finlay and McGibbon have long been associated with the area.

Garden (pronounced with the emphasis on the second syllable) is probably the best known of the old baronies because it has survived to modern times as an estate in the hands of the Stirling family. William Wilson suggested that the name could have had the same *gart* root as Shirgarton and indicated that it may therefore mean that Garden was a small enclosed cultivated field or area when contrasted with Gartmore, a similar, but larger estate. However, he also pointed out that the early spelling in Acts of Parliament and elsewhere was actually *carden* or *cardun*, which suggests a quite different etymology. He explained that the stem Gaelic phrase is 'Calhair – divna' (pronounced exactly Card (y) e n), which means 'the fort of defence or shelter' and which would give it a similar probable origin to the other nearby estates of Cardross and Carbeth.[17] This explanation seems likely, but it is worth recalling that the 'car' prefix indicates a Brythonic rather than Gaelic derivation, but of similar meaning. The notion of the name being linked to an ancient British fortress is to some extent supported by the existence of yet another keir on the estate. The keir brae of Garden stands to the east of the present mansion. For centuries it was called the Peel of Garden and it was located on a peninsula that rose from a morass or loch drained long ago and now known as the Meadow. Around the Peel was a rampart or berm-kyn and a ditch and it was entered via a drawbridge. The traditional description would certainly seem to be of a 'Dark Age' castle.

Sir Duncan Forrester, who was Comptroller of the King's Household under James IV, was probably the Baron of Garden whose attempt to deprive the child John Buchanan of Arnprior of his inheritance was recounted at the beginning of this chapter. By the end of the 16th century, however, the Forresters had sold the estate to Sir Archibald Stirling of Keir whose descendants have provided the lairds ever since.

The modern mansion of Garden was constructed in 1824 to the

design of the architect William Stirling. It incorporated at the rear an older house built in 1749 and is now notable for its classical dimensions and for a fine Greek porch supported by Gothic columns.

The westernmost barony of Kippen was Buchlyvie, extending from the location of the present village of the same name to Balgair Muir in the south. In earlier times it was spelled in a variety of ways – Bochlyfi, Bochlyvie, Bucklyvie, Bollchlyvie and Ballchlavie. Origins for the name have been variously suggested, but none seems very convincing. Grahams of Fintry were early lairds and in a charter of 1541 King James V granted the 'lands of Bochlyfi Grahame in the Lordship of Menteith and county of Perth . . . which the King, also for good service and money paid, erected into the Barony of Bochlyvie . . .'[18] (Two spellings in the one charter indicates the havoc created by the name for the early royal writers, a confusion probably shared by strangers ever since.)

The Baron of Buchlyvie was, of course, immortalised in a 'Scottish Popular Rhyme' which Sir Walter Scott included at the head of a chapter of his novel *Rob Roy*:

> Baron o' Buchlyvie
> May the foul fiend drive ye,
> And a' tae pieces rive ye,
> For biggin sic a toon,
> Whaur ther's neither horse meat
> Nor man's meat, nor a chair to sit doon.

The baron referred to in this verse is believed to be Sir Andrew Graham, second son of the Marquis of Montrose, who is said to have founded the village (as distinct from the barony) in 1680.[19] No doubt the original author of the rhyme had been struck by the poverty of the place. However, another equally bitter traditional ballad, 'The De'il o' Buchlyvie', has come down to us and it was credited to one Watty McOwat whose stepfather was a Buchlyvie 'cock-laird' (presumably a contemptuous term for a small poultry keeper). McOwat had been driven from his home by his stepfather and apprenticed as harp bearer (or general dogsbody) to a wandering minstrel named Dawson.

One evening Dawson and McOwat were providing the entertainment by the fireside at the laird of Broich's house when the latter enquired as to why the boy had taken up such a beggarly trade. McOwat explained that his stepfather ('Davie Souple-shanks, wha is a wee daft whiles') had acted the part of a dancing satyr (mythical part man part goat) at a great banquet before the court at Stirling Castle. On that occasion Watty had been forced to act as servant to the dancers and he had become ashamed of his parent's continual boasting of his dancing prowess. In revenge, the boy had made up some disparaging rhymes that his stepfather had enjoyed at first, before the mocking laughter of friends and neighbours had turned his amusement to rage. When the wandering minstrel Dawson had come past, the boy had been given to him with 'naething but a gowf in the lug'.

The laird of Broich then demanded to hear one of Watty's songs, whereupon the lad strummed his harp and sang:

The De'il o' Buchlyvie

Nae doubt ye'll hae heard how daft Davie McOwat
Cam' hame like a de'il, wi' an auld horn bouat;
His feet they were cloven, horns stuck through his bonnet
That fley'd a' the neibours whenever they looked on it;
The bairns flew like bees in a fright to their hivie,
For na'er sic a de'il was e'er seen in Buchlyvie.

We had de'ils o' our ain in plenty to grue at,
Without makin' a new deil o' Davie McOwat,
We hae de'ils at the scornin', and de'ils at blasphemin';
We hae de'ils at the cursin', and de'ils at nicknamin';
But for cloots and for horns, and jaws fit to rive ye,
Sic a deil never cam' to the toon o' Buchlyvie.

We hae de'ils that that will lie wi' ony de'il breathing;
We're a' de'ils for drink when we get it for naething;
We tak' a' we can, we gie unco' little,
For no'ane'll part wi' the reek o' his spittle;
The shoul we ne'er use, wi' the rake we will rive you;
So we'll fen without ony mae de'ils in Buchlyvie.

Though han'less and clootless, wi' nae tail to smite ye,
Like leeches when yaup, fu' sair can we bite ye.
In our meal-pock nae new de'il will e'er get his nieve in,
For among us the auld de'il could scarce get ai leevin'.
Tae keep a' that's gude tae ourselves we contrive aye –
For that is the creed o' the toon o' Buchlyvie.

But de'ils wi' Court favour we never look blue at,
Then let's drink to our new de'il, daft Davie McOwat,
And lang may he wag baith his tail and his bairdie
Without skaith or scorning frae lord or frae lairdie!
Let him get but the Queen at our fauts to connive aye –
He'll be the best de'il for the toon o' Buchlyvie.

Now I've tell't ye ilk failin', I've telt ye ilk faut;
Stick mair to your moilin', and less to your maut;
And aiblins ye'll find it far better and wiser
Than traikin' and drinkin' wi' Davie, the guizer;
And never to wanthrift may ony de'il drive ye,
Is the wish o' wee Watty, the Bard o' Buchlyvie.[20]

(Glossary: *De'il* – devil; *bouat* – lantern; *fley'd* – frightened; *grue* – shiver or shudder; *scornin'* – mocking; *cloots* – cloven hoofs; *unco'* – very; *reek* – smell; *shoul* – shovel; *fen* – manage; *smite* – strike or hit; *yaup* – empty or hungry; *meal-pock* – pouch for carrying oatmeal; *nieve* – fist; *leevin'* – scrap; *gude* – good; *bairdie* – beard; *skaith* – harm or damage; *ilk* – every; *failin'* – failure; *faut* – fault; *moilin* – buttermilk; *maut* – whisky; *aiblins* – perhaps; *traikin'* – wandering; *guizer* – disguised wandering entertainer; *wanthrift* – poverty.)

The sour tone of this song, in which the citizens of Buchlyvie are accused of almost all the vices, and the shared words suggest that the wandering singer Watty McOwat was probably also the author of the more famous 'Baron o' Buchlyvie'.

Perhaps inevitably from time to time there were disputes between the various lairds of the baronies. One such quarrel apparently led to serious bloodshed, and it concerned a conflict between Dasher and Arnprior that seems to have occurred about 1534, and therefore may have involved John Buchanan, King of Kippen. The Dasher laird would have been a Leckie and at one time this family was very strong and warlike having even contended on occasion with the Grahams of Boquhan and their powerful Menteith kinsmen.

Since the two baronies concerned were not immediate neighbours, it is hard at first to see why they may have been in dispute. However, it appears that the cause of the problem was a disagreement over the course of the stream that flows out from Loch Laggan and runs down to the Forth. There is a spring or underground brook that empties itself into the loch, the level of which never falls despite it being the apparent source of the stream in question. One or another or both of the barons wished to divert the course of the burn, presumably to make it run through their lands. (The burn that runs down the east side of Kippen through the lands of Dasher sometimes becomes little more than a trickle, so it may be that a dry season provoked the laird into the idea of looking for an additional water supply.)

Tempers became heated with the result that there was a battle a little north of the loch (near the old quarry) at a place known thereafter as Bloody Mires. Evidently there was considerable loss of life. In the 1850s a James Buchan of Arnprior, while making a road over a marsh in the area near The Firs, uncovered two swords and a stirrup and spur, suggesting that at least some of the fighting may have been on horseback. Hearing of the conflict, King James V intervened and ordered that the burn should not pass through either of the baronies, but instead should be channelled down to the Forth through the Broich. The consequence of this decision was that a little later there was sufficient water passing down the Broich to construct an important meal mill driven by a water wheel.[21]

As mentioned above, the Leckies may also have fought with the Grahams of Boquhan. Nimmo, the early historian of Stirlingshire, apparently examined a document prepared by one of the late 18th-century lairds, General Fletcher Campbell of Boquhan and Saltoun, in which the latter claimed to have heard an old lady of the estate sing a ballad that celebrated what was known as 'the battle of Ballochleam'. Sadly, the words of the ballad now seem to be lost. However, possible evidence for this battle was uncovered in one of the fields of Ballochleam farm close to the burn, where an elderly tenant dug up not only some spear points and bits of brass armour, but 'a great quantity of different bones'. He evidently stopped his digging for fear 'that he might raise up the plague'. Whether these relics actually related to the conflict between the Leckies and the Grahams, or to some other ancient dispute, it is impossible to say.[22]

It will have been noted that Boquhan was not one of the baronies of Kippen. The parish boundary was the Boquhan Burn and, therefore, although located only a mile or so from the village, since the mansion and home farm were traditionally on the east side of the stream, the estate has been regarded as being in Gargunnock parish. In fact, of course, some of the lands lie west of the burn and Boquhan lairds have often played an important part in the history of Kippen.

Various explanations of the name Boquhan have been suggested.

Mr Wilson offered the Gaelic *mocuan*, meaning a plain of the sea or ocean, which would obviously relate the place to the appearance of the carse. This notion did not convince William Chrystal who indicated an alternative – a combination of *both* (a house or dwelling) and *can* (the rent or tribute), so that Boquhan might have been the place where the payment was received from tenants. In his *Place-Names of Stirlingshire*, Johnston made another Gaelic suggestion, *bothbhan*, the 'white house', which seems quite possible.[23]

The mediaeval Boquhan Tower was located further up the burn on lands belonging to the farm of Auld Hall, and close to the line of the old Dumbarton Road. Obviously this stronghold would have gained in importance from its proximity to the fords and the road. By the Middle Ages the tower had been abandoned and in 1760 some of its remains were 'dug up', including an iron 'yett' (portcullis) and grated windows.[24]

One of the earliest Barons of Boquhan to whom this castle belonged was one John de Grahame, who was of the same family as the Earls of Menteith. Much later Lady Margaret Graham of Menteith became the second wife of the 4th Earl of Argyll and her son, Sir Colin Campbell, inherited Boquhan. On the death of his older half-brother Sir Colin became the 6th Earl in 1573. Subsequently Boquhan was leased to a family named Cunninghame. However, the last of this family, Miss Mary Cunninghame, had no successor, and therefore, early in the 18th century the estate passed to Henry Fletcher, second son of Lord Milton. As was common in such circumstances, a clause in the will obliged the inheritor to change his name, in this case to the Argyll family name of Campbell. Henry Campbell also died without children, so that the two estates, Saltoun (in East Lothian) and Boquhan, passed to his brother, the above-mentioned Lt General John Fletcher-Campbell. In this way Boquhan came into the hands of a family renowned for progressive agricultural reform and improvement.[25]

Up to the 18th century farming in Kippen parish would have been very traditional. The peat moss from Boquhan to Ford Head and in the immediate area of the Frews was probably not very deep and was cleared at quite an early stage. However, elsewhere most of the cultivation occurred in what was known as the 'dry-field' on the rising ground as it shelved up from the carse in each of the baronies. The method would have involved repeated strip or 'run-rig' cropping of the better, but small 'in-field' with 'bear' (coarse barley) and oats, tilling the 'out-field' less frequently and sometimes with little preparation, and grazing the livestock on the rough moorland. Until the end of the 17th century there would have been no recognisable village, but rather cottages clustered round a number of farmtouns. The short, ploughed strips would have followed the direction of the sloping ground to give some basic drainage, and this cultivated area would gradually have extended up from the carse towards Kippen Muir. Priority in farming, however, would have been given to cattle and sheep rearing for the very good reason that it was easier to protect livestock from the depredations of raiders of one kind or another. Whereas crops were liable to be burnt, animals might, in an emergency, be driven out of harm's way.[26]

3

JAMES URE OF SHIRGARTON AND THE COVENANTERS OF THE VALE OF MENTEITH

The unification of Scotland into one kingdom did not, of course, end the cultural divisions within the country. In southern Scotland the dominant language gradually became English, but spoken in the Old Scots dialect (exemplified in Watty McOwatt's 'Deil o' Buchlyvie'). However, in the Highlands Gaelic remained for long the main tongue. This was the most obvious mark of a deep cultural divide to which the 14th-century writer, John of Fordun, alluded when he claimed that 'the manners and customs of the Scots vary with the diversity of their speech'. In his view, whereas the people of the east coast and the Lowlands were

> of domestic and civilised habits, trusty, patient and urbane, decent in their attire, affable and peaceful, devout in Divine worship yet always prone to resist a wrong at the hands of their enemies. The highlanders and people of the islands, on the other hand, are a savage and untamed nation, rude and independent, given to rapine, easy-living, of a docile and warm disposition, comely in person but unsightly in dress, hostile to the English people and language and owing to diversity of speech, even to their own nation, and exceedingly cruel.[1]

As far as this ethnic and cultural divide was concerned once again Kippen was for centuries at or close to the boundary, being (because of the mosslands) on a sharply defined stretch of the northern frontier of the Lowlands. Inevitably, therefore, this position and the relationships that it produced, coloured much of the history of the district.

An interesting example of the nature of the typical problem emerges from the Stirling presbytery records of the 1580s. Walter Buchanan, a brother of the laird of Arnprior had returned from a trip to Europe during which he had married a Flemish woman. The presbytery was deeply suspicious because she came from a country where Protestants were subject to attack and suppression 'be sword and fyr'. Since his return Buchanan had not attended the sacraments in Kippen church and it was believed that this was because he was afraid that if he became known as a Protestant his wife's property in Flanders would be liable to seizure by the local Catholic authorities. Presbytery repeatedly demanded that he attend church services, but Buchanan replied that he was unable to do so since the area of 'Kippen quhair he dwellis is undir sic feir of brokin heland men' that he was unable to leave his home unguarded.[2]

(A 'broken Highland man' was one who had been excluded by his clan chieftain or who was a member of a clan that had been destroyed by rivals. Sometimes, as in the case of the Macgregors from 1603, the term was also applied to members of a clan that had been outlawed by the Crown and forbidden to use the name. If a 'broken' Highlander could not find an alternative protector he and his family could face the loss of traditional dwelling rights and extreme poverty. (It was this desperate state that could often make such men especially dangerous and hated by Lowlanders.)

Like many others in his day, Walter Buchanan may well have been somewhat ambivalent in his religious loyalty and may, therefore, have been glad of a reason for explaining his absence from church. However, his excuse was one that would have been readily understood by local people at the time, for the risk of raids from the Highlands was a constant fear which exerted a powerful influence on attitudes in the Kippen district.

This aspect of the history of Kippen became most significant in the second half of the 17th century and was no doubt a factor in the life of the covenanting laird, James Ure of Shirgarton. To understand the outlook and conduct of Ure, and his friends and neighbours and their wives and families, it is, of course, necessary to know something of the complex history of the religious and political events of his lifetime. A full study of that subject cannot be provided here and interested readers are therefore advised to look elsewhere.[3] However, a brief account of the context is required. At the outset it should be made clear that the issues went far beyond religious controversy, involved thorny economic and political problems, and concerned some of the most fundamental questions about the future direction of the development of Scottish (and perhaps British and, ultimately Western) society.

The Reformation in Scotland was a long drawn out process that extended from 1560 through to 1690. Not until the latter year did the Church of Scotland emerge in its classic Presbyterian form, with a structure based on elders, ministers, kirk sessions, presbyteries and General Assembly. The initial Reformation led by John Knox was certainly Calvinist, but not necessarily anti-episcopalian and it occurred during a period when the monarchy was exceptionally weak. The twenty-year-old Mary, Queen of Scots was presented with a *fait accompli* when she assumed her adult duties in 1561 and her infant son James VI was at first equally powerless when he succeeded his mother in Scotland. As a consequence, the first phase was relatively peaceful and there was nothing like the bloodshed of Tudor England. The Scottish Reformation was guided by two main principles – first, the parish should be the basic, primary unit of church life; and second, the laity should be allowed a large measure of participation in the running of the church in order to prevent a return to the old priestly abuses. Against the will of Knox, it also involved a large and steadily growing transfer of former church lands from the monasteries and abbeys to lairds of various degrees of wealth.

Had the early situation been sustained there might have been relatively little subsequent trouble. However, leaders of the Scottish Church came to adopt a position which in some spheres asserted independence from, or indeed superiority over, the powers of the state. The most formidable political thinker and scholar of the day was George Buchanan of Killearn, Moderator of the General Assembly and historian. In his *De Iure Regni apud Scotus* (1579) he gave to the Scots Presbyterians the concept of the 'limited sovereignty' of governments, arguing that kings or other rulers exist by the will and for the good of the people. The logical conclusion of that position, of course, was that a sovereign who misruled or who abused authority was ultimately accountable to the people and could if necessary be removed and replaced. The accession of the adult James to the English throne in 1603 made such claims a recipe for almost inevitable conflict, since the Scottish Church was now confronted not only by a king who had become much more powerful, but one who believed that he ruled by 'divine right'. Moreover the king was now also constitutionally head of the Episcopalian Church of England.

James was a wily individual who well understood his native countrymen. Hence when he insisted on reintroducing bishops to the Scottish Church in 1610 he compromised by installing them as permanent presidents of presbyteries. This worked well enough during his lifetime and seems to have enjoyed broad support from the dominant factions in Scottish society. Charles I, however, was far less sensitive and made clear his desire to assimilate the practices of the Church in Scotland with those of the Church of England. He also repeatedly threatened to restore all the old church lands and this seriously challenged the interests of many lairds in various parts of Scotland, including some in the Vale of Menteith. A key problem was that the old system for the financial support of the Church by teinds (church tax) had become hopelessly absorbed into the system of ordinary rents on which the landholders now depended for income. In addition, the influential town merchant classes were equally hostile to the effect of the king's policies on levels of municipal tax.

Charles obliged the Scots to accept a new prayer book and this seemed to hark back to the mass and to older Catholic practices and provided the spark to ignite the conflict. In 1638 the estates of Scotland gathered in Edinburgh to sign a national protest, the National Covenant, signed one day by the nobility and barons and on the next by the ministers and burgesses. It pledged the resistance of the Scots to any change in their forms of worship not previously approved by free assemblies and parliaments.

The signatories to the Covenant were careful to declare the loyalty of the people to the Crown, but Charles reacted by treating all who had signed as rebels and by preparing to march an army into Scotland. However, he was persuaded to draw back and, for the first time in twenty years, to call a General Assembly, which, to his horror, promptly abolished bishops and asserted its Presbyterian principles. Threatened now by royal military force, the Covenanters formed their own first army and prepared to resist. It was not a difficult task, for the Europe of the day was being scourged by war and many of the Scots who had found employment in various continental armies now rushed home to play their parts.

At this point the Scottish problem began to merge into the larger background of the English civil war. At first this worked to the advantage of the Covenanters who, in 1643, entered into a Solemn League and Covenant with the English parliamentarians. This not only gave to the Scots their adherence to the 'Westminster Confession' of faith, but effectively committed both groups to the pursuit of constitutional monarchy and parliamentary government and, indeed, 'firm peace and union' between Scotland and England. The Covenanting army marched south and intervened (decisively) in the war in the north of England.

As the Covenanters became aligned with the parliamentary cause so this tested the loyalties of those who drew the line at making war against the king. Most importantly, James Graham, Earl of Montrose, who had started out as a leading signatory of the Covenant and had in fact given to the Covenanting soldiers their hallmark blue bonnet ribbons and sash, now joined the Royalists. Having failed to gain much support in southern Scotland apart from among his own estates and kinsmen, in August 1644 he raised the royal standard in the Highlands and rapidly gathered an army which was joined by a contingent from Ireland under the command of Alasdair MacColla (Macdonald). The Highlands had been little affected by the Reformation up to this stage and ancient clan loyalties and rivalries were far more important factors than religion in rallying Highland support to Montrose's side. But in addition the Highland clan chieftains of the day were almost uniformly characterised by their chronic poverty and extensive debts and were keenly alert to the possibilities of well organised military raids on more prosperous southern communities.[4] To understand Highland society at this time the key point to grasp is that population levels were now constantly overstraining the capacity of the traditional economy of most of the area, and cattle raiding and armed robbery were virtually endemic.

Montrose's forces were quite small, rarely more than a few thousand, but with the main Covenanting army committed to the war in the north of England, for the next few months he played havoc with the forces brought against him. Personally a civilised and gallant man, Montrose found that it was not easy to control his troops, as was demonstrated in September when the city of Aberdeen was cruelly sacked and subjected to 'three days of pillage, rape and murder'[5].

The war now assumed something of the character of a clan feud. The Covenanting forces in Scotland were commanded by the 8th Earl of Argyll. As a soldier he was no match for the dashing Montrose and inevitably he and his lands and possessions became the target of many envious clansmen with a score to settle against the Campbells. In the winter of 1644–1645 Argyll itself was invaded and one of Alasdair MacColla's men boasted that 'we left neither house nor hold unburned, nor corn, nor cattle, that belonged to the whole name of Campbell'.[6]

So far Montrose had made little impact on the Lowlands, but in August 1645 his Highlanders came south, sacked and burned Castle Campbell at Dollar, ravaged some of Argyll's property in Clackmannanshire and then avoided Stirling and crossed the Forth at the Fords of Frew. They then paused 'to rest' for two days. Apparently most of this rest period was spent in the Campsies on some of Montrose's land at Dundaff Muir near Loch Carron.[7] What happened to the country people of the Kippen district and particularly of the Campbell lands of Boquhan as the Highland army passed through has not been recorded, but it is probably enough to say that henceforth most of the community of Kippen were passionately and irrevocably committed to the Covenanting cause.

After a victory at Kilsyth (followed by the indiscriminate killing of all but a few hundred of the defeated Covenanters), Montrose's Highlanders were finally trapped by the main Covenanting army which had come hurrying back from England. Under the command of General David Leslie these troops contained a high proportion of experienced soldiers rather than the largely civilian militia that had provided most of the opposition thus far, and at Philiphaugh on the night of 12th September most of the Highland army was surrounded and destroyed. In an act that indelibly blackened the reputation of the Covenanters many of the Highlanders and Irishmen and their camp followers who attempted to surrender were simply slaughtered, and this may be a measure of the fear and loathing that the latter inspired among Lowlanders at the time.

The alliance between the Scots and the English parliamentarians did not last, but the complex circumstances which led to the Cromwellian invasion of Scotland go beyond the requirements of the present narrative. Suffice it to say here that in 1653 Cromwell abolished the General Assembly, but forced a measure of religious toleration on the Scots, and he did not interfere greatly with Presbyterian practices. Despite the fact that he had routed Scottish armies, many Covenanters (particularly Argyll's friends) were not unduly dismayed by Cromwell's government, because he provided the country with the most fundamental requirement of peace and security. The price of the war in Scotland had been heavy both in financial and in human terms and had been marked, for example, by a severe outbreak of the plague. Now, however, Cromwell established powerful garrisons at strategic points across the country and notably at Ayr, Leith, Inverlochy and Inverness, and by 1655 it was being boasted that a man could safely 'ride all over Scotland with £100 in his pocket, which he could not have done these five hundred years'.[8] Small wonder that when (following Cromwell's death), in the winter of 1659–1660, General Monck rode south to initiate the return of Charles II, he took with him petitions from the Scottish commissioners of shires and burghs to maintain the union between Scotland and England, but on better terms.[9] The plea was ignored and the restoration of Charles to his father's throne in 1660 had the effect of restoring Scottish independence almost by default and against the wishes of many Lowland Scots.

Although he did not at first compel major changes in forms of worship, Charles II did insist on the return of bishops as being necessary to royal government, and presbyteries were abolished by proclamation because of 'the unsuitableness thereof to his Majesty's monarchical estate'.[10] Nonconformists could be committed to prison. The king also required a measure of revenge on his father's erstwhile opponents. The Earl of Argyll was charged with treason and executed on 27th May, 1661, and he was followed to the scaffold on 1st June by James Guthrie, minister of Stirling, and one of the leading Covenanting preachers.

The changes introduced by Charles were acceptable to the Scottish aristocracy, many members of which had in any case been switching towards episcopacy in order to bring 'Church government to a submission to the civil power'. The notion of power and influence diffusing down through society was not one that naturally commended itself to many members of the nobility nor to the small but important group of wealthy town burgesses. So long as their lands were not threatened and taxation was not excessive, these groups were broadly supportive of the royal policies. However, there is little doubt that in restoring rule by bishops the wishes of the overwhelming majority of Lowland Scots were 'overridden in the interests of royal autocracy'.[11] From this point on the main Covenanting support was drawn from the small lairds, the ministers and the lower classes in the community.

About 400 dissenting ministers were now driven from their manses and parishes (almost all south of the Tay) and patrons were instructed to nominate alternative pastors. In some cases lairds with Presbyterian sympathies refused to do so and responsibility for finding ministers therefore devolved to the newly installed bishops and the Crown. The intruded replacement ministers were referred to with contempt as 'king's curates' and they seem sometimes to have been highly unsuitable in various respects. Often they were individuals who had been unable previously to find a parish, and the contemporary historian Gilbert Burnet described them as 'ignorant to a reproach and many of them were openly vicious. They were a disgrace to orders, and the sacred functions: and were indeed the dregs and refuse of northern parts.'[12] Since Burnet was also deeply critical of many of the Presbyterian ministers for their ignorance, he may be considered a fairly objective if caustic observer. Certainly his description of the curates seems not inappropriate to the experience of Kippen under the care of one such individual. What has to be remembered, of course, is that in these days a manse, a glebe, a relatively good income and a leading place in the community came with the position as parish minister and those who sought such a living were not always primarily influenced by deep religious convictions.

Many of the curates could only be inducted into their new charges with military support. But finding a church and parish for a curate was one thing, finding a congregation quite another. In many communities the people declined to attend church and instead worshipped at services run by displaced ministers, either in neighbouring parishes, in private homes or at open air 'conventicles'. As a result, in 1663 these forms of worship were outlawed, but in many parts of the south and west in particular huge numbers continued to attend such services.

The Privy Council (the dominant aristocratic instrument of the king's government in Scotland) passed an Act popularly known as the 'Bishop's Drag-net' which made it seditious for any minister to preach without permission and made all persons who failed to attend their own parish church liable to fines or beatings. If they had no money to pay such fines poor men might have their coats impounded while women were sometimes stripped of their precious plaids. In some instances troops were sent to churches to check the identities of worshippers and to fine those who failed to obey the law, but there were still many ways for the people to show their resistance. For example, the story is told of one 'curate' who, annoyed at being confronted by empty pews on a Sunday, sent a threatening message to all the women of the parish promising to inform against them if they did not attend church. On the following Sunday many did turn up, but each with an infant in her arms. As soon as the service commenced first one and then another child began to cry until the whole company joined in a loud chorus of screams and wails so that the voice of the preacher was drowned out. 'He stormed and cursed', but could do nothing.[13]

During the years 1619 to 1665 the Kippen minister had been Henry Levingstone, who may well have been a member of the family of the Glentirran lairds and a relative of the Earl of Callander. Given the length of his ministry he obviously became an old man and was therefore probably left undisturbed in his latter years. Little is known of his successor, Edward Blair, the first episcopal 'curate' who died in 1673, but Robert Young who was installed later that year with the consent of Lord Cardross, soon proved himself to be bitterly hostile to the local Covenanters.

For some time Covenanting preachers had been active in the area. Two ministers, John Law and Thomas Forrester (formerly minister at Alva), who had been forcibly ejected from their churches, had been in the habit of holding open-air or private house services in various parts of the district. They then clandestinely ordained three others, John King at Port of Menteith, George Barclay at Gargunnock and Archibald Riddell, third son of Sir Walter Riddell, at Kippen, to provide services of worship to their followers.[14]

As has been noted, by this stage most of the leading members of the aristocracy were supportive of the king and of episcopacy, while the Covenanters drew their backing from small lairds and the common country people, particularly in the western Lowlands. In Kippen and the Vale of Menteith, although there is no doubt that most of the lairds and their tenants were Covenanters, the situation was slightly different in that they also had a degree of aristocratic leadership. At this time the Grahams of Menteith were in decline and deeply in debt, hence the leading position in the district was taken by Henry Erskine, 3rd Lord Cardross and a member of a notable Presbyterian family.

The barony of Cardross formerly belonged to the Abbey of Cambuskenneth, but in 1606 James VI recognised the claims to ownership of the Earl of Mar who bestowed it on his third son, the latter becoming first Lord Cardross. Along with the Cardross barony went other former Cambuskenneth estates, including 'the landis of East Garden, the landis of Kepe, the landis of East Poldarie, the landis of Wester Poldarie, the myln of Arnprior . . . the Kirk landis of Kippen, the Kirk of Kippen – parsonage and vicarage with all prebendaries and chaplanreis, in all time coming'.[14] Clearly, therefore, as far as Kippen was concerned, through the 17th century the Earls of Cardross provided the senior leadership.

In the early 1670s Lord Cardross's initial position seems to have been fairly moderate and, as we have seen, he promoted curate Young's installation at Kippen kirk. However, his attitude began to harden when confronted by the injustice of the Government's repression. His wife was Katherine, second daughter and heiress of Sir James Stewart of Uphall and Kirkhill near Linlithgow. She supported John King and on one occasion in 1675 held a house conventicle at Cardross when her husband was away from home. Despite his protests, as a punishment for his wife's offence, in August of that year he was fined £1000 by the Scottish Privy Council and troops were billeted for a time in his house. Soon thereafter he was again fined (on this occasion £112 10s) because his tenants had attended two local conventicles. As a result of his suspected Covenanting sympathies, he was then imprisoned in Edinburgh Castle from 1675 until July 1679, during which period he was fined a further £3000 (half his valued rental income) because Katherine had dared to have one of their children baptised by a nonconformist minister. A month before his release in 1679, troops marched out of their way to ransack the estates in West Lothian that he had inherited via his wife. Early in 1680 he attended the court in London to plead with King Charles for redress, but he was soon forced to conclude that it was impossible to expect any justice from the existing régime. In despair he decided to emigrate and sailed to North America, where he founded a plantation at Charleston Neck, North Carolina. This, however, was an ill-starred venture, for he and some of the other colonists were attacked by Spaniards and, with considerable loss of life, driven from the settlement. Cardross then returned to Europe where he sought service in Holland in the army of William of Orange. In 1685, to clear his debts his Scottish estates were sold at a public roup, but purchased by the Earl of Mar in the seemingly forlorn hope that one day his affairs might improve.[15]

We will return to Cardross's subsequent role, but suffice it to say for the moment that many of the Covenanters of Menteith looked to him as their natural leader. As far as Kippen was concerned some of his direct influence may also have come via his sister Margaret, who was married to William Cunninghame, laird of Boquhan. However, it should also be pointed out that the lairds of the district formed a fairly tight-knit group and one of the factors which united them was that, like the Earl, many were in the possession of baronies which had previously belonged to the former church authorities. They therefore probably felt particularly threatened by the Episcopalian bishops.

An example of another Kippen Covenanting laird was John Knox of the barony of Arnmanuel. Reputed to be of the same family as the early leader of the Scottish Reformation, this Knox permitted many field services to be held on his land, either at the so-called 'preaching howe' – the little valley above the Broich, but belonging to Angus Stepp farm – or further up on the moor at Gribloch at a place close to Loch Laggan. No doubt Mr Riddell and his colleagues also conducted worship in the private houses of other sympathetic lairds.

In different parts of the country, and to the fury of the authorised church establishment, the open-air 'conventicles' attracted huge numbers of people. Young appears to have been incensed by the non-attendance at his services of many of his nominal parishioners and he may also have been experiencing other difficulties. At this time the old mediaeval church building was in very poor condition and the Earl of Callander, a staunch Episcopalian, had lent money to enable repairs to be made, but required repayment of his loan.[16] The local lairds and their people may have been less than happy to provide for the financial support of a church that they were reluctant to attend. For whatever reason Young was quick to denounce and inform on his opponents. On 5th August, 1675 several of the tenants of the Cardross estate were fined for their attendance at house conventicles at which John King had frequently been the preacher.[17]

Soldiers in disguise were sent from Stirling to arrest King whom they detained at Cardoss. However, the alarm quickly spread among the people who came rushing to attempt his rescue. The soldiers hastened to bring him 'east of the mosses', but they were intercepted at Boquhapple near Thornhill by a party coming across from Kippen. Whether any of the soldiers was hurt is not known, but a local man named Norrie was killed before Mr King was freed, in an incident that foreshadowed what was to come.[18] (This was presumably the event that led to Lord Cardoss' arrest and imprisonment in Edinburgh Castle.)

If Mr King was successfully released, less fortunate was Mr Riddell and some of those who attended one of his services near Loch Laggan. Riddell and David Connell of Buchlyvie were among those apprehended and imprisoned at Leith prior to intended deportation to the colonies. Other worshippers were fined, and had their horses, cattle and other goods seized.[19]

In 1676 a large conventicle was held at Kippen during which a Communion service was conducted by three ministers, Law, Hugh Smith of Eastwood and Matthew Crawford. By this stage the authorities were becoming more violent in their attempts to suppress the field services. The latter were particularly prevalent in the south-west of the country where small lairds and owner-occupying tenants could follow their religious beliefs without the fear of eviction by landlords. Elsewhere, tenants risked their homes and livelihoods. Indeed, since soldiers were frequently used in an effort to break up services, worshippers increasingly began to bring weapons with them, at first to deter interference. Gradually, however, such conventicles came to be seen by the authorities as armed gatherings of at least potential rebels.

The King's Privy Council now introduced two measures in an attempt to secure obedience. First an 'indulgence' was introduced whereby ejected ministers who accepted certain conditions – notably agreeing to swear to recognise the king's sovereignty over religious matters – were allowed to exercise the functions of ministry in certain limited localities. Forty or so ministers agreed to these terms, but the overwhelming majority refused to submit.

The second initiative was much more severe. In December 1677 the Government turned to the Highlands to obtain troops willing to suppress the Covenanters. This indeed, was effectively an admission of the impossibility of raising sufficient numbers of soldiers in the Lowlands who were prepared to undertake such tasks. The so-called 'Highland Host' was recruited and 6000 Highlanders and 3000 Lowland militia were marched into Ayrshire, Dumfriesshire and elsewhere in south-west Scotland, quartered on the recalcitrant people and used to enforce fines and other punishments. In some cases whole estates were seized and money and lands frequently passed into the possession of members of the Government and their friends. Other landlords were compelled to sign bonds of surety for the future conduct of their tenants. When the Highlanders were withdrawn in the spring of the following year they left behind a bitter, looted and impoverished community, thirsting for revenge.

Armed insurrection was now obviously close and required only a spark to ignite the conflict. It occurred in 1679. The most detested churchman in Lowland Scotland was probably Archbishop Sharpe of St Andrews. It was not that he was an especially evil man, but he was seen by many Covenanters as a turncoat who had sold himself out to the king and the ruling aristocracy in return for personal preferment. He had originally been a Covenanter and had been charged by his colleagues with the task of negotiating with the king and members of the Government at the time of the restoration. He was regarded with particular contempt for his abandonment of Presbyterianism and for his acceptance of the archbishopric. He had also been active in organising the persecution of dissidents and had instigated the vicious torture of opponents to secure information. Sharpe now submitted to the Privy Council an edict making it lawful, or rather a duty, for any officer down to the rank of sergeant to kill, without trial, any man carrying arms who was believed to be going to or from a conventicle. Despite the reluctance of some members of council, this act was approved and sent to London for royal signature.

In Fife the local sheriff-depute, named Carmichael, had a particularly bad reputation for abusing Covenanting suspects. One of his frequent tactics apparently was to try to force women to betray their husbands, sometimes by burning tapers between their bound fingers so that their flesh was scorched back to the bone. On 3rd May a group of six men led by one Hackston of Rathillet set out to trap Carmichael on the St Andrews road. Later they claimed no intention of harming him, but stated that they wished so to frighten him as to force him to leave the district. As it happened they failed to locate Carmichael and instead came up with Sharpe in his carriage. Hackston tried to dissuade the others from violence, but the Archbishop was brutally murdered. The action was unpremeditated, was not part of any concerted plan and was generally disapproved of by the wider community. However, violent repression was now a certainty and Covenanters across southern Scotland looked to how best they might defend themselves.[20]

Following the murder, the six scattered and some fled to the west. One, John Balfour of Kinloch, reached Kippen, where he spent the night with James Ure at Shirgarton. There is, of course, no reason to believe that Ure knew anything of the murder, at least until Balfour's arrival at his house. (In his novel, *Old Mortality*, Sir Walter Scott mistakenly described this man as Balfour of Burley, and later writers tended to follow this error by assuming that he was the contemporary figure, John Balfour of Burleigh, who in fact was not a Covenanter.)

A group of 80 or so armed Covenanters (including Balfour) gathered at Rutherglen on 29th May and nailed to the cross a declaration denouncing all that had happened since the restoration of Charles. The Council's response was to send a party of dragoons under John Graham of Claverhouse (later Viscount Dundee) to destroy the rebels. Claverhouse's men succeeded in capturing a few individuals, including the Menteith minister John King, but when the soldiers attempted to break up a large conventicle at Loudon Hill they found themselves confronted by 100 well-armed men together with another 200 or so with pitchforks and other improvised weapons. The soldiers foolishly opened fire on this crowd, but at the ensuing 'Battle of Drumclog' they were routed and Claverhouse only just escaped with his life. It was not a great battle – two officers and about 40 soldiers were killed on the one side and five or six Covenanters on the other, but civil disobedience had now clearly given way to armed insurrection.

What would have happened had Lord Cardross not been incarcerated in Edinburgh Castle at this critical juncture can only be a matter for conjecture, but it is just possible that he may have advised caution and kept the men of the upper Forth valley out of the conflict. In his absence, less powerful individuals may have felt themselves swept along by forces beyond their control.

As has been mentioned, James Ure had succeeded his father to the Shirgarton estate. His mother had been married before and his half-brother was another Covenanter named Peter Rollo. Ure's date of birth is uncertain, but it appears to have been about 1650, which would make him aged about 30 when he found himself caught up by these events. He was married to Mary Graham and by 1679 they already had five children, each having been baptised by a Covenanting minister.[21]

The news that the West Country men were up in arms spread rapidly and, of course, soon reached Kippen. According to Ure's 'Narrative' of these events, Robert Young had repeatedly informed the authorities against him and, in consequence, his house had been ransacked by soldiers on several occasions. (As it happens, by Ure's day the Shirgarton estate contained some land which had formerly belonged to Cambuskenneth and this former church land was coveted by Young and may have been the real reason for his vindictiveness against Ure.) In any event, Ure now felt that he had no choice but to flee and to join the rebels. Two years later, when he was tried in his absence, a boatman at the Frew, William Millar, gave evidence that he had seen Ure 'whom he knew very well, riding to Glasgow on a white horse, armed with sword and pistols, and a partie of the rebells at his back on foot: some of them had swords and guns, and some not'.[22]

Covenanters now gathered and formed something like an army at Rutherglen before moving on to Hamilton. Ure says that there were in fact 52 men with him when he left Kippen, but that they were joined in the next few days by a further 150 or so.[23] Others continued to appear so that eventually more than 280 had gathered from the Kippen district (including, of course, men from Gargunnock, Buchlyvie and Menteith). Obviously with such a hastily assembled scratch army there was no regular structure of command on which to draw and lack of overall leadership was to prove a crippling handicap. However, the Kippen men spontaneously elected Ure to be their captain. Given that the total population of the district was then unlikely to have exceeded 4000, the remarkable thing is clearly the sheer number of men who had followed him and been prepared to risk lives and homes in the Covenanting cause. This leaves no room for doubt about the sympathies of the community in the Vale of Menteith.

Over the next few days the leading figures among the Covenanters fell to squabbling bitterly among themselves. Nominally their commander was one Robert Hamilton of Preston, but he was able to exercise little control over some of the other leaders. Essentially the argument seems to have been between the moderates, who considered themselves loyal to the Crown and who were willing to seek a compromise, and the extremists who favoured outright rebellion and no accommodation with the authorities. Ure, a moderate, seems to have found the continual argument distressing, particularly since it was taking place in the face of an approaching royal army. He concentrated on seeing that his men were as well prepared and equipped as possible. He had ensured that his initial contingent had brought some gunpowder with them and while they waited at Monklands he 'cast the ball' (melted lead in a furnace and poured out musket balls). Most of his men were reasonably well armed – 'those that wanted, I got them pike, so that our company was upward of two hundred well appointed, two parts with guns, and the third part with pikes'. As time passed some of the less resolute volunteers began to slip away, but Ure managed to procure some of their weapons for his unarmed men. He was horrified at the lack of preparation being made elsewhere and claims that beyond his own men 'there were few in the army that had powder and shot to shoot twice'.[24]

Ure was also enraged by an example of misconduct unwittingly assisted by some of his men. While in Glasgow a group had been on guard when they were approached by 'a knave', a 'wool finer' who claimed to know of a house where several weapons were hidden. The officer of the guard detailed four men to accompany the informant to the house, but when they arrived they were instructed to wait outside while the 'wool finer' entered and obtained the weapons. In fact this man was a thief and he robbed the householder at sword point, stealing his money, but obtaining no weapons. Next morning, the householder, named Walkinshaw, who happened to be a relative of Ure's wife, came and complained. Later Ure wrote, 'I thought very much shame, because they were my men.' He arrested the thief who was by now drunk, recovered as much of the money as remained, and caused the offender to be nailed by 'his lugg' (ear) to the gallows at Hamilton.[25]

Although not one of the senior figures in the Covenanting army, Ure was obviously a highly respected individual and he was present during some of the squabbles of the commanders, which he observed with disgust. On one occasion he was sufficiently provoked to intervene and has, therefore, left us with a clear statement of his views. He told Robert Hamilton and the others that 'I had a wife and five children, and that I had a little bit of an estate, and that I was come to hazard all and my life, to get the yoke of prelacy and supremacy removed; but for ought that I saw, they [the extremists] intended to tyrannise over our consciences and lead us to a worse snare nor we were into . . .'

He offended the more aggressive group by condemning their 'odious . . . naughty principles' and particularly rejected their disloyalty to the King: 'I desired them to forbear their reflecting language against the king . . . I told them, I would hear none such doctrine, and that it gave offence to many.'

He joined with some others to submit to the leadership a printed declaration calling for an end to the quarrelling and dispute until a parliament and general assembly were in place to provide constitutional government.[26]

By this stage, however, the Covenanters were in real danger. A royal army containing English and Highland troops had been assembled under the command of King Charles's illegitimate son, James, Duke of Monmouth and Buccleuch, and it now drew close. The Covenanting army of about 4000 was west of the river Clyde while the Duke, with his 10,000 mainly regular soldiers, approached from the east. They met at Bothwell Bridge.

Two companies under Hackston had been on guard at the bridge, but strangely had failed to mine it with explosives to be detonated in an emergency. However, they called on Ure's assistance at which he brought the Kippen men forward. He says that he drew his men up by the river directly in front of the bridge and was supported by a company from Lennox on his left, and one from Glasgow on his right. Two hundred men from Galloway also came up, 'but they had no other arms but pikes and halberts, with four pair of colours, and took ground on our right hand furthest from the enemy. There came one troop of their horse and drew up behind us and then our canon was drawn down, being a field piece.'

There were no mountings for the other two available cannon which were thereby rendered useless. Unbelievably the overwhelming bulk of the Covenanting army remained some distance off watching as events unfolded at the bridge.[27]

On the morning of 22nd June the royal army began to advance on the bridge. There was a brief skirmish between musketeers during which one of the Kippen men was injured in the foot while several of the duke's troopers were also either wounded or killed . . . 'I never saw them rise again.' Then for an hour there was a pause while negotiations took place, with a minister named David Hume speaking for the Covenanters. The Duke, however, demanded unconditional surrender, to which the rebels were afraid to submit, fearing reprisals once they had disarmed.

The royal troops now brought up five cannons and opened fire, killing two horses. This fire was returned with some accuracy, at which the gunners fled and caused some disturbance among a neighbouring troop of dragoons. Seeing the abandoned cannon, Ure wished to advance to seize them, 'but if I had gone without command, if they should have turned on me, there would none have relieved me'. In other words, a successful attempt to secure the abandoned enemy guns would have been a major achievement, but he could not rely on support if he had been counter-attacked while on the other side of the bridge. Indeed he was probably wise to hold his ground because the apparent abandonment of the guns may have been a ruse to draw his force out of position.

The gunners returned, recommenced fire and were joined by 500 or so redcoats under 'My Lord Lithgow's son' so that a sharp fight now developed. Ure says that gradually the other Covenanting companies withdrew as their ammunition was used up, but that he and his men for a time continued to retain their end of the bridge. (Ure's narrative was subsequently annotated by Robert Hamilton who claims that the company that held on was led by a man named Fowler, but since Ure was actually at the bridge while Hamilton was back with the main army and not exactly covering himself with glory, Ure's would seem to be the more reliable account. Indeed, Ure seems to have been an honest man of deep religious principle and since he must have known that his description of these events would be read by others who had been present, there is no reason to doubt the veracity of his record.) Appeals for help and fresh ammunition merely brought a foolish instruction from Hamilton to the rest of the army to fall back .

In the 19th century a Prussian general, Karl Gustov von Rudloff, examined the Battle of Bothwell Bridge and wrote of Hamilton's instruction to withdraw that

> nothing could have been more senseless than such a command; but as the division, now without the means of defence, was without support, they were compelled unwillingly to obey. But even yet their courage made itself conspicuous in a valorous deed. Finding as they retreated that a detachment of the royal army was already on the south side of the river, they suddenly wheeled about and attacked them so vigorously in a hand-to-hand conflict, that they drove them back and regained possession of the important position. But after almost instinctively having pointed out the way, if not to triumph at least to safety, being unsupported, they were compelled to fall back on the main army, still idly looking on.[28]

Ure's description of this incident is as follows. As he and his men withdrew

> Lithgow's son was the first that came over the bridge with three hundred foot and a troop of horse in his rear. So they advanced

towards us, on which I desired our men to fall about and let them see that we were not flying: so I went back. There followed me at first about thirty-four of my men; the rest advanced after them. The enemy fired about one hundred muskets on us: we clapped [flung themselves down], and so escaped all hazard of that fire, and immediately advanced again still forward, resolving not to fire till we were in their bosom. They seeing us advance so resolutely, their horse retired first, and then their foot, so that there were none on this side of the gate [probably a toll gate in the middle of the bridge]. Upon which retreat we made fire upon them, and the rest of my men coming down fired also. The enemy faced, and fired at me from the other side, and from the bridge, upwards of five hundred shot; likewise their cannon played. With the first shot they killed two men to me, and there was another killed with a musket; and as I saw none coming to assist, I was forced to retire to the moor to the rest. On my retiring there was some of theirs pursued, and killed a man that was wounded on the bridge. I caused my party to face about, and [again] chased them back; but they outran us to their party.[29]

By this courageous action the Kippen men and those that were with them were able to withdraw in good order. Ure's resentment at the poor quality of the Covenanting leadership is clear; 'in all this hot dispute, our commanders never owned us. As for Robert Hamilton, I never saw him' after the negotiations were broken off. Fortunately, however, fatal casualties among Ure's men in this action were slight, probably not more than about ten killed. But the bridge was now open and the entire royal army was therefore able to cross, and at its leisure to form up and advance towards the Covenanters.

In the absence of orders, Ure now brought the Kippen men up beside a force commanded by a Major Joseph Learmont who asked him to protect the left flank. The company was therefore disposed in a little hollow by a burn with the 'picked men' (skirmishers) spread out to the side to prevent the position from being outflanked by enemy cavalry. When he had arranged his men in this order, Ure jumped on his horse and moved out in front to study the approaching army: 'What number they were I know not, but I am sure they were three times our number; so I rode alongst their battle [front line] within shot of them a great way, and came back alongst to our men again; and so I came encouraging them what I could, for I saw none to do it. After this I rode to my men down the brae side.'[30]

As the duke's army advanced so they brought forward some cannon, the sight of which caused some of the Covenanting irregulars immediately opposite to panic. As they rushed to flee they ran among their own mounted troops and in turn some of the horses bolted and the panic spread. At this point the attack developed. A squadron of dragoons charged at the Kippen men who opened fire and held them off for a short time. However, most of the left of the Covenanting army now broke into complete flight, isolating the company. 'The right hand stood a little, but not so long as to put on a pair of gloves.' In these circumstances Ure had little option – 'I cried to my men to make away.'

It was now more or less every man for himself. A loyal servant brought up Ure's horse and he was 'beholden' to its speed and stamina in making his escape. Many others were not so lucky. While the critical fight at the bridge had cost only a few lives, in the course of their flight the Covenanters were harried mercilessly by the royal cavalry, particularly by Claverhouse's dragoons, and about 400 were killed. A further 1200, including an unknown number of the Kippen men, were captured and many of them would have been killed at once had Monmouth not personally intervened. A chivalrous and charming man and the acknowledged champion of English nonconformists, he insisted on clemency for those who surrendered, although for so doing he was soundly berated by some of his senior officers, including Sir Tam Dalzell of the Binns.

Before moving on, it is perhaps worth reflecting for a moment on the conduct of Ure and the Kippen contingent at the Battle of Bothwell Brig. Ure records in his 'Narrative' that he and his men had been at the bridge from three in the morning until about six and that the final defeat had occurred about eight o'clock. He also seems to imply that the troop from Kippen and district accounted for almost one third of the Covenanting soldiers who were equipped with guns and he proudly declares that in the whole army 'there were not better like men, and better armed men, than our company were'.

Two questions immediately spring to mind. First, why was the Kippen company so well equipped? Part of the answer presumably is down to Ure's own personal care and prudent efforts on behalf of his men. However, to provide upwards of 200 muskets would have been no easy matter for a provincial laird and one can only assume that most of the men had brought their own weapons. The fact that, unlike most of the other volunteers, they possessed firearms in the first place is probably explicable by their normal everyday need for continuous vigilance against Highland raiders. Many of the men, including Ure, had probably served from time to time in the local watches organised to identify and resist Highland cattle thieves, and it is known that in the earlier 1670s arms had indeed been distributed to watch keepers in the area.[31]

The second question concerns Ure himself. As the 'well attested account'[32] makes clear, he seems to have led his men with an extraordinary degree of cool skill and authority. Even if he was being less than modest, his actions in bringing his company to the critical position, in resisting the temptation to be drawn out of place, and in holding on under fire from a superior force, would all in themselves excite admiration. However, the conduct of the withdrawal from the bridge – leading the turnabout to push the enemy back, causing his men to go to ground to avoid enemy fire, making them hold their own fire until they were in close contact, repeatedly making them display good order and collective discipline in the face of the enemy so that they could retire without being molested – and his disposition of his men in sheltered ground with skirmishers out to protect his flank, all indicate a trained, knowledgeable soldier thinking clearly in a crisis. There is no evidence that Ure himself had previously been a soldier. However, we do know that his father had, from 1644, been a member of the 'Committee of War' for the county of Perth. This James Ure may well have fought during the first of the Covenanting wars and it seems possible that he passed on his knowledge to his son. Moreover it seems quite probable that in the years leading up to 1679, Ure had spent some time (either clandestinely or as a member of the watch) training with his men. His election as their commander does not look to have been in the least fortuitous and their own conduct in the battle deservedly earned his proud approval.

As has been mentioned, Monmouth insisted on initial clemency, but punishments were inevitably inflicted on the captured Covenanters. Sixteen were hanged, including a number of ministers, one of whom was John King of Cardross. A further 250 were to be shipped to servitude in the West Indies, but the vessel in which they were being conveyed sank off the Orkneys so that all but a handful were drowned. Many of the other prisoners, including some of Ure's men, suffered great privations, being confined for more than five months in Greyfriars' churchyard in Edinburgh. Eventually 400 or so were released after signing a bond of surety pledging their future good conduct.

Unfortunately, that was not the end of the matter, for Covenanters were now being hunted down and suppressed with increasing ferocity. For a time, under the influence of Monmouth, a fairly moderate policy was pursued, but this did not stop the dragooning and the fining of the Covenanters, the most fanatical of which became known as the 'Society People' or Cameronians. (The famous British Army regiment which eventually descended from this group, for centuries acknowledged their origins by carrying their rifles to church and posting sentries outside.)

Gradually the tempo of the repression increased and from 1684 the country entered what became known as the 'killing times' as Covenanters were hunted down. About 100 were formally executed, but many more were cut down by soldiers in the field. Many were arrested, were subjected to beatings and so on and had their goods and lands appropriated. The most severe repression actually followed an attempted rising by the 9th Earl of Argyll in 1685. He had been in exile abroad for several years, and his intervention proved little more than a short lived fiasco, but its suppression did something to create a bond of loyalty between the new King James and the anti-Campbell clans of the western Highlands. Indeed, the arrest and subsequent execution of the second successive Earl of Argyll was to provide something of the foundation for the later Jacobite cause in the Highlands.

After Bothwell Brig, Ure and some of his men managed to make their way back to Kippen, but he was soon being hunted down by government troops. A lion-herald appeared at Shirgarton and posted a summons for him to appear at court. Since he did not surrender himself, witnesses were called to prove that he had been with the rebels, and then a forfeiture of all his goods was passed. His rents and moveable possessions were seized and his house raided on as many as 30 separate occasions. For some months he hid out among his tenants, but troopers were quartered on them and he had to take to the moors. A reward of £100 (a small fortune at the time) was offered to anyone 'who will bring in the said James Ure dead or alive'.[33]

At the beginning of 1682 Ure, together with a number of others, was tried in his absence. The charges against him accused him of the murder of two soldiers, but no evidence was presented as to who they were nor was evidence submitted in respect of the circumstances under which such a crime had been committed. Also he was accused of complicity in the Sharpe murder and in other events with which he had no connection whatsoever. The only witness called against him was the boatman Millar, who, as we have seen, described seeing him going off with his men before Bothwell Brig. Nevertheless, on 17th January, he was found guilty, and together with the others sentenced 'to be executed to the death as traitors, when they shall be apprehended; their names, memory, and honours to be extinct – that their posterity may never have place nor be able to bruik or joyse any honour, office, and etc and to have forfaulted all and sundry their lands, and etc'.[34]

As the hunt for Ure intensified he and a few of his closest companions decided to flee to Ireland. However, Curate Young got wind of this and informed the authorities who despatched some soldiers together with a man called Methven who knew Ure to the harbours at Cartsdike and Greenock to search the Ireland-bound ships. As luck would have it Ure was at a quayside inn when the troopers boarded his ship and he thereby managed to evade capture.

During his absence his family suffered grievously, but was given great support by the surrounding community. Soldiers continued to raid Shirgarton and laid waste to his crops and sometimes to those belonging to his tenants. The tenants could not dare to be caught paying his rents (chiefly in the form of grain), but in fact they continued secretly to set them aside and to inform his wife as to where these contributions might be collected by her most trusted friends. In this way Mary was able to provide for herself and her children. In addition, some of his wealthier friends bought all of his forfeited property and allowed her to continue to live on in Shirgarton House.

Ure was not, of course, the only local Covenanter to be persecuted. The Kippen preacher, Archibald Riddell, for instance, had an extraordinary career. As was mentioned earlier, he had been intended for deportation, but had eventually been released in London and had made his way back to Scotland. In 1679 he was twice arrested for preaching, once at Haddington, and jailed at Jedburgh. In 1681 he was released from prison to see his dying mother, and during this visit he conducted a service at Kippen and baptised several infants. He was duly reported to the authorities (presumably by Young or his associates), rearrested and, together with a considerable number of other Covenanting preachers, con-fined in the prison on the Bass Rock in the Firth of Forth. In 1685 he was transported to America, where the locals welcomed him and he spent time preaching to congregations at New Bridge, Long Island, and Woodbridge, New Jersey. He remained at the latter church until 1689 when he attempted to return to Scotland, but on the voyage his ship was captured by a French 'man of war'. He and his son were taken to France and for 19 months held captive in an old hulk moored at Toulon. For another year they were imprisoned together with hundreds of others in a castle at Dinan. Finally in an exchange involving a number of Catholic priests they were released by the French government and allowed to return to Scotland. Interestingly, Mr Riddell's name appears on the roll of ministers of Kippen church under the date 1691, but if he ever was formally inducted to the church, it cannot have been for long, for in that year he was presented in the parish of Wemyss.[35]

Sometime about 1683 another field conventicle was held at Gribloch. Word had spread of this meeting and soldiers arrived and arrested many of the worshippers, including Ure's mother (a woman in her seventies), his half brother, Peter Rollo, Donald Connell of Broich and his wife, Margaret Philip, and Margaret Macklinn, whose husband was Arthur Dougall, the miller of Newmiln. The latter may well have been one of Ure's staunchest men. The prisoners were taken and at first crowded together at the Tolbooth gaol in Glasgow. The overcrowding and stress were too much for old Mrs Ure, who fell ill, but the jailers ignored pleas for assistance and she died among the crowd. The other prisoners were then taken to Leith before being sent on to the ancient Dunnottar Castle near Stonehaven where they were held for many months under appalling conditions.[36] More than 110 male and female prisoners were packed into a single vault and their state was described by two wives in a petition for relief submitted to the Privy Council.

> Where there is little or no day light at all, and contrarie to all modestie, men and women promiscuouslie togither, and fourtie and two more in another roume in the same condition, and no person allowed to come near them with meat or drink, but such bread and drink as scarce any rationall creature can live upon, and yet at extraordinary rates, being twentie pennies each pynt of ale, which is not worth a plack the pint, and the peck of sandie dustie meal is offered to them at eighteen shillings per peck. And not so much as a drink of water allowed to be carryed to them, whereby they are not only in a starving condition, but must inevitably incur a plague or other fearful diseases.[37]

Eventually several of these prisoners were sentenced to be shipped to the colonies, but Donald Connell and his wife, and perhaps some of the others, seem to have been able to secure sufficient money to persuade the ship's captain to land them at Leith.

After having been in Ireland for about six months, Ure returned to Kippen and hid out at Shirgarton and it appears that he was so well protected that for some months he remained undetected. During this time he evidently stayed several nights at the house. Mary became pregnant, and eventually this could not be concealed so that his presence in the area became known. Strenuous efforts were made by the authorities to apprehend him, but he remained free.

Much of the time he seems to have hidden on the Shirgarton stretch of the moor at what is now called Wright Park and down in the wood at the back of the Boquhan estate. Apparently Mary joined him there on many nights and there may have been others also staying with him. 'Covenanters Cave', above the Hole of Sneath on the Boquhan Burn, obviously takes its name from one hiding place behind the waterfall. (The soft stone face of the overhang of the fall and the front of the cave have worn away so that it now looks much less deep and impressive than it did in earlier times.) Dougald's (or Dougall's) Tour (tower) was a lookout point from where guard could be kept and was possibly named after Arthur Dougall or his son John. The winter of 1685 was particularly cold and on some mornings James and Mary awoke with their hair frozen to the ground and their clothes stuck together. Nearby friends and tenants looked after Ure and one such was Duncan Chrystal who had the cottage at Muirend, the stone walls of which still stand. Sometimes he was hidden there in a corn store.[38]

On other occasions, of course, Ure was able to stay closer to home, but he had many narrow escapes. For example, it is said that a party of dragoons was once sent over the hill from Glasgow to attempt his capture. Coming across from Campsie and Fintry the troopers stopped to refresh themselves at an inn at the Lernock toll. One of the servants at the inn had been a maid at Shirgarton and she overheard some of the soldiers' conversation that left her in no doubt as to the intended object of the raid. She managed to slip away from the inn undetected and ran all the way over the moor and down to Kippen, bursting in to Shirgarton House with the cry, 'The soldiers are coming!' As Ure fled from the house, so the clatter of galloping hooves could be heard above Cauldhame. Fortunately it was late summer or early autumn and he was able to rush out and lie down amid the 'victual' (tall corn), leaving the soldiers to search in vain.

No doubt such stories gained in the telling, but it is equally clear that Ure was a considerable hero to the district and that the locals came to relish shielding him from the authorities. Another story, for example, tells how one day he was working in a field with some of his men when soldiers were spotted cantering straight towards him. 'I am catcht this time,' he cried in despair. However, a quick-thinking companion promptly flung himself onto a horse and kicked its ribs to send it off in a flat gallop in the opposite direction. Without stopping the soldiers were drawn into pursuit and Ure and the others were able to watch as they went careering past. By the time they realised they were after the wrong game their target was long gone.

It was said that he developed a kind of sixth sense for when soldiers would come in search of him and that at times he would waken in the night having dreamed that they were approaching. Several times he was said to have fled only minutes before the cottage where he lay was raided so that the troopers found the bedclothes still warm. Then 'they would rage exceedingly' and sometimes arrest the tenant who had provided his shelter.[39]

In 1686, shortly after her child was born, Mary was herself arrested with several others and charged with 'going to conventicles' on the moor above Kippen and 'conversing' with her outlawed husband. She was imprisoned in Edinburgh for 14 days and, in a petition to the Council, said that she had seven children, with one 'sucking on her breist'. She had been 'brought in prisoner to the Tolbooth of Cannegett, where she has lyen in a most miserable condition with her poor infant, having neither coal nor candle and thereby reduced to a starving condition'. Friends rallied to her aid and secured her release on bail at a cost of 2000 merks (about £112). A few days later she appeared in court 'with her child in her arms', but, on the intervention of the laird of Blairdrummond, Chamberlain to the Earl of Perth, the Council declined to examine her and she was discharged. Meanwhile, James, desperate with anxiety, travelled to Edinburgh in disguise only to discover to his relief and joy that she had been released. (Interestingly, both she and the wife of Robert Harvie of Gribloch of Arnmanuel bravely continued to refuse to confess to any wrongdoing, although such statements were wrung from some of the others. In one confession it was said that of the 60 or so attending the conventicle only the outlawed Ure had been carrying weapons – presumably because he was still the one most in danger from the authorities.)[40]

During Ure's period as an outlaw curate Young sought to take advantage of his predicament by annexing to the glebe a piece of Shirgarton land known as 'the beddal's half-acre' (almost certainly what is now the Helensfield paddock). As we have seen, many of the baronies of the district contained former church lands, and this little field appears formerly to have been allotted to the mediaeval 'beddal', the monk or clerk responsible for maintaining the fabric of church buildings. When Cambuskenneth land passed into the hands of secular lairds, title to the beddal's land (and perhaps duties) was obtained (probably from the Earl of Mar) by the Forresters of Culmore and Poldar. Eventually the field was feued to the Ures and incorporated into the Shirgarton estate.

Seeing his chance, in 1680 Young secured an order from the Bishop and Synod of Dunblane disbarring Ure from the rights of the beddalship and seized the field. However, despite being a fugitive, Ure continued to defend his property. For instance, one harvest time early in the morning and together with his tenants, he crept into the field, sheared the corn and carried the crop off before Young could intervene.[41] As we shall see, this was by no means the last time that Ure would have to resist the claims of a covetous clergyman.

For most of the 1680s the prospects for the Covenanters in general and for James Ure in particular appeared to be very poor. However, the reign of King James VII (and II) brought unexpected relief. James was a Roman Catholic, and not surprisingly he attempted to have the repressive anti-Catholic laws removed. In fact, it was estimated that there were scarcely 2000 Roman Catholics in Scotland at that time, but the legal restrictions made it difficult for priests to recruit converts and, of course, the King was concerned not just with the problems of Scotland, but with those of England and Ireland as well. James, therefore, repeatedly attempted to reform the situation. His problem was, however, that it was very difficult to introduce religious toleration for Catholics while maintaining fierce pressure on what he described to his Privy Councillors as 'those enemies of Christianity . . . the field conventiclers, whom we recommend to you to root out with all the severities of our laws'.[42]

Nevertheless, despite holding such a low opinion of the Presbyterian dissenters, by June 1687 the king accepted that he had to give way on the general principles of toleration if he was to obtain Catholic emancipation. As a result a proclamation was issued announcing that henceforth all the king's subjects would be allowed 'to meet to serve God after their own way, be it in private houses, chapels, or places purposely hired or built for that use'.[43] Up to that point hopes of a restoration of Presbyterianism had seemed remote, but immediately the situation was transformed. The aristocratic members of the Privy Council had realised full well the latent preference for the Presbyterian system in Lowland Scotland and some members refused to sign the letter acknowledging the royal proclamation. As a consequence, by his decision King James forfeited significant aristocratic Scottish Episcopalian support. However, Covenanters and other Presbyterians all over the Lowlands now moved swiftly to set up their own churches.

At the end of July of that year Ure, together with many other fugitive Covenanters, found that the charges of treason against him were removed and that he was once more a free man.[44] One of his first actions thereafter was to combine with Cunninghame of Boquhan, Leckie of Dasher and other Kippen lairds to create a meeting house or temporary church and this is believed to have been located at what became known as 'Music Hall'. The appointed minister was George Barclay who was provided with 'a good manse'. Evidently, almost the whole population of the parish transferred themselves to his ministry, 'none staying with the curate but a few Jacobite lairds and their adherents', which was precisely the kind of outcome that the Privy Councillors had feared.[45] (The only identifiable Kippen laird suspected of Jacobite sympathies was Livingstone of Glentirran, although there may have been one or two others from the Buchlyvie area and connected to the Marquis of Montrose's estate. Buchlyvie did not, of course, have its own church at this time. That said, Donald Connell, Portioner of Buchlyvie, was one of Ure's staunchest supporters.)

If matters had improved dramatically for Ure and his friends, the complete revolution was brought about by events in England. Catholic emancipation and the birth of a new royal prince in June 1688 seemed to pose an immense threat to a large section of the English ruling aristocracy, who responded by encouraging the claims to the English throne of William of Orange. When the latter landed at Torbay in November of that year King James soon took flight.

Although over the years many influential Scots, such as Cardross, had joined William's entourage in Holland to obtain refuge from religious persecution, few Scots had taken part in the initial revolution. However, it was quickly clear that the foundations of the government in Scotland were now feeble. Moreover, James had called the Scottish army into England (where it accomplished nothing) and there was, therefore, no force left to the Privy Council to maintain its hold on the country. Across the Lowlands Covenanters moved swiftly to take control into their own hands.

To this stage the story of James Ure of Shirgarton is fairly easy to follow because much of it was recorded in his own 'Narrative' of Bothwell Brig and in the notes of the early-19th-century historian, Thomas McCrie, based on the writings of Wodrow and others. These sources form the main basis for the account set out in the preceding pages. However, little of Ure's subsequent life has so far been brought together and it is now appropriate to address that omission. In many ways it is an even more remarkable and interesting tale.

4

THE FIRST JACOBITE WAR
AND THE MYTH OF ROB
ROY MACGREGOR

The second half of the 17th century was by no means entirely given over to strife and struggle as far as the Kingdom of Kippen was concerned. In fact it was during these years that the modern villages began to take shape.

Up to this point, the baronies had largely been peopled by tenants who lived in farmtouns or in more isolated cottages on the moors. In addition, summer pastures would have been found at shielings on the Gargunnock and Fintry Hills. But it was at this time that the attempt was being made to establish more obviously commercial centres. Fairs had long been held – St Mauvais' annual fair on 26th October was mentioned earlier – but such fairs were originally little more than holidays or semi-religious festivals, during which some merrymaking would have been accompanied by the exchange of surplus commodities and products. Increasingly, however, the latter activity became more important.

In 1663 the heritors and parishioners of Kippen had sought approval from the Estates of Parliament to hold two yearly fairs. The 'supplication' explained that the local people

> ly at a far distance from any mercat toun, whereby they are much prejudged – put to great expences in going to fairs for buyeing of their necessaries, which otherwayes they would not be put to if there were fairs appointed to be holden at any place within the said bounds, and therefore humbly desireing two fairs yearly might be allowed them to be keepit at the said Kirk of Kippen as the supplication bears, which being taken into consideration, the King with advice and consent of his Estates of Parliament, doth hereby give and grant to the heritors and parichoners of Kippen or where the same shall be situat heirafter, in any place of the said paroche, one fair in May the other in October yearly in all time comeing – with all privileges and liberties belonging thereto.[1]

The two fairs must have soon been found to be inadequate, for in 1686 William Leckie, the laird of Dasher, obtained a further Act of the Estates of Parliament receiving permission to hold three annual fairs as well as three markets on the first three Wednesdays of December on the 'Castlehill of Dasher'.[2] The April fair was apparently known as the 'Gowk' fair, taking its name from the tradition of the April Gowk (fool), and one wonders precisely how that was celebrated at the time.

It was undoubtedly these attempts to establish thriving markets that produced the layout of the heart of the old village. The wide street front extending from the church yard up to Castlehill would have been the location for most of the fairs and it was set out in such a way as to provide room for the stalls and carts of the traders and cottagers. At what stage some of the cottages now lining the street were first built is unclear, but certainly most of the contemporary buildings are on the site of older dwellings that date from this period.

Buchlyvie developed in a very similar way at about the same time. By this stage the barony seems to have been under the feudal superiority of the Marquis of Montrose whose estate at Drymen was close by, and in 1672 a charter was granted by Charles II creating 'a Free Burgh of Barony, to be called Buchlyvie-Grahame'.[3] Thereafter, it too developed around a wide main street intended to accommodate markets.

However, the most important of the local markets were undoubtedly those held in March, May, June and August on the south side of Kippen Muir at Balgair. These were essentially cattle markets held at a convenient meeting point for drovers and buyers from the Lowlands and the Highlands. The June market became particularly notable. Cattle being brought south to Balgair could be driven round the western end of the mosses, or, in dry weather cross over a ford at Cardross. As a consequence of the latter trail Arnprior also began to develop as a hamlet at this time with the corner cottage (at the top of the Port road) evidently originating as a drovers' alehouse and the road leading up the hill from the nursery school towards Balgair became known as the Fair Loan. The main drovers' route, of course, was by the Fords of Frew and cattle were driven by that way either to Balgair or on over the Campsies by way of Ballochleam, Burnfoot, and Denny to the famous Falkirk Tryst.[4] After being sold the cattle would be taken on by the Lowland drovers to Glasgow or Edinburgh or south to Carlisle and the English markets.

Given these various efforts to develop commercial activity in the district, it will be clear that at the end of the 17th century the lairds of the area had every reason to desire a settled resolution to the political and religious conflicts that dominated the period. In addition, it should be noted that by this time some of the most accessible parts of the moss lands of the valley floor had been drained and cleared, and thoughtful lairds and their tenants would have realised that under the moss good, flat, clay soil lay waiting for cultivation. The key requirements to encourage large-scale improvement in the area must have appeared to be prolonged peace and some kind of guarantee against Highland brigandage.

As William of Orange began to consolidate his grip on the crown of England it was at first by no means certain that James VII would also be toppled from the Scottish throne. However, in late December the latter fled to France and it soon became obvious that his almost entirely unrepresentative Scottish government, 'a strange mixture of rogues and converts (of convenience) to Roman Catholicism', had become virtually powerless.[5] In Edinburgh the mob rioted and sacked the Chapel Royal at Holyrood. On Christmas Eve the Privy Council wrote to William inviting him to call a free Parliament, and in January 1689 this was followed by a request from a gathering of Scottish notables urging him to assume the administration of government and to summon a Convention. The declaration calling the Convention was duly issued early in February.

The Convention of Estates, or Parliament, was not, of course, democratic in any modern sense, being largely dominated by members of the peerage, but it did include an elected element in the burgh representatives, and everywhere across Lowland Scotland the burghs returned Presbyterian sympathisers. To the fury of its Viscount, even the burgh of Dundee elected a staunch Presbyterian to attend the first session of the Convention on 14th March.[6]

John Graham of Claverhouse – appointed 1st Viscount Dundee in 1688 – and many of the other Jacobite Episcopalians had hoped that their personal influence would be sufficient to maintain the existing régime, but as far as the Scottish Lowlands were concerned this was now seen to be an illusion. Indeed, Dundee, or 'Bloody Clavers' as he had become known for his ruthless persecution of the Covenanters, had good cause to fear for his life and therefore kept his dragoons close to hand. The Duke of Gordon, the Governor of Edinburgh Castle, was also a Jacobite, but his garrison was small and through January and February the Edinburgh citizens prevented it from being reinforced.

It was probable that when it first gathered in mid-March the Convention would be subjected to military intimidation, and to guard against that risk about 1000 armed Covenanters from all over the west of Scotland descended on Edinburgh and placed themselves under the nominal command of the Earl of Leven. Clearly, they themselves represented an intimidating force, but the truth is that they critically neutralised the presence of Dundee's troopers and the other soldiers of James's army which had come straggling back to Scotland, and they thus enabled the Convention to conduct its business in relative security.

James Ure and a number of his followers were among those who had armed themselves and rushed to Edinburgh. He later described how he had attached the Kippen company to a unit led by Lord Newbottle and, at his own expense, kept his men as part of the guard blockading the castle and protecting the Convention.[7] He received his reward for these services when he (and Donald Connell of Buchlyvie) were listed among those named by the Convention as having all the 'decreits' and penalties imposed on them by the previous régime removed and declared null and void.[8]

Indeed, all Ure's possessions and position were rapidly restored. When Shirgarton had been seized and sold by the court it had been bought and held for him by his friends who had allowed Mary and her family to live on in the house. Notwithstanding the forfeiture now being declared illegal and having title to the estate returned to him, Ure appears to have ensured that all his friends were repaid in full.[9]

When William had landed in England he had brought with him many Scots exiles who, as soon as conditions permitted, had hurried north, desperate to retrieve their own fortunes. Among the latter, of course, was Henry, Lord Cardross, whose loyal supporters in the Vale of Menteith welcomed him with delight. But by far the most important of the returning aristocrats was Archibald Campbell, 10th Earl (later 1st Duke) of Argyll. Both now took up their places in the Convention and Argyll's restoration in particular caused fear and trepidation among those Highland chieftains who had seized Campbell lands and had exploited the weakness of the Earl and his predecessors over the preceding decades. This Earl was a strange, chameleon-like character who, before fleeing into exile, had publicly opposed his father's abortive rising in 1685 and had even offered to convert to Catholicism to please James. When he returned with William he was once more a Protestant, but his real single-minded purpose was always to regain his hereditary powers and possessions.

On 16th March, when it was becoming clear that the Convention was going to declare its support for the joint monarchy of William and his Queen Mary (James's daughter), Dundee gathered his troop of Dragoons and fled from Edinburgh with the intention of rousing the Highlands for James. Within a matter of hours many of the western Covenanters had ceased to be irregulars and had formed a regiment 800 strong, under Lord Leven's command, to maintain the investment of the castle garrison and to prepare for war. (This regiment was to become the famous British army regiment, the King's Own Scottish Borderers.) A day or two later contingents of William's army led by Major General Hugh Mackay began to land at Leith and with their arrival most of the Covenanting volunteers were dismissed to return to their homes.

Ure and the others from the Kippen area had not joined Leven's regiment because, of course, they were well aware that another Highland war of the kind that had occurred during the Montrose period 50 years earlier, would be almost certain to place their homes and lands in immediate danger. Indeed, in the first instance, while the extent of the threat was still uncertain, the Convention called out the fencible men and the local militia, to organise a defence against a sudden attack from the north. On 30th March Ure was designated as a captain in the western regiment of the Perthshire militia and it is notable that other Kippen lairds – William Cunninghame of Boquhan, Sir Alexander Livingstone of Glentirran and William Leckie of Dasher – were similarly designated captains in the Stirlingshire militia.[10] Cardross, Ure and Livingstone were also among those appointed as commissioners to set and gather taxes in the counties of Perth and Stirling respectively in order to assist in providing the finance to enable the Convention to prosecute the war.

The militia regiments were purely defensive organisations of irregulars and were not really capable of significant operations, so it was evident that something else would be required if it became necessary to fight a serious war. King William, as Stadtholder of Holland, was rarely at peace with his powerful neighbour, Louis XIV of France. He was soon also to be involved in a war against James in Ireland, and there was always the (increasingly unlikely) possibility of an English counter-revolution. In consequence William could not afford to send much of his army to Scotland. Three Scottish regiments of the Anglo-Dutch Brigade, totalling about 1100 men, together with a handful of English cavalry, provided the nucleus. Otherwise William's supporters in Scotland had themselves to provide General Mackay with the troops needed to defeat a Highland rising.[11]

Dundee did not find it so very easy to gather an army. Most Lowland Episcopalians understandably were unwilling to plunge

Scotland back into the uncertainty and dangers of civil war and, therefore, remained neutral if, in many cases, uncomfortable. The Highlanders generally were more supportive, particularly the clans which were hostile to Argyll and the 'broken' clansmen, such as the Macgregors, who were always alert to the possibilities of plunder. Elsewhere, many of the chieftains were reluctant to show their hands too quickly. However, by early May Dundee had gathered about 2000 or so clansmen under his command; others were expected to join his colours before long, and James had promised to send a contingent from Ireland. It was also expected that some of the Williamite soldiers who had previously served James would change sides at the first convenient opportunity.

To assist with the establishment of the proper field army needed to quell the rising, the Convention of Estates ordered the recruitment and formation of a number of regiments, including three of particular interest in the context of the Kippen district. Lord Cardross was authorised to recruit a company of 300 dragoons to be organised into six troops of 50 men. In addition, he was given authority to raise on behalf of the 18-year-old Earl of Angus a regiment of infantry to be recruited mainly on the Douglas estates in Lanarkshire and to be commanded by another returning exile, William Cleland, who had fought alongside Ure at Bothwell Bridge. (Angus himself did not join his regiment until several years later.) Finally, Argyll's offer to raise a regiment from his own estates was accepted and Argyll himself became one of the commanders in the field.[12]

To have gathered a substantial army from the Covenanting heartlands of south-west Scotland would have been a fairly simple matter, for there many men were only too willing to avenge themselves for the long years of humiliation and particularly nurtured bitter memories of the 'Highland Host' of 1678. Indeed, on the occasions when real danger seemed to threaten such men did flock to volunteer their services. However, the members of William's administration were anxious not only to avoid the costs of the upkeep of an excessively large army; they were also conscious of the real risks of distributing weapons to thousands of men well capable of exacting revenge on their former aristocratic Lowland oppressors. As a result, recruiting in the west country was deliberately restricted. Nevertheless, the three regiments mentioned above, as well as Leven's, all had many Covenanters in their ranks.

It is also worth noting that the Argyll and Angus regiments of infantry and Cardross's dragoons provided a critical, influential military power-base during the course of the war. Noblemen such as

Argyll and Cardross and lesser Presbyterian gentry such as Ure, who had suffered at the hands of the previous government, and whose wealth and lands were constantly vulnerable because of their proximity to the lawless turbulence of Highland society, had broad, but clear objectives. First, of course, they wanted to re-establish their personal fortunes and create a basis for developing the wealth-creating potential of their lands. Second, they wanted to promote a government, at least tolerably sympathetic to their religious beliefs, but with sufficient power and authority to establish genuine security and to bring the clans under more permanent control. And finally, having known persecution, exile and poverty, they wanted to ensure that in the future the political pendulum would not swing back in such a way as to threaten them ever again. Many of the men concerned felt that ultimately such objectives could only really be attained through union between Scotland and England which was why, although they soon found aspects of the rule of William and Mary to be objectionable, they remained committed to their support. On the other hand they continued to gather as much strength as possible into their own hands while overtly providing troops for the Crown.

Dragoons had horses, and therefore, had rapid manoeuvrability, but they were more heavily armed than conventional cavalry and are really more accurately described as mounted infantry. The troopers were typically equipped with a flintlock musket and bayonet and a brace of pistols. The horses were locally obtained by a levy on the counties of Fife, Stirlingshire and Perthshire and were sturdy animals, capable of carrying a good weight and tolerant of Scottish conditions. (Interestingly, at the time English cavalry operating in Scotland tended to suffer severely from the rapid deterioration of their animals.) Cardross's 300 dragoons were certainly almost entirely found from Menteith, the Kippen district, Strathendrick and perhaps the Earl's Lothian estates. The muster rolls of 1690 show such familiar local names as Charles and John Cunninghame, Thomas and Hugh Leckie, Thomas and James Steel, Thomas and William Carson, Robert and Duncan Dow, James and John Harvie, George Spowart, John Yule, John Neel, Walter Coubrough, Robert and David Davidson, William Paterson, John Adam, Alexander Glen, James Muir, James Miller, Will Moore, John Brown, George Wilson and William Lennie.[13] Similarly one or two companies in each of the infantry regiments of both Angus and Argyll were also found from the district.

Argyll's proved to be the regiment that was slowest to form, taking more than a year to gather to its full capacity. This was probably because most of the men had to be raised from a levy of the Argyll clansmen of the western Highlands, and it involved the awkward task of welding together a force mainly of Gaelic-speaking Highlanders with a minority of Lowlanders of a strong Covenanting tradition. To attempt to train the battalion to a fighting condition, in May of 1689, 16 experienced men were transferred from a regiment of the Anglo-Dutch Brigade to form a core of sergeants and corporals.[14]

It is Argyll's regiment that provides one of the most remarkable stories of the period. Robert Wodrow was responsible for obtaining Ure's *Narrative of Bothwell Bridge* shortly after 1700 and there is no doubt that he communicated directly with Ure and was familiar with the latter's career. He recorded the episode of Ure bringing his men to help to guard the Convention of Estates and wrote that 'afterwards he was captain-lieutenant in Argyle's regiment, where he was very useful against the Highlanders'.[15]

In the regimental muster rolls there is no record of an officer named James Ure. However, in the Register of the Privy Council of Scotland on several occasions the quartermaster of the regiment is noted as one John McUre.[16] In August 1691 John McUre petitioned the Council and told it that not only was he quartermaster and paymaster of the Earl of Argyll's regiment, but that in the spring of 1689 he had brought his own men to Edinburgh, placing them under 'my Lord Newbotl's command, where he served as a sentinell upon his owne charges frae the downsitting of the Conventione till they were dismist by Mgr-General McKayes arrival'.[17]

There is little question, therefore, that James Ure of Shirgarton and John McUre, captain quartermaster of Argyll's Regiment were one and the same person. Why did he adopt a *nom de guerre*? The answer is quite straightforward. Ure, who had succeeded in remaining one jump ahead of authority for more than a decade was certainly a well known 'romantic' figure in the Vale of Menteith and in the straths to the north. However, as a key regimental quartermaster – the buyer of arms and supplies for Argyll's soldiers – he was bound also to become an identifiable figure in the commercial capitals of Edinburgh and Glasgow and, indeed, London. He would soon have been marked out by the numerous Jacobite spies frequenting the docks and military supply centres. Once identified he and his estate would have been at real risk from raids from the north. As events were to prove, this was a genuine danger, and Williamite lairds in Perthshire and Stirlingshire were frequently specifically targeted by Jacobite marauding parties.[18] The simple device of a change of name when discharging a particular task – which could, of course, not subsequently be openly acknowledged – probably provided a useful cloak in an age before photography and when most Highlanders could not read or write English. In this instance, it was not entirely successful, but for a number of reasons he was forced to maintain the deception.

In many ways Ure was an ideal quartermaster for the regiment. As we have seen, not only had he proved himself to be a skilful and resourceful soldier familiar with survival under Scottish conditions, but before Bothwell Bridge he had demonstrated himself to be adept at equipping troops. Moreover, during the long years when he had been forced to live as a fugitive on the margins between the Lowlands and the Highlands it is probable that he had become a fluent Gaelic speaker. He would have been as capable as anyone of commanding the confidence and trust of both Lowland and Highland officers and men. It is no surprise, therefore, that he should have been recruited by, or offered his services to, Argyll, particularly since some of his own men may have been among those who enlisted in the regiment. Once again the muster rolls (for April 1691) are revealing and, in addition to the host of Campbells, MacDiarmids, MacNichols and other Argyll clansmen in the Highland companies, the Lowland companies show John Syme, John Keir, Alexander Knox, Archibald Ure, Alexander and Robert Forrester, Mungo Stirling, John, Walter and Patrick Buchanan, James Dougall, William Carrick, Alexander, William and Duncan Graham, William Yule, Huw Hay, Donald McCowan, John Johnstone, Thomas Younger, John Muir, John Gunn, Duncan Clark, Thomas Wright, Duncan McCallum and John Dow – all names which resonate of long-standing families of the Kippen district.[19]

For offering to raise this regiment Argyll was soon rewarded when William restored his title to his forfeited estates, but inevitably it took time to re-establish the Earl's authority in the remoter glens and islands.

One of the initial fears of General Mackay and the Convention was of Jacobite reinforcements landing from Ireland (as had happened during the Montrose war), and to guard against this possibility Argyll's, Angus's, most of the Cardross dragoons and some other troops were ordered to the west early in July 1689.[20] Despite the rawness of his soldiers, and his fears of exhausting the resources of the countryside around Inveraray, this probably suited Argyll in his efforts to retrieve his properties. In any event, it was to be a fortunate deployment in that it enabled those concerned to avoid being caught up in the first bloody encounter of the war.

As Mackay advanced north of Perth with his army, Dundee realised that he had to secure some immediate gains if his campaign of recruitment in the Highlands was to stand any chance of success. Although somewhat outnumbered, he therefore launched his 2000 clansmen into the attack as Mackay's five infantry battalions (including Leven's) slowly decanted from the pass of Killiecrankie and advanced up the valley of the River Garry. Apparently Mackay's men had been issued with a new type of badly designed 'plug' bayonet which was intended to be engaged by being thrust or 'plugged' into the muzzles of the soldiers' muskets. While preventing the guns from being reloaded and fired again, the bayonets did not even make effective pikes, since the hilts tended to snap off in contact and, once used, were often difficult to withdraw.[21] This was a disastrous handicap for largely inexperienced troops in a close contact engagement with Highlanders whose tactics were famously one volley followed by a furious charge to bring on hand-to-hand combat.

The slaughter was dreadful, with perhaps 1200 soldiers being killed while as many fled, some to be picked off and murdered by Atholl clansmen as small groups tried to escape to safety. Interestingly Leven's was one of the battalions that did not break despite being badly mauled, and it assisted Mackay to rally the remnants of his army and retire through the night to Drummond Castle.

Dundee's men had gained a stunning victory, but had not, of course, emerged unscathed from so violent an encounter. It has been estimated that perhaps a third of the Highlanders were killed, the flintlock musket proving very effective when used as a straightforward firearm. Most importantly, Dundee himself was shot down, and apparently his body was immediately stripped and robbed by a party of Cameron clansmen,[22] an incident which, if true, provides an interesting commentary on what the Highlanders really felt about a leader who was subsequently to be portrayed by Jacobite romantics as 'Bonnie Dundee' and 'the last and best of Scots'.

The rout of Mackay's army seemed at first to leave the whole of southern Scotland open to attack and it took some time for news of Dundee's death to spread. Indeed, as clansmen staggered home laden with the booty of the army's baggage train so other doubting clan chiefs took heart and pledged their support for King James.

In the crisis Argyll's men were swiftly brought back to protect central Scotland while Mackay reorganised his other forces. On 2nd August two troops of Cardross's dragoons were ordered to Cardross, Kippen and Gargunnock to form a screen on the south bank of the

Forth, while Angus's regiment was deployed to guard Doune and Dunblane. The still self-confident Mackay, however, refused to panic or to accept help from the western Covenanters and merely called for the temporary deployment in southern Scotland of two English regiments.[23]

Argyll's regiment was still not really in a fit state to fight and at this stage it remained part of an enlarged garrison at Stirling. However, a few days later the Council ordered Angus's north to Dunkeld and Cardross's mounted troops to Perth where they were placed under General Ramsay's command.

Angus's was a remarkable battalion made up mainly of Covenanting 'madd men, not to be governed', but also including some soldiers recruited on a more normal basis. They were dubbed the Cameronians, taking the name in memory of Richard Cameron, the former leader of one of the most fanatical of the Covenanting sects. As yet the men had no uniforms, were difficult to control because they were under arms more in consequence of their desire to protect their religious freedoms than from any sense of loyalty to a king or government, and they were in low spirits. They particularly objected to the failure to provide them with proper clothing and they were disgusted by the profane behaviour of some of their officers. During their recent march to the west and back they had lost a significant number from their ranks through desertion and Colonel Cleland and his colleagues were hard pressed to hold them together. This was the unpromising beginning of what was eventually to develop into a famous regiment of the British Army.

The advance of the battalion to Dunkeld was a strange deployment apparently intended to prevent raids from Atholl into the Perthshire lowlands and to provide a base from which to launch later operations into the glens. Since Mackay was now concentrating most of his troops to the south and east of the Highlands, this one regiment of 700 or so men was extremely isolated. The more paranoid of the Cameronians in fact believed that they were being deliberately exposed by the Council, presided over at that time by the Duke of Hamilton who, resenting the harassment of Episcopalian clergy by some of the soldiers, had actually called for the regiment to be disbanded.

Assuming that the main Jacobite army was still recruiting in the north-east Highlands and that the threats were, therefore, purely local, the commander at Perth, General Ramsay, at first instructed Cardross to take 250 of his dragoons to join the Cameronians at Dunkeld. Indeed, for much of the war the two regiments were to operate together and in proximity, which was fairly appropriate since the men were very much of a similar mind. For example, in July two of the troopers, Thomas Turnbull and Samuel Welsh, had written formally to Lord Cardross to complain that 'the greater part of the troops who are engaged being persons of a principle', they objected to having to serve not only with 'profane' men, but even with some who had previously been guilty of persecuting Covenanters. They particularly condemned the recruitment of troopers who were 'guilty of all the debauchery common to man', as well as the bad example being set by the ill-mannered and uncouth personal conduct of one of the officers.[24]

When Dundee was killed, command of the Jacobite army passed to Major General Alexander Cannon, a Galloway man and professional soldier who had spent most of his career to this point in King James' army, where he had become Colonel of the Queen's Regiment. Together with a number of other officers he had been sent over from Ireland and in the aftermath of Killiecrankie he had taken charge. Initially he had been unable to prevent many of the clansmen from dispersing to their homes with their plunder, but gradually his forces had concentrated once more and by the beginning of August he had a substantial army gathering in Strathbogie.

The intrusion of the Cameronians to Dunkeld roused the resentment of the local clansmen. A fiery cross summoned several hundred men from Atholl and Strathtay and they were soon joined by a contingent of 120 Stewarts from Appin, a similar number of Macgregors under Donald Macgregor of Glengyle, father of the soon-to-be-famous Rob Roy, and a company of Macdonalds from Glencoe. At this point Cannon suddenly led his men down through the eastern Highlands and consolidated almost the entire Jacobite army in Strathtay. Estimates of its strength varied from under 3000 to the 5000 quoted by prisoners. Certainly in numerical terms it was a substantially more powerful army than had swept to success at Killiecrankie. Moreover, by his swift movement south Cannon had left Mackay and his men trailing far to the east, and the Jacobite general was entitled to believe that he had gained a perfect opportunity to annihilate the isolated garrison at Dunkeld.

As the evidence of the concentration of the clans along the upper Tay began to filter through, Ramsay ordered Cardross to withdraw to Perth. The latter, as the senior officer on the spot, at first declined and instead led a mixed party of dragoons and Cameronians up the strath to try to establish the precise nature of the forces gathering above Dunkeld, a task which would have been impossible without his horsemen. During a day of successful skirmishing while avoiding ambushes a number of Highlanders were killed and captured before contact was finally made with the vanguard of Cannon's approaching army, at which point, realising that he was now in the presence of the full Jacobite strength, Cardross rapidly fell back to Dunkeld. To his fury he then again received peremptory orders from Ramsay insisting that he withdraw the dragoons to Perth, but no similar instruction was given to the Cameronians.

Ramsay later claimed that the order to withdraw was given because the only mounted unit left to him by General Mackay was that of Cardross, and that he could not afford to have it cut off from his main infantry force at Perth. The decision has been described as a major error, but this is by no means clear. In fact, the small regiment of dragoons had already performed one of the classic functions of cavalry by identifying and giving warning of the approach of the main enemy field-force, and since it was the only troop of its type available to the General it does not seem unreasonable for him to have insisted on its temporary retirement to a safer position. Even the failure to order a similar withdrawal by the Cameronians may not deserve too severe censure. Subsequent events were certainly to suggest that they may have had better prospects from fighting from a position in the town of Dunkeld than if they had been caught retreating through open country.

Although still only 28 years old, Colonel Cleland was a skilful, experienced and resourceful soldier and he had spent the previous few days reinforcing the buildings of Dunkeld and constructing defensive dykes. In addition, because his men were short of bullets he had sent squads to strip the roof of Dunkeld House and to melt the recovered lead into musket balls. Inevitably, however, when they saw the dragoons departing, many Cameronians felt that they had been betrayed and threatened to mutiny and Cleland himself 'charged those retiring dragoons with the loss and blood of that regiment'. But he quietened his men and persuaded them to stay by threatening to shoot his own horse to demonstrate his personal resolve to share their fate.

Cleland had studied Killiecrankie and understood the importance of breaking up and absorbing the shock of the Highland charge. He therefore arranged some of his men into advanced skirmishing parties and showed the soldiers how to retreat in small groups from one prepared position to another so that the impetus of the attack would be lost. Even so the situation must have seemed fairly hopeless.

On the morning of 21st August the Highlanders descended from the hills above Dunkeld and, as they approached, the Cameronians are reported to have sung another psalm – perhaps

> If that the Lord had not our cause maintained
> When cruel men against us furiously
> Rose up in wrath, to make of us their prey[25]

and prepared the ammunition.

The Highland army advanced confidently and sent out mounted troops to cut off any possible retreat to the east. The main attack then broke first on a little hill north-east of the town where the defenders were a party under Captain Hay who, as planned, fell back slowly from dyke to dyke. In the fierce fighting he had his legs broken, but his men retreated in good order. The Highlanders now pushed in from all sides, but repeatedly found themselves brought to a halt before prepared positions and at street barricades between the houses. This was not the kind of fighting to which they were accustomed and when, on some occasions, they entered the cottages for shelter, the Cameronians blocked the doors and torched the thatched roofs.

Many of the soldiers were badly equipped and, for example, the musketeers had neither swords nor bayonets. However, Cleland had so mixed his force that those with guns were shielded by others with old-fashioned pikes and halberds and interestingly this was very similar to the tactics adopted ten years earlier by Ure at Bothwell Bridge. The musketeers were, therefore, enabled to reload and fire again and again at close range into the mass of the Highlanders. At the height of the battle Cleland and his second-in-command were both killed, but Captain George Munro continued to organise the defence and about 100 of the men retreated into the cathedral from where they maintained their resistance while others fought from the surrounding streets and houses.

By about 11 a.m. the regiment's powder was running out and Munro and his colleagues were evidently preparing to make a last suicidal stand at Dunkeld House, when abruptly the Highlanders fell back, refusing to renew the assault on the 'mad and desperate men' who had fought them to a standstill. For a time the clansmen remained in the hills to the north-west of the town, while the Cameronians set about repairing the breaches in their defensive system, not hesitating to use church pews in the process. They then sang more psalms and waited for the next attack.

When Cardross and his men had reached Perth the Earl protested to Ramsay at having been withdrawn and the General, now aware that reinforcements were hastening up from Stirling and rushing down through Strathmore, agreed to release the dragoons to speed back to Dunkeld. Later that evening Ramsay himself followed with his infantry.

In the afternoon as Cardross's horsemen approached the town the Highlanders melted away before them, retreating up the Tay valley, abandoning both their dead and their plunder. They left behind perhaps 300 killed. On the Cameronian side Cleland, his major, a captain and a lieutenant were killed, together with a score or more of the men, the exact number being obscured by the desertions which occurred both before and after the action at Dunkeld. A few days later Mackay, now with a large army, advanced into Blair and compelled the Atholl men to surrender their arms. Some soldiers of the Highland companies of Argyll's regiment (which had been among the troops that had hurried from Stirling) – and the Earl himself – behaved badly on this occasion, exacting some revenge for the ravaging of Argyll in 1685.

The strange truth is that Dunkeld can almost be described as one of the forgotten battles of the Jacobite wars. Most Scots have at least heard of Killiecrankie and Sheriffmuir and, of course, they know of Culloden, and yet the remarkable truth is that in many ways Dunkeld was more decisive than any of these more famous battles. In one morning, a single scratch battalion of Cameronians had confronted virtually the entire Highland army and fought it to a standstill. The poet of the Macdonalds of Glencoe might sneer that the 'stalwart young men' of the clans had been 'felled by bullets fired by cowherds' hiding behind walls, but the fact remained that the legend of the invincible ferocity of the Highland warriors, established in the time of the great Montrose, had been laid permanently to rest. Now it had been demonstrated that properly handled Lowland troops could be every bit as resilient and valiant as the Highlanders and that there was no real prospect of any major Jacobite success if the effort depended solely on an army raised in the Highlands. Never again, in the present war, were James' leaders able to gather a force of anything approaching similar strength and it was obvious to all that as a general, Cannon was no Montrose. In the next few weeks many of the lesser Highland chiefs slipped down to Edinburgh to submit. Indeed, it can argued that after Dunkeld all the various Jacobite enterprises were in truth not much more than the occasional spectacular flares of dying embers.[26]

The war now changed its character, becoming much more of what, in the 20th century, would be familiar as a guerrilla war. It is true that there was one more significant action when, on 1st May,

1690, Sir Thomas Livingston surprised Cannon and about 1400 Highlanders as they rested in camp at Cromdale in Strathspey. Charging straight down with his 400 dragoons Livingston swept through the Highlanders, killing perhaps 300–400 of them and forcing Cannon and the survivors to flee for their lives. Apart from this rout on the 'Houghs of Cromdale', however, the war became, on the Jacobite side, largely a matter of raiding parties, striking by stealth and surprise and melting away before proper forces could be brought against them. On the Williamite side, the response was more one of establishing garrisons to protect the most vulnerable areas while maintaining pressure to compel the recalcitrant clans to submit.

It was clear to everyone that in a military sense the Jacobites could not win a war in Scotland. Their only real hope was that the English would become disillusioned with the prolonged conflict on the Continent in support of the Dutch and that as a result there would be an English counter-revolution. Also there was the possibility that James, perhaps with the help of French troops, might obtain a victory in Ireland, thus releasing forces to invade Scotland. That none of these things was going to happen was actually fairly certain from the summer of 1690 when William's army decisively overcame the Irish Jacobites at the Boyne and when the defeat of the Anglo-Dutch fleet off Beachy Head resulted in neither an invasion by French troops nor in a rising in England. Nevertheless the war in the various theatres rumbled on for many months.

In Scotland the raiding parties were driven not just by Highland Jacobite fervour, but perhaps more importantly by economic desperation. Severe weather in May 1689 had resulted in a very poor harvest in most of the country and the following year was not much better. In addition, the war significantly disrupted the vital cattle trade so that by the early 1690s many of the Highland communities were close to starvation. In some cases, therefore, it was hard to distinguish between acts of war and simply the large-scale organised theft of food supplies. Inevitably, of course, Cannon instructed his supporters to conduct as many raids on the Lowlands as possible in order to keep the Government's forces stretched and committed to guard duties.

Following Dunkeld, very early in September a group 140 strong, led by Macgregor of Glengyle and possibly including Rob Roy, raided into Menteith and stole about 160 cows. The reivers declared that they were acting on Cannon's instructions and targeted only Lord Cardross's tenants.[27] Three of the latter, John Mroll (More?), John Anderson and Thomas Ure, described the episode in the following statement:

Donald Glass McGregor and his younger son . . . came with a considerable number of men being estimate to be about seven score to Cardross ground through the mosses . . . drove away an fold of cows belonging to John Harvey, being thirty-eight cows of them, and an fold of cows from John Anderson and Thomas Ure being forty of them, and from John Mroll twelf cows, twelf cows from Jany Somervell and William Morrison, thirty cows, from John Ure twenty cows. The half sixty broke from them before they got them carried a mile away, and the country rose and pursued them till they came to Arky [Achray].

. . . The rebells sayd to the country folke that it was not for their own sake but for their masters and that Major General Mackay raided on them a greater prejudice not long before, and that they had Cannon's order for what they did, and the sayd Donald McGregor and most of them with him were sayd to be at both the engadgments at Gilliecrankie and Dunkeld.[28]

Obviously in withdrawing after Dunkeld Macgregor had kept his men together and raided south into Menteith. What is interesting is their open insistence to the tenants that this was not just straight-forward theft and that they were acting on Cannon's orders. Apparently they were accompanied by two Lowland Jacobites specifically to identify Cardross's tenants. How far this sally penetrated into the Vale is unclear, but about this time a family called Ure, but not immediately connected to the Covenanter, were tenants at Lintmill above Arnprior and that may have been from where some of the cattle were taken. In that case the raiders would have come straight through the Cardross lands for a distance of about three miles. It is notable that the Highlanders quickly lost a good number of the stolen animals and that the people from the surrounding area came rushing and chased them across the mosses and perhaps as far as Loch Achray.

It was probably in a direct response to this raid that a chain of garrisons was immediately established to protect the Lowlands of Perthshire and Stirlingshire and these were stationed at Blair, Weem, Drummond Castle, Cambusmore, Cardross, Drumquassle near Loch Lomond and, specifically to annoy the Macgregors, at Finlarig.[29]

On 16th September the Privy Council instructed the heritors (land owners) of the parishes of Port of Menteith, Kippen, Gargunnock, Fintry, Balfron, Drymen, Aberfoyle, Campsie and Killearn to assist Lord Cardross to maintain the garrison at Cardross for six months by supplying 'fyre and candle, bedds, bedding, pottes, pannes and uttincils . . . necessar according to the number of soldiers in the said garrison'.[30]

Meanwhile in Kippen itself curate Robert Young had finally been forced from office. Congregations from all over the Lowlands had been petitioning the Council to discharge Episcopalian priests and on 3rd October such a petition was submitted on behalf of the people of Kippen by an elder called Andrew Kerr. Alleged against Young were

> the hail forsaids crymes of drunkenness, profaneing the sabeth day by busking fish hooks thereon, stricking and blooding of his neighbours thereon, speaking profane and baudie language, curssing and swearing thereon, as particularlie invocating that the devill would put ane hook in his bellie if any should sheer his corn till he was secured of his tents [had been paid his teind or tenth share – church tax] and of his using the airt of magick with his Bible and a key, and his disponeing of and making use of the poors money to his own use, with many gross and abominable crymes . . .

But if the above noted conduct did not provide sufficient cause to remove Young, the petition informed the Council that he had refused to discharge the duty of reading from the pulpit a proclamation issued by the Convention of Estates. When he was instructed to do so by two of the lairds, Mr William Leckie of Dasher and James Edmistoune of Broich, he had replied that 'tho' others could eat swine's flesh yet he would eat non of it' . . . On 20th April last he preached yet he prayed not for King William and Queen Mary'. And he refused to read orders for raising the militia, instructed elders not to pay the cess (local tax) and rejoiced 'at the report of the loss at Gilliecrankie, saying it was good news that Claverhouse had won the day'.

In his defence Young claimed not to have received the Convention's proclamation and that he had only preached in his own home. Nevertheless, the Council ordered him to be deprived of the church, manse and glebe and 'letters of horning' were issued against his ordination, meaning that he was deprived of his licence to preach in an established church.

Similarly curate Patrick Bell was removed from the church at Port of Menteith with Lord Cardross presenting the petition, and John Edmistone was forced out of Gargunnock, with the petition in this case being made on behalf of the parish by William Cunninghame of Boquhan.[31]

(In passing, the Jacobitism of the Episcopalian church in Scotland left King William little option but to give backing to the Scottish Presbyterians, even though neither he nor, in particular, Queen Mary, had any sympathy with the latter's religious views and practices. Moreover, a real problem for the joint monarchs was that most of the senior Lowland aristocracy, on whom they would instinctively have drawn to form their administration, were typically Episcopalian. The King and Queen, therefore, had to perform an awkward balancing act combining broad support for the Presbyterian Scots while striving to include many moderate Episcopalians in office. Nevertheless, in June 1690 the Episcopalian form of church government in Scotland was abolished, the Presbyterian system and General Assemblies were authorised and parishes were encouraged to reinstate ministers ousted by the previous régime.)

Despite the presence of the garrisons, over the next few months there continued to be many raids in strength, perhaps mainly because of the desperate food shortage in the Jacobite Highlands. Indeed, a few days after the first raid on Cardross a number of Macdonalds of Keppoch and Glencoe, probably also making their bitter way back from Dunkeld, had savagely pillaged Glenlyon.

Macdonalds of Glencoe were also among a party of 500 Highlanders which, in November, descended on the Kilmoronock estate south-east of Loch Lomond of the Williamite laird, William Cochrane. Against such a force the garrison at Drumquassle could do nothing but retreat into a defensive position and watch while the property was ransacked.[32]

Other raids further to the west provoked outrage and induced the Council to organise a system of warning beacons to alert both garrisons and the local militia when a raid threatened. In addition, Argyll took his regiment back to Argyllshire both to raise more auxiliaries and so to threaten the western Highlanders as to prevent them from taking part in other thrusts into the Lowlands.

In January of 1690 the Macgregors foolishly attempted a second raid on Kilmoronock, which is perhaps a measure of the desperation to which clans were being driven that winter, but on this occasion their leader, Donald Macgregor of Glengyle, was himself captured, to be subsequently imprisoned in Edinburgh.

Notwithstanding the triumph at Cromdale on 1st May, 1690 was an unpleasant year for the Williamites. The Jacobites could not win, but they could pick the time and place for raids into the central Lowlands and the small garrisons must often have felt that they were chasing shadows and sometimes being drawn into ambushes. In addition, the Government, increasingly conscious of its inability to meet the costs of maintaining so many soldiers under arms, severely restricted General Mackay's ability to conduct offensive operations. The raids, therefore, continued – more frequently on the lands of Highland lairds who had submitted, but also into the Lowlands.

As far as the Vale of Menteith was concerned, big raids, largely spearheaded by Macgregors, and possibly with Cannon and his colleague General Thomas Buchan personally present, took place in July and August of 1690. In July attacks were concentrated particularly on the lands of known Williamite lairds both north and south of the Forth and when, on one occasion, a small troop of dragoons stumbled on raiding Highlanders above Doune and attempted to interfere, the troopers were chased back almost to Stirling.[33] About this time 14,000 angry western Covenanters again assembled and offered their services to the Government which declined and instead strengthened the garrison at Stirling and ordered General Mackay, then campaigning in Strathspey, to keep more of his army in central Scotland.

Towards the end of August it was reported that 'about 130 Macgregors – who are a pack of thieves and robbers of long standing – and other rebels, that committed daily depredations in the shires of Menteith and Doune, carrying away all the cows and sheep that came their way' had raided again through Cardross. When they were spotted, 24 of the Cardross dragoons sallied out to intercept them, but were drawn into a trap and in the ensuing clash, 14 dragoons were killed, while five others, including their Captain Ramsay were captured and taken hostage. The Highlanders then resumed the attack on the neighbouring estates, gathering and driving off some herds. However, six dragoons had escaped back to Cardross and the garrison commander sent a courier racing for assistance. He reached Dunblane where the Cameronian regiment was then based together with Captain Rollo's troop of Cardross's dragoons.

The Cameronians were now commanded by a Menteith man, Colonel Fullerton, and he hurried west with two companies of the regiment together with the dragoons. As the Highlanders were withdrawing (probably north from the Frews and up through the valley of the Teith) so the troops intercepted them and a short, bloody battle ensued. Forty or so of the Macgregors and their allies were killed; about the same number, including most of their officers, were captured and the rest fled into the mountains. All of the hostages were rescued (although Captain Ramsay soon died of his wounds) and the stolen cattle and other animals were all recovered.[34]

In his account of James Ure's career, Wodrow wrote that because of his activities for Argyll's regiment, Cannon and Buchan had sent a raiding party to harry Shirgarton. Ure had been away at the time, but Mary had bravely organised the servants, called in some of the tenants and had successfully defended the house against an attack, although she had been unable to prevent some of the stock from being driven off.[35] If indeed, as was indicated previously, Ure's house was located on the position of the red sandstone cottage (the former farm steading) at Shirgarton farm it would have been an eminently defensible building commanding the crest of the ridge above the present Fore Road. Certainly Ure, with his ready access to weapons, would have ensured that his family and friends were all well armed for such an emergency, and in the circumstances the Highlanders would have found themselves confronted by a difficult nut to crack. Exactly when this incident occurred it is impossible to say, but it could well have been part of the raid of August 1690. If so the repulse at Shirgarton might have been disastrous for the Macgregors, since the delay could have given Fullerton and his Cameronians and Rollo's troop of the dragoons the time they required to rush west to intercept and destroy the raiding party. In any event, whether or not it was on this occasion, the attack on Shirgarton was not the last time that Mary would prove herself to be a doughty fighter when the need arose.

Despite this reverse, early in September the Jacobite General Buchan brought down about 300 men drawn from the central Highlands and collected 200 more from Glen Dochart and Balquhidder, before advancing towards Dunblane. News of the approach of this group reached the Stirling garrison commander, the Earl of Drumlanrig, who assumed that the Vale of Menteith was the intended Jacobite target, perhaps in the attempt to gain some revenge for the recent defeat of the Macgregors. He advanced along the Vale with a large army while Argyll brought his regiment rushing south from Perth. Alerted by sympathisers that he was walking into a trap, Buchan turned on his tracks and hastily retreated through Balquhidder, and within the next few days his men evaporated into the Highlands.[36] In the following weeks, from all directions government soldiers marched through the glens forcing the chieftains to pledge loyalty and seized or destroyed some of the crops of those who declined. In addition, a significant garrison was now established at a specially constructed fort at Inverlochy (Fort William) under the command of the veteran Colonel John Hill, further extending the pressure on the western Highlanders.

Although Buchan and Cannon remained at large, the Highlands were now in a fairly desperate condition and sheer poverty drove much of the raiding through the winter of 1690–1691. It was very difficult now to bring large raiding parties, but smaller groups came and, if they could not drive off whole herds, they continued to steal some animals as well as ransacking houses. Such raids – while still typically directed against known Williamites – were impossible to distinguish from common armed robbery. The commander-in-chief, General Mackay, was quite clear that the Highlanders remaining under arms only had the purpose of committing organised theft. In September of 1690 he had written that the disarming of the Highlanders and the destruction of the crops in the glens of parts of Inverness-shire had effectively ended resistance there and, in his view, 'the braes of Menteith, Bochwitter and other Highlands thereabout ought to be treated the same way; but since it is so near the government, I would not order it without their good finding'.[37] In other words, he was reluctant to treat the southern Highlands with the severe measures that he used further north.

The garrison at Cardross, which had no longer seemed necessary by the late autumn, was restored in January because of the continued minor activity in Menteith and in the neighbourhood of Blair Drummond and Doune.[38] However, it was now evident to local lairds that the neighbouring Highlands were starving and that some employment was necessary to help to sustain these communities; and it was also clear that the Government was increasingly unwilling and unable to support the cost of the garrisons. In February, therefore, a group of lairds, including John Buchanan of Arnprior, Robert Adam of Middleboig and William Cochrane of Kilmaronock, obtained authority from the Privy Council to establish a traditional watch to suppress cattle raiding. The watch-keepers could call out the militia when necessary, had the duty of retrieving stolen livestock and, of course, were bound in law themselves to keep the king's peace. Buchanan and the others told the Council that

> their ground and tenants are dayly harassed and oppressed by the incursions of thieves and broken men from the Highlands, querby the petitioners ground is laid waste and now are utterly destroyed and disabled either to subsist with themselves and families or to pay supplyes to the government imposed by authority.

Accordingly they wished to engage John (Iain) Macgregor of Glengyle (an elder brother of Rob Roy) and Archibald Macgregor of Kilmanan to organise the watch. Permission was granted for this arrangement and it suggests that the need was becoming obvious for co-operation along this part of the Lowland–Highland border in order to restore essential farming and to rebuild food supplies.

It is into this broad context that has to be set a frequently retold incident of 1691, known as the 'Hership' – or devastation – of Kippen which established much of the legend of Rob Roy Macgregor. The tale probably gained something through oral story telling in the 18th century, and it was perhaps first set down in written form in a few vague sentences by John Campbell in his contribution on Kippen Parish for the first *Statistical Account* (1799). It was then reproduced in the 19th century by various writers, including a brief reference in Sir Walter Scott's notes accompanying his 1817 novel *Rob Roy* and by A.H. Miller in his *History of Rob Roy* (1883). Amelia G.M. MacGregor retold the story in her two-volume *History of the Clan Gregor* (1901) and it has been repeated by various modern writers including Hamilton Howlett (1950) and most recently W.H. Murray in his *Rob Roy MacGregor* (1982), the book which inspired the film, *Rob Roy*, starring Liam Neeson. Briefly the story is as follows:

Acting on the instructions of King James (via Buchan?) 'to plunder the rebel whigs', after the harvest of 1691, the 20-year-old Rob gathered his fully armed men in Balquhidder and brought them down to Menteith where he planned to steal a herd of cattle belonging to Sir James Livingstone of Bedlormie, the latter being a scion of the family of the Earl of Callander. W.H. Murray suggests that Rob embarked on this raid because he was grief stricken at the death of his mother, and in despair at his father's continued imprisonment in Edinburgh. He was particularly enraged when, in September, his father's rents had been seized by government troops enforcing a court order intended to compel payment of prison expenses. According to Murray, 'he would take back what his clan had lost, and take it from a lowland Whig'.[39]

Rob had gained information that Livingstone's 'valuable' herd of cattle would be driven through Balfron and Kippen to Stirling and he planned to intercept it at Buchlyvie. The Macgregors came through the mosses and took up position in Buchlyvie where they waited several hours watching for the herd. Meanwhile the Buchlyvie country people, alarmed at the arrival in their midst of so many Highlanders, sent out to both Balfron and Kippen asking for help in tackling the reivers. As the locals hurried in from the fields with still no sign of the herd the precincts of the village became uncomfortable with the two sides niggling at one another, so Rob decided to move on to the south to encamp for the night on Kippen Muir. He was followed by the Buchlyvie men.

'The villagers of Kippen meanwhile had been aroused by exaggerated reports of the foray and were rapidly advancing towards Buchlyvie armed with such agricultural weapons as their agricultural pursuits supplied.'[40] (Murray suggests that these would have been 'toothed sickles, flails, cudgels and one or two straight handled scythes'.[41])

Rob and his men thus found themselves between two groups of countrymen eager to attack them, but with whom they had no quarrel. Rob attempted to avoid a fight 'knowing that the imperfect weapons that they had brought against him were unequally matched with the claymores of his own hardy mountaineers'. At this point, however, the herd for which he had been waiting all day now slowly approached and he therefore sent his men rushing to seize it. The Kippen men attempted to protect the herd and pushed the Highlanders back, but in the ensuing struggle, in order to avoid bloodshed, the Highlanders at first used only the flat of their swords. The Kippen men pushed harder and finally, in frustration, the raiders began to use their weapons in earnest whereupon 'the helpless Lowlanders fled', leaving the poor cowherd to be quickly cut down.

Rob split his force and sent one group to take the herd back to Balquhidder by way of Aberfoyle. However, his 'fierce Highland passions' had now been inflamed and he decided to teach his foolish assailants a lesson. Therefore that evening he descended on Kippen with the remainder of his party. There he found the village 'almost deserted, the panic that had seized upon its defenders had not abated, and they were afraid to return to their homes'. Confronted by such 'cowardice' he seized the cattle from every byre as a punishment and drove this second herd across the Fords of Frew and so north. Before they left, the Macgregors also burned down some buildings, including Kippen church, and it is has even been suggested by one author that at the Frews they were intercepted by a company of dragoons from Cardross which was too small to stop their withdrawal.[42] All writers agree that Livingstone's was a valuable herd and one suggests 200 head for the numbers of cattle stolen. Whatever the true figure, it is generally claimed that it was an impressive raid and that the 'Hership of Kippen' did much to establish the legend of the young Rob Roy. Murray concludes that it 'made a deep impression on the public mind as a bold isolated act, and on Whig ministers of the Crown, for the Highland line was supposed to be under the army's control'.[43]

In the context of the Highland war the use of the word 'isolated' to describe this raid seems somewhat odd, and it is interesting that none of the tellers of this tale supplies much hard evidence. Indeed, Hamilton Howlett, in 1950, wrote quite explicitly that there was not 'a scrap of contemporary evidence to back it up'. There 'is not the least evidence that Rob Roy or his clan had anything to do with the celebrated "Hership of Kippen" in September 1691, but the exploit has been attributed to him, and it is one that he would gladly have attempted, had he dared'.[44]

In fact, there is actually some circumstantial evidence for the raid, but it is interesting to consider the tale as it has come down to us. First, it simply does not ring true. Given what had happened to the Macgregors and their allies when they raided the area in strength a year earlier, the idea that they could simply have loitered about for a day or planned to spend the night camped on the moor is, all other things being equal, absurd. Also extraordinary is the notion that the people of the district were a bunch of yokels with neither the real weapons nor the knowledge of how to fight. Similarly, the idea seems incredible that men who would brutally hack down and murder an innocent cowherd would, in order to avoid bloodshed, somehow use only the flat of their swords against opponents who came at them wielding scythes, cudgels and flails.

Moreover, there are two other problems with this story. First, it is worth repeating that at the time Rob's brother and his cousin were contracted to organise the watch against cattle raiding and, under normal circumstances, the Lowland lairds would certainly have ensured that they were both completely destroyed had any serious raid taken place at the hands of young Rob. Second, at the presumed time of the raid, Rob's father was rotting in jail in Edinburgh. For Rob to have attempted such a venture, therefore, must surely have risked ending any prospect of his father's release.

As has been indicated, the evidence for this episode is intriguingly thin and mainly circumstantial. However, set properly in context it does seem possible to work out approximately what happened, and the real story of the 'Hership of Kippen' may be very much more interesting than the legend.

By the early part of 1691 it was fairly clear that while many of the Highlanders had still not formally submitted and remained difficult to control, the flames of war were dying down. General Mackay was relieved of his command and sent to assist the king's troops in Ireland and was replaced as commander-in-chief in Scotland by General Sir Thomas Livingston, the victor of Cromdale.

At the time William was desperately anxious to transfer to the war in Flanders some of his Scottish soldiers, including Angus's Cameronians, with their fine fighting reputation. Accordingly, four reorganised and strengthened regiments left Scotland in January. In addition, however, the Scottish government was now bankrupt and could not raise the revenues to pay its debts. To reduce expenditure the king ordered the amalgamation of three regiments to provide Hill's garrison at Fort William and the disbandment of one regiment of infantry and Cardross's dragoons. (These changes reduced the army in Scotland to three Scottish regiments of dragoons, four of infantry, including Argyll's – by now one of the best equipped forces in the army – and a number of 'independent' companies and two English regiments.)[45]

Like almost all of the other troops, Cardross's dragoons had not been paid for many months and, as with every other regiment, they had run up debts in most of the parts of the country in which they had been stationed over the past two years. Indeed, the Treasury did not even have sufficient funds available to give the men one month's pay on demobilisation.[46] When, in early January, it was decided to disband the dragoons they were discretely instructed to return from their present position near Aberdeen and to march 'troop be troop' to Stirling. This was presumably to prevent the regiment of horses and men from using up or pillaging the entire supplies of winter forage of every community through which they passed on the way south. Once in Stirling, the order instructed that each troop should hand over 'to the keeper of His Majesty's magazines . . . their armes upon his receipt'.[47] In the event, this order was disobeyed and the dragoons retired to their homes in and around the Vale with their arms and equipment still intact. Perhaps part of the fear was that if the weapons and horses were surrendered, Cardross and his men would never have received their arrears of pay nor have had their debts cleared.

Moreover, there was nothing that the Government could do about their defiance. As late as June Lord Cardross wrote to the Privy Council demanding payment of the debts and indicating his intention of voluntarily keeping the regiment together for the time being. 'Lord Cardross offers upon full payment of the arrears due to the said regiment to find sufficient bale beyond exception for repayment of whatsoever shall be found resting be the said regiment to the county, and in the mean tyme that he and they shall serve their Majesties the space forsaid without pay'.[48]

The Council (of which Cardross was, of course, himself a member) remitted the offer to the Treasury, but in July he was complaining that he and his officers could not get on with their ordinary affairs because they were constantly being hounded for payment of the regiment's debts.[49]

No doubt the main reason for the retention of the weapons was to provide some kind of security in order to have a prospect of having their debts cleared. However, it is also worth repeating that Argyll's, Angus's and Cardross's dragoons in particular had provided an important military power base to some of the leading Presbyterian Whigs including especially the Earl of Argyll and Cardross himself.

With the Cameronians now despatched to Flanders the retention for a time of the other two units may have had an especial political significance. It is interesting that at this point Cardross also managed to get himself appointed colonel of the militias of both Edinburgh and Linlithgow.

Initially most of the costs incurred in the maintenance of the dragoons and their horses had fallen on the lairds and their tenants of Stirlingshire and southern Perthshire. Through Gargunnock and Kippen and along the Vale of Menteith and beyond to Lomond and Strathblane the country people were owed money and were themselves experiencing hard times made worse through the succession of poor harvests and the raiding of 1690. When the dragoons returned to their homes in the early spring with news of the order to disband their regiment many of the landowners and their tenants realised that the money owed to them might never be paid. At the end of March an angry crowd of lairds descended on Stirling, demanded to see the new commander-in-chief and, when they received no satisfaction from him, seem to have allowed their anger to get out of hand, perhaps falling into violence. For whatever precise reason, General Livingston had his soldiers arrest a number of the lairds and imprison them in the Tolbooth of Stirling.

The list makes impressive reading:

> John Buchanan of Arnpryer, Douglas Buchanan of Gartengableth, Walter Grhame of Gartuir elder, James Grhame younger thereof, John Buchanan of Carbeth, John Buchanan of Craigaterne, Andrew Buchanan of Gartarten, Arthur MacFarlane also of Gartarten, Mr William Leckie of Delshores (Dasher), James Edmonstone of Broich, Thomas Grhame of Douchray, John Buchanan of Auchinmair, Robert Grhame of Gleny, Henry Grhame of Boquhapple, John Grhame of Killernie, Edward Buchanan of Spittle and Douglas Buchanan of Gartincaber.

In other words, a very high proportion of the lairds and tenant farmers of the district.[50]

When Livingston reported his action to the Privy Council on 28th March and asked for instructions he was ordered to release the men who were to submit 'bonds with sufficient cautioners' (bonds guaranteed by other men of means) which would be forfeited if the offenders breached the peace in future. The men were to present themselves to the Council on 16th April with their bonds and if any failed to do so those of them who were landowners would be liable to fines of up to the value of three years of their rents and the lesser men would be fined 2000 merks. Sir Thomas was instructed to obtain advice from Lord Cardross and Sir Colin Campbell of Aberuchill as to the credit-worthiness of the proposed cautioners (guarantors) of the bonds.

Beyond doubt, to have received such a weight of restraint on their future conduct the men must have severely rabbled the General, and this can only be seen as a measure of their anger. In the event, 'because it was seed time and expensive for them to attend Edinburgh' the lairds and their farmers were allowed to present their bonds to Livingston at Stirling, and duly did so. Most of the cautioners were found from neighbouring lairds, and interestingly one of the two who guaranteed the largest amount was James Ure of Shirgarton who stood bond for no less than £3000 on the future conduct of Thomas Graham of Duchray. This suggests not only that Thomas Graham had committed some act of particular outrage, but also that he must have had some special relationship with Ure. Perhaps indeed he may have been Mary's brother, in which case her father would have been the previous laird of Duchray, John Graham. If so, that might explain some of her fighting mettle, for the Grahams of Castle Duchray (located west of Aberfoyle, deep in what is now Lochard Forest) were a notably wild family, and enjoyed a reputation for giving and taking hard knocks. This reputation probably mainly derived from the adventures associated with living almost exactly on the boundary between Highlands and Lowlands, but the family had also famously feuded with the Earls of Menteith.[51]

Reviewing the situation, therefore, it is clear that by the summer of 1691, along the Vale of Menteith and on through Strathendrick and Strathblane, there was a host of lairds and tenant farmers, all of whom were owed significant amounts of money. They had not been paid for the supplies provided to maintain the dragoons and other army units for much of the previous two years. They felt cheated; some had been pillaged, many had orders standing over them for their future conduct, while their friends and neighbours were liable to huge financial penalties if they fell foul of the authorities again. Inevitably, therefore, the area was seething with discontent. Added to that, the dragoons were still unofficially being held in the district complete with their horses and weapons. Finally, for almost the entire year of 1691 Argyll's regiment, commanded from day to day by a local Stirlingshire man, Major Robert Duncanson of Fassokie, had been quartered at Stirling with companies manning the Forth and Perthshire garrisons in rotation. This regiment, including its two locally recruited companies, was also grossly underpaid, trailing a host of debts and frequently short of adequate rations.[52] These are all matters which have to be kept in mind when examining the context for the 'Hership of Kippen'.

There are, however, some broader issues that should also be considered. Some of the principal moderate Highland aristocrats and their Lowland allies were now certain that the Jacobite cause was lost, at least for the time being, and they therefore attempted to secure a deal or more congenial settlement with King William. In particular, John Campbell of Glenorchy, Earl of Breadalbane (in some ways Argyll's chief Campbell rival), led the attempt to obtain an agreement whereby in return for some cash payments the Highlanders would take an oath of allegiance. As a matter of honour, however, before making their submissions the chieftains wanted King James formally to release them in order to make their peace with William. Hence it took months to conclude the deal. An armistice or 'cessation' was therefore agreed, and it was to be maintained until 1st October, by which time the chieftains were required to have taken the oath, whereupon they would be pardoned for their previous actions. (This deadline was later extended to 1st January, 1692.)

William, in Flanders, and still more Queen Mary in London, who was responsible for many of the day-to-day decisions, became fairly enthusiastic for this initiative as a means of bringing the irritating conflict in Scotland to a reasonable conclusion. Moreover, Breadalbane also proposed to control the clans in future with a locally raised 4000-strong Highland Watch, largely under his command, and this would relieve more royal troops for the war in Flanders. Finally, however, the settlement would enable a more 'Episcopalian' aristocratic administration to be formed to bring the Scottish and English governments into closer alignment. From William's point of view such an outcome was desirable for, as he told Bishop Rose of Edinburgh, he now understood that 'the great body of the nobility and gentry are for Episcopacy, and 'tis the trading and inferior sort are for Presbytery'.[53]

In consequence of these proposals, through the summer of 1691 the Presbyterian majority on the Scottish Privy Council and their allies across the Lowlands were suddenly confronted with the nightmare of a return to power of an 'Episcopalian' administration largely made up of individuals whom they regarded as 'crypto-Jacobites'. In addition, if Breadalbane's plan were accepted, such a government would have significant military muscle in the form of a powerful force that looked suspiciously like a permanent 'Highland Host'. Paul Hopkins argues that it was for this reason that during this period the Presbyterians were bent on undermining both the cessation and William's confidence in the Episcopalians.[54]

Set in context, therefore, it should already be clear that the traditional tale of the Hership of Kippen is mainly nonsense. Had the Macgregors attempted a 'normal' raid in the summer or early autumn of 1691, they would not have been able to loiter about before walking off with two herds. Indeed, with Cardross's dragoons at their homes in Kippen and around the valley, Argyll's infantry garrisoning Cardross, Doune and Stirling, and bitterly angry farmers throughout the length and breadth of the district, it is most unlikely that the raiders would have been confronted just by cudgels and scythes or that many of them would have returned safely to Balquhidder.

However, the context does indicate two possible explanations for what happened. The first is fairly straightforward. The Earl of Cardross and the lairds wanted to recover their debts, but without risking their bonds or the money of their guarantors. Almost certainly the owner of the herd was not Sir James Livingstone of Bedlormie, but Sir Alexander Livingstone of Glentirran, which would explain why the herd was in the neighbourhood of Kippen in the first place. Sir Alexander, who had been awarded his knighthood of Nova Scotia in 1685, was the illegitimate son of the 2nd Earl of Callander and the leading Episcopalian of the district.[55] Sir James and Sir Alexander were actually briefly related through the short-lived marriage of Sir Alexander's stepmother, Mary, to Sir James, and the two men may well have co-operated and in so doing caused the confusion over the ownership of the herd. Since Sir James owned an estate at Westquarter near Falkirk, it is quite possible that Sir Alexander's herd had been taken there to be secure from the raiding which had threatened Menteith through 1690. By the summer of 1691 it may have seemed safe to bring the cattle back to Glentirran by driving them over the moors from Falkirk via Carron and Fintry, so passing Balgair on the way to Kippen.

This explanation, therefore, suggests that a secret deal had been struck between some of the Kippen lairds (probably including Cardross himself) and the Macgregor watch-keepers to have young Rob bring across a party to intercept and steal the herd. The cattle would then have been taken north, reset, and sold at various markets, with the proceeds being shared out among the plotters. In targeting the property of an Episcopalian laird the organisers of the theft would have been doing no more than repeating the tactics of the Highlanders who had directed their attentions so frequently on known Williamites. Obviously John and Archibald Macgregor could not do the raid themselves without risking their jobs, the task therefore being given to John's younger brother. Similarly, the dragoons and Argyll's men would have been kept well out of the way. Those countrymen who did turn up to jostle the raiders may have done so either in ignorance or in order to make a pretence, but either way this would explain why only the flat sides of swords were used, why the 'defenders' quickly retreated and why the village was found to be deserted. The burning of the church was a nice touch to add a bit of colour, since this would have been the old half-ruined mediaeval church which had been abandoned three years earlier by all of the congregation except the Episcopalians. Interestingly a brand new church – the gable end of which still stands in the church yard – was opened later that same year. Finally, the real reward for the Macgregors – apart perhaps from a share of the loot – would have been that Cardross and his friends would have promised to persuade the Privy Council to release Rob's father Donald. This release was duly obtained on 1st October, and all the prison expenses waived.[56]

This explanation, then, would explain the Hership purely as a scam, by means of which the local lairds recouped some of their losses. To do so they would have connived at the theft of a herd from what they considered to be a neo-Jacobite Episcopalian neighbour, while in return for their help the Macgregors obtained Donald of Glengyle's freedom. (In passing, James Ure almost certainly had a hand in just such a venture. Wodrow recorded that Ure 'observed the righteousness of providence, in making some of his persecutors taste of the cup he had drunk so deep of', and McCrie also states that Ure 'continued zealous to his principles against the Jacobite lairds . . . with whom he had many encounters'.[57] It seems clear, therefore, that he had his revenge on some of the local Episcopalians who had co-operated in his persecution, and Sir Alexander Livingstone seems a very likely candidate for this type of punishment.)

The second possible explanation of the Hership is rather more sinister. Most of the facets of the raid would have been exactly as described above, but in this case the intention behind the plot would not just have been to retrieve money which people felt to be due to them. The main purpose of the supposed outrage may have been partly deliberately to destabilise and sabotage the settlement being brokered by the Earl of Breadalbane by engineering an apparent gross breach of the truce. In this case, the fact that the herd probably belonged to Sir Alexander Livingstone of Glentirran becomes even more interesting, since he was a cousin of the Earl of Linlithgow, one of the principal Lowland Episcopalians at that time actually negotiating with King William in support of Breadalbane's plan.

One of the problems in evaluating this case is that it has not proved possible to establish the precise date of the Hership. Tradition locates it in September, but there is absolutely no confirmation of this. Indeed, the only circumstantial information is a report which indicates a raid south of the Forth in late July.[58] If indeed this was the occasion of the 'attack' on Kippen, then the sequence is fascinating.

Early that month General Sir Thomas Livingston (a staunch Presbyterian, unrelated to Sir Alexander) was allowed by the Council to inform Argyll of the planned truce or cessation. On the 14th the Earl replied, bitterly protesting against any such agreement, but his letter was 'layd asyde without answering'.[59] A day or two later the Scottish Privy Council authorised Livingston to move his army closer to the Highlands as a threat, but taking care not to bring on an actual conflict. Then on 29th July the Council recalled Livingston and wrote to Queen Mary as follows: 'Wee have given order to Sir Thomas Livingston to stop the march of the troops towards the Highlands till farder order, *notwithstanding a new insolence committed there* . . .'[60] Three weeks later, on 17th August, William wrote from Flanders authorising the Council to issue a proclamation restoring those rebels who took the oath of allegiance, offering to extend the deadline and ordering the army to return to its winter quarters. Towards the end of this letter, however, the king's tone changed abruptly from one of reconciliation to one of harsh anger. He condemned specifically the thieving activities of the Macgregors, and instructed the Council to issue a proclamation 'certifying our good subjects of the dainger they incurr by intertaining that clan' and requiring all landlords on whose land Macgregors resided to provide sureties against any depredations which they might commit in future. Inevitably within a few months many landlords were anxious to evict all Macgregors from their properties.[61]

If the Kippen raid was the 'new insolence' that took place towards the end of July and was intended to destabilise the agreement, the possibility is that Argyll and Cardross may have been the real puppet-masters behind the plot, perhaps with Ure acting as their agent. They may have hoped to arouse the king's fury by convincing him that Highland raiders had broken the truce. Paul Hopkins, without shedding specific light on the raid, nevertheless concludes that in explaining the King's ire against the Macgregors 'possibly the decisive event was Rob Roy's first major exploit, the "Hership of Kippen"', and certainly if it took place in late July it would appear to fit the time-frame.[62] In addition, it is undoubtedly curious that while

General Livingston and some of the others wished finally to pacify the Highlands through the example of a ruthless punitive operation (a view which came to be shared by the king himself), no such expedition was mounted against the Macgregors, and instead Donald of Glengyle was released from jail and his expenses waived. This suggests that despite the king's outrage, Donald and his kinsmen had some very powerful protectors. Rather it was another clan of cattle thieves, the poor Macdonalds of Glencoe, which received the punishment when, on the instructions of General Livingston, a Highland company of Argyll's regiment entered their glen on 13th February, 1692 and committed the notorious massacre which has haunted the Highlands ever since.

Because of the deceptive nature of the Hership we may never know for certain precisely what happened, although the second explanation offered above seems likely to be very close to the truth. However, from the point of view of many of Rob's men, who were probably completely unaware of the source of his instructions, and also perhaps from the perceptions of the similarly ignorant country people who watched the events unfold in and around Buchlyvie and Kippen, the Hership may well have seemed to be just as it has come down to us in the traditional tale. None of the real plotters could tell the truth, of course, and hence the romantic legend of Rob Roy Macgregor, the brave and bold Highland reiver, was launched by an elaborate confidence trick and theft organised by Lowlanders against a Jacobite sympathising laird.

In passing, another Kippen tale that helped to build up the myth of Rob is also worth setting briefly in context. In the recent film, in a complete travesty of the truth, Henry Cunninghame of Boquhan is depicted as a talented, but very sleazy 'English' swordsman who was the tool of an evil Duke of Montrose. Both characterisations are nonsense. However, in W.H. Murray's book the story is repeated of Cunninghame, 'a Lowland fop, whose affectation was an effeminate delicacy of manner, dress and speech', quarrelling with Rob in the corner pub at Arnprior. Cunninghame's sword was hidden by a friend anxious 'to save the poor boy from quick slaughter', but in his rage the Kippen man searched out a rusty old sword in a corner of the inn, and after just one pass, such was the fury of Cunninghame's challenge that Rob turned and ran away.[63] In some traditions, he fled through the pub window. Indeed, some of this may not be so far from the truth. However, it is appropriate to point out that Henry Cunninghame was the son of Margaret, Lord Cardross's sister and a brother of one of the officers of the dragoons. Far from being a feckless youth, he was well regarded, and on one occasion Cardross attempted to obtain for him the post of 'Clerk of the Exchequer or Treasurie'.[64] Undoubtedly if Rob got into a dispute with this young man – and wanted to get back to his home in one piece – he did well to take to his heels whether or not the latter was a competent swordsman.

As is the brutal nature of civil wars, the first Jacobite war in Scotland brought immense distress to the country. Apart from the loss of life on both sides, the Highlands and many near areas of the Lowlands were devastated by the repeated raiding and by the looting and plundering of soldiers and Highland reivers alike. In addition, the administration of the country was bankrupt because of the impossibility of finding sufficient tax income in Scotland and because the separate English government regarded the matter purely as a Scottish problem. James Ure did not escape the miserable consequences.

As was mentioned previously, it took many months for Argyll's regiment, with its mixture of Highland and Lowland companies, to be brought up to its full fighting strength of 13 companies, and for the first year the Earl himself funded the entire cost out of his own purse. Understandably, this burden gave him cause for bitter complaint. However, by 1691 the unit was as well organised and equipped as any in the army.

The soldiers' uniforms apparently consisted of red coats with yellow facings, loose grey breeches tied with ribbons below the knee, yellow stockings and high-fronted, steel buckled black shoes. Beneath their coats the men had long tartan waistcoats and by the second winter of the war their rough woollen plaids had been replaced by greatcoats. On their heads they wore blue bonnets with a badge embroidered in London to the design of a Huguenot exile and consisting of an earl's coronet combined with the boar's head of Argyll. Most of the clothing was apparently made in London on Ure's instructions and shipped to Leith.

The soldiers were equipped to the standard of the best contemporary English regiments. Each company had 60 men, one third bearing pikes and the remainder equipped with first class flintlock muskets. The troopers also had a 'hanger', a sword encased in a black leather scabbard which hung from their left side. On the right side of the belt was carried the 'patrontash', a cartridge box containing twelve rounds of powder and ball, and behind hung a modern bayonet. The latter was capable of being locked onto the musket barrel, thus enabling the gun to be fired or used as a pike as the situation required.

Clearly Ure had accomplished his task very well and even the equipment of the regimental surgeon had not been neglected. John Prebble tells us that 'Argyll was childishly pleased with his regiment when he saw it drawn up on parade at Perth or Stirling'. The Earl wrote to Lord Melville boasting that 'scarce any new regiment can be in better order than mine'.[65]

Nevertheless, despite being armed to a high standard and clothed in a manner far beyond their normal civilian expectations, the men were often extremely unhappy, particularly when their wages did not appear and when food supplies became scarce. At one point in May 1690, when there was neither money for their pay nor to buy their food, the soldiers dropped their weapons and mutinied, and it was Ure that was faced with the crisis. Perhaps the Earl was at William's court in Flanders at the time or possibly he had simply absented himself because he could no longer afford to foot the bills. In any event, Ure was confronted with a situation where the regiment was about to disintegrate, and this would have been disastrous both for the prosecution of the war and for the Earl's honour and reputation. To avoid these disasters, on his own personal credit Ure borrowed £733 5s 9d sterling from Edinburgh lenders and used this money to defuse the crisis. As he later told the Privy Council: 'when the regiment brock and threw doune their armes for want of bread, the petitioner by said advanced money did keep them togither in their Majesties' service, as is nottour to all the officers of the regiment and attested by the major thereof, his declarations subscribed be him on the fifteenth day of May 1690'.[66]

Since one pound sterling was 12 times the value of a pound Scots, this was a huge amount of debt for a country laird to take on his own shoulders. Even so, when a similar disaster threatened a few weeks later, he borrowed another £100, again on his personal credit.

This situation, of course, could not go on indefinitely, and by January 1691 Ure was in trouble. The wife of a Glasgow merchant took action against Major Archibald Rollo (perhaps Ure's kinsman) of the regiment, seeking to have the latter's wages arrested for non-payment of a bill of £14 18s in respect of supplies, the account being made out in the quartermaster's name. The problem at this stage was referred to the Treasury.[67]

Six months later Ure was arrested and imprisoned in the Tolbooth of the Canongate of Edinburgh. Far from advancing the money to deal with the regiment's debts the Lords of the Treasury had declined to take any action until they discovered how much income was going to be raised from taxation. The other regiments funded from the

Scottish budget were in much the same plight as Argyll's, and to
address the general problems of the Government's lack of money
they had decided to introduce the notoriously inefficient 'hearth tax'.
On 16th August Ure found himself imprisoned on the initiative of
some of the money-lenders from whom he had obtained his borrowings in order to keep the regiment going.

The timing of this arrest again provides some further room for
speculation. Was the situation simply as it appears to be from a
straightforward reading of the records? Or could it perhaps be that
Sir Alexander Livingstone, Lord Linlithgow and some of their friends
had become suspicious of the true nature of the Hership of Kippen
and regarded Ure as one of the ringleaders? Did Ure's imprisonment
in mid-August have as much to do with the loss of a valuable herd in
late July as with the regiment's unpaid bills?

In any event, on 27th August Ure petitioned the Privy Council to
order his release and demonstrated how outrageously he had been
treated. Not surprisingly the Council did order his release, but they
also upheld the validity of the claims made against him and the
regiment and again referred the matter to the Treasury. This effectively meant that his creditors could continue to keep him in jail until
a means was agreed of discharging the debts.

All told, Argyll had spent about £12,000 on his soldiers' pay,
clothing and weapons and £7478 was still owed to him by the
Government. The Earl was perfectly willing that Ure's share of the
debt should be met as a priority and the Lords of the Treasury now
awarded Ure the proceeds of the hearth tax for the county of
Lanarkshire in order to raise the necessary money. However, to act for
him in collecting this tax Ure had to appoint a constable, James
Melvill of Cassangray (one of his creditors), and ten other substitutes.

On 9th April 1692 Ure once again petitioned the Council for his
release. Melvill claimed that the collection of the tax had only
yielded £800, and that by the time his fees and costs had been
deducted, there was insufficient left to pay all of Ure's bills. Unless
the debts owed to Melvill were paid in full the latter was unwilling to
agree to Ure's release. Once again, the Council ordered Ure to be set
free provided he could find an acceptable guarantor and urged the
Treasury to provide the money. Ure's proposed 'cautioner' was the
Provost of Glasgow.[68]

At this point the trail of the affair seems to disappear from the
records, but by this stage King William had decided to deploy
Argyll's regiment to the war in Flanders. To the fury of the chief
commissioner of the English Treasury this transfer meant that the

costs of the regiment's upkeep became his problem. In order to obtain the Earl's consent to sending his men overseas, in May 1692 Argyll therefore had his debts paid by the English government together with some interest, which presumably meant that Ure too finally had the burden removed.[69]

(As a matter of interest, Argyll's regiment was taken to Flanders under the command of Robert Jackson, formerly colonel of Lord Cardross's dragoons, and it acquitted itself with considerable distinction. In one action in 1693 it drove the French from a defensive position between the rivers Scheldt and Lys at D'Otignies and Captain Thomas Drummond's company of grenadiers in particular covered itself in glory when it held on against a force 'thirty times their number'. Nevertheless, unlike the Cameronians, the regiment was disbanded in 1697 at the end of the war.[70])

Poor Ure had suffered grievously during his nine months of imprisonment. The jail itself he described as 'noisome' and he blamed it for the 'distemper' which had broken out on his skin. His creditors had pursued him so relentlessly that he had scarcely been able to obtain sufficient food, and in his absence his estate had been neglected. More tragically his family had been 'afflicted with fevers and other sickness whereoff four of them have died which adds greatly to his distress'.[71]

Nevertheless we are told by Wodrow that, despite 'all his sore sufferings', James Ure did live on into old age, surviving to see the defeat of the second Jacobite rising in 1715, and finally dying in peace in his own home, 'much lamented by all the good people that had been acquaint with him'.

As an old man he had one more battle to fight, for in 1708 and again in 1710 the minister, Michael Potter, had attempted to renew Curate Young's old claim to the 'Beddal's half acre' paddock. At this time Potter had the advantage in that his father, also Michael Potter, was moderator of the Presbytery of Dunblane and he arranged an official visit to Kippen to address the problem. Potter junior pointed out that his glebe had a road passing through it and that consequently it did not contain the full four acres to which he was entitled. He demanded that both pieces of land be measured and that the shortfall in the glebe should be made good by the addition of the paddock. Throughout the legal part of this action, both during the visitation and in court, Ure was defended by his son James, by now a lawyer and soon to become a Writer to the Signet.

When the Presbytery and officials came to Kippen to consider the problem in October 1710 they arranged to have the glebe measured.

This was done by the literal use of poles and chains and the usable area of the field was found to be 'two acres and three roods and fourteen falls, so that it wants ane acre and twenty-six falls of ground to make its complete four acres'. The accuracy of the measurement was bitterly contested by the Ures who pointed out that some of the land used by the minister had not been included in the calculation. They also rejected the notion that the church authorities could make good any shortfall by seizing the paddock, at that time being leased to one of Ure's tenants, James Rennie. Nevertheless, the Presbytery ordered the little field to be measured and this precipitated what might be termed the 'battle of the half acre'.

Mary Ure and her daughters Christian and Agnes and daughter-in-law, Elizabeth Montgomery and Lillias Baillie, and Abigail Miller and [Anne?] Dougall, both married to other Ure men, together with some servants and a number of other women, appeared on the scene and prevented further progress with the measuring. At first it seems merely to have been a question of pulling up pegs and generally disrupting the process. However, according to the Presbytery minute, when challenged by the official Mary said 'that she would not suffer him nor any man to measure the land and thereupon flew upon him'. The men now attempted to carry out the measuring by force and by physically holding the poles and staves in position, but the women retaliated, and under a hail of stones the members of the Presbytery were driven to seek shelter in the church. Ure and his son meanwhile prudently absented themselves from the scene and ignored the ministers' messages demanding that the women be restrained.[72]

The decision was now made to postpone the action for a month to permit tempers to cool and this gave the younger James Ure the time to take action in the Court of Session. Here the judges' finding was that the Presbytery could not unilaterally appropriate Ure's land and that if such were permitted it would threaten the many owners of former church lands all over Scotland. Decisions on questions of this kind were matters for the civil courts and not for the church authorities.[73] Effectively this removed the challenge throughout the remaining years of Ure's life. However, it did leave the problem that the minister's glebe was smaller than was required by church regulations. Perhaps because of some residual resentment at his initiation of the process, nothing seems to have been done to address this matter during the remainder of Mr Potter's ministry in Kippen. But a little later, in 1756, a 'line of substitutes was settled' which allowed the minister's field to be increased to the stipulated four acres. Some other Shirgarton land was made available in order to enable ground to the north and east to be incorporated into the glebe. In addition, it was further extended in useful size when the old road (which used to run up past the mediaeval church) and its verges were made redundant and returned to cultivation. (This latter development may have followed the construction of the new military (or Dumbarton) road, the lane that runs from Rennies Loan down to Little Broich.) As a result of these changes, by the later 18th century the glebe measured almost five acres. However, despite now possessing a field substantially larger than the size specified by the church, some later ministers still occasionally remained puzzled. Perhaps they found it difficult to understand that something popularly known as 'the Beddal's half Acre' did not belong to the church, and that, as with Ladylands farm, it was simply a fragment of former mediaeval church lands which had passed into secular hands.

Before leaving the story of James Ure of Shirgarton, it is perhaps worth reflecting briefly on the significance of the events through which he lived and in which he played a not inconsiderable part. It has sometimes been claimed with some justice that Scottish history has undergone a 'Highlanding' process, through which the past of the Highlands and the past of Scotland as a whole have come to be seen as one and the same thing.[74] In this way, for example, the Jacobite wars came to be depicted not so much as civil wars, but as conflicts between Scotland and England. Moreover, while a misty aura came to surround the memory of the ancient Highland clan society as it faded into the past, the Lowlanders of the period were remembered with little more than grudging contempt. A typical example of the attitude was provided by R.B. Cunninghame Graham when he described the Lowlanders as 'bodachs' – small, unimportant people who were 'dull . . . and . . . uninteresting', mere clodhoppers – in contrast to the much more exciting, romantic Highlanders with their passionate conflicts and whimsical Gaelic culture.[75] Nineteenth-century writers, most notably Sir Walter Scott (and monarchs, particularly Queen Victoria), also searching for the symbols of a Scottish identity, furthered the process and, with the help of the British Army, even managed to convert a highly stylised artificial version of male Highland dress into something which is now taken to be Scottish. In fact, of course, to Lowland Scots of Ure's generation and beyond, the old homespun woollen plaid of the Highlanders, forerunner of the modern kilt, was an object regarded with disdain and contempt. It was no accident that the plaid was discarded in favour of breeches, red jacket and greatcoat when Ure equipped the mixed Highlanders and Lowlanders of Argyll's regiment.

During the huge social and economic changes that overtook Scotland in the 18th and 19th centuries much of the history of the earlier period was forgotten, neglected and corrupted in the telling. Lowland Scots, as with the Highlanders, migrated in huge numbers to the growing cities of central Scotland and England or to North America, Australia and New Zealand, while incoming Irish migrants also changed much of the cultural balance of the Scottish population. As a result the achievement of Ure's generation of Lowlanders was more forgotten than celebrated. In addition, many modern historians have not been comfortable with Presbyterianism, often associating it with repression, narrowness of mind and bigotry. For example, even so formidable a scholar as Paul Hopkins can scarcely write the word Presbyterian without relating it to an adjective such as 'extremist', when the truth is that at the time Presbyterians were neither more nor less extreme than their political or religious opponents.

Undoubtedly frequently motivated as much by personal economic self interest as by religious beliefs, the reality is that the Covenanters also struggled to assert a set of principles which left an invaluable legacy to later generations. Their persecution taught them the importance of the freedom to worship according to individual conscience. Their support of a form of church government through representative general assemblies led them to believe in parliamentary government, perhaps headed by a constitutional monarch, but with authority restricted by a concept of limited sovereignty which acknowledged the ultimate interests of the people as a whole. They struggled to diffuse power and influence throughout an ever-widening spectrum of society. And some of their most important leaders pursued permanent internal peace and security by promoting the political unity of the British Isles.

In advancing such beliefs the Presbyterians of Lowland Scotland of the late 17th century prepared the way for much of the economic, intellectual, social and political progress of the following years. They were far more in tune with the requirements of the emerging modern world than were their Highland counterparts and they can accurately be described as the fathers or grandfathers of the Scottish Enlightenment. By contrast, for all the romantic veneer that came to surround the Highlanders, their violent, lawless and poverty-stricken way of life had little genuine relevance to the future. It is, therefore, a real irony that it is a Highland rascal, a fairly unpleasant character, Rob Roy, the contributor of little or nothing of significant value, who is celebrated by modern Scotland in books and films and whose statue takes pride of place in the royal burgh of Stirling. On the other hand, the memory of his contemporary, James Ure of Shirgarton, whose life embodied many features of an authentic Scottish Lowland hero, is preserved by little more than a name on a stone in an overgrown corner of a disused country churchyard.

5

KIPPEN IN THE 18TH AND 19TH CENTURIES

Neither of the Jacobite risings of 1715 and 1745 made much immediate impact on Kippen although on both occasions the Fords of Frew played a part in the train of events. However, the risings were to leave important legacies to the district.

In 1715 the Highlanders and Episcopalians of the North-East rallying behind the Earl of Mar to the standard of James Stuart, 'the Old Pretender', found themselves confronted by government forces which were pitifully weak, but led by a splendid general. John Campbell, 2nd Duke of Argyll, who came to be known to his clansmen and admirers as 'Red John of the Battles', was perhaps second only to the great Duke of Marlborough as the most renowned British soldier of the age. In 1707, as a politician, the young Argyll had played a major part in unifying the parliaments of Scotland and England and, in his military career, he had distinguished himself in some of Marlborough's campaigns in northern Europe. When the rising occurred, despite the lack of troops in Scotland, he determined to hold Stirling until reinforcements could be brought north.

At the beginning of the rebellion the Government had little more than 1500 regular soldiers in garrisons scattered throughout Scotland. Mar quickly raised perhaps 12,000 troops, mostly from the Highlands and north-east, but hesitated to bring them south of the Forth, instead waiting to see if there would be uprisings in support of Prince James elsewhere in the country. However, by the late autumn the Earl had finally nerved himself to begin his attack, and he started to march down from Perth with his main force with the intention of crossing over the Forth at the Frews. Because the northerners did not know the route over the fords, it was apparently hoped that Rob Roy Macgregor would lead the way, although the latter was not greatly trusted, particularly since he was believed to have some personal allegiance to Argyll.[1]

The Duke had made good use of the extra time given by his

opponent's procrastination. He concentrated the available soldiers at Stirling and called out the militia to take the places of the various key Lowland garrisons. For example, the dragoons that had been covering the Frews were ordered to join his main force while their guard duties were taken over by a considerable company of militia. The militia as a whole were described by a French Jacobite observer as 'nearly all Presbyterians and for this reason regarded as enemies of the Pretender and strongly attached to the Duke of Argyll whose forebears have always been the chiefs of this sect. They vulgarly call themselves 'Cameronians'.[2] There can be little doubt that many of the Kippen men, with their local knowledge, would have been with the group barring the way at the Frews.

As Mar advanced south, so Argyll decided to intercept his progress on the moors above Dunblane and the two armies clashed at Sheriffmuir on 13th October. More than 9000 Jacobites far outnumbered the 3500 or so soldiers led by Argyll, but the battle was superficially inconclusive. One wing of the government army was driven into flight, but the troops immediately under Argyll's command similarly routed their direct Highland opponents. At the end of the day, Argyll had lost perhaps 600 of his men, while 800 or so rebels were killed. According to Sir Walter Scott, Rob Roy and his men watched the struggle, but declined to intervene, presumably not being entirely sure on which side their bread would be best buttered.[3] Despite being an apparent draw, in outcome the battle was actually decisive in that it effectively ended the rebellion, the Jacobite army disintegrating in the course of the bitter winter months that followed. Early in February 1716 James slipped sadly away to France.

The rising of 1745 was, of course, much more dramatic, although strangely Prince Charles Edward Stuart rarely, if ever, mustered as many men in his army as had followed his father's banner. On this occasion, however, with the prince personally at their head, the Highlanders moved with rather more alacrity. Again, to begin with they were faced by fewer than 3000 troops in Scotland, this time under very indifferent leadership.

By 1745 attitudes may have changed significantly so that active Jacobitism in Scotland was now rather more confined to the Highlands. Even the lairds of the north-eastern areas which had given support to his father, were now at first much more reluctant to become involved, and this partly explains why Charles had with him little more than 2000 men when, on 13th September he advanced to the Fords of Frew. It is very interesting to note that this time the Lowlanders were far slower to organise themselves to resist. It seems that as the 18th century had advanced so the notion of a rebellion to restore the Stuarts had become more and more fanciful to southern Scots and the danger from the Highlands had seemed to recede. In consequence, far from rushing to take up arms, in 1745 many Lowlanders at first watched the progress of Charles and his men with almost paralysed astonishment.

The Frews were guarded by a company of dragoons under a Colonel Gardner, but the regular soldiers did not know the area and did not realise that there were a number of crossing points which required to be covered (which suggests that no local men were involved). When it was suddenly realised that Highlanders were appearing behind them, Gardner and his men beat a rapid retreat and the Jacobites were able to come over without resistance. Charles was intent on a prompt advance to Edinburgh and turned at once to the east, hence Kippen appears to have remained undisturbed by his troops. He spent his first night south of the Forth at Leckie House near Gargunnock.

This is not the place to recount the astonishing story of how, excited by his initial success, more Jacobites rallied to the Prince, and proceeded to terrify and amaze the country. A detailed account of their rapid victory at Prestonpans, their march deep into the heart England, their weary, despairing retreat from Derby, and the gallant check which they inflicted on their pursuers at Falkirk, would take more space than can be justified here. It is sufficient to record that, as they retreated north on the way to their sad fate at Culloden, Charles' army once more passed over the Frews.

On this occasion, on 1st February, 1746, the fords were again guarded by a small company of government dragoons. With the Duke of Cumberland's main army already approaching the outskirts of Stirling, there was nothing to be gained from contesting the passage, and the dragoons withdrew, contenting themselves with casting caltrops into the bed of the stream on the main crossing point. Caltrops were metal balls with four spikes and were designed to disable horses. There is also a tradition that one of the local blacksmiths added to the hazard by throwing some sets of iron harrows into the water. However, it appears that most of the Highlanders crossed at a different place and were not at all inconvenienced by the traps, although there is a suggestion that some of the horses pulling artillery pieces were hurt and that, as a result, cannons were lost in the river. This is not certain since a magazine temporarily stored in the church at St Ninian's had accidentally blown up a few days previously, and the weapons may have been destroyed at that time. But, whatever the reason for the loss, the lack of the field artillery was to prove serious at Culloden.[4]

To the west of Boquhan there is a stone well on which was inscribed 'Prince's Well, 1790'. Whether Charles Edward stopped there to drink either on his way south or north, it is impossible to say. However, it is believed that during the retreat together with a number of his officers the 'Young Pretender' did dine at the old Boquhan House.

Given the lack of support in mainland Britain south of the Forth, the '45 Rebellion had not the remotest chance of real success, despite its dramatic course. Nevertheless, it did provide endless inspiration to the following generation of romantic writers, poets and singers. However, some parts of the country, including Kippen, were actually left a rather more substantial and practical legacy. In the aftermath of the rising of 1715, between 1726 and 1737, under the guidance of General George Wade, the army had constructed an extensive network of 250 miles of road across the Highlands in order to enable troops to move rapidly between the more important strategic locations. 'If you'd seen these roads before they were made, You'd get down on your knees and bless General Wade', ran the old rhyme in celebration. After the '45 this process was greatly extended, with a further 600 miles of roadway and many fine bridges being constructed. 'They did the Royal Engineers much credit, for they were the best roads in the United Kingdom.'[5]

This activity touched Kippen in the period 1745–1755 with the completion of the Stirling to Dumbarton military road, which in places was made by building on and improving existing lanes. The road came through Gargunnock, past the Burnton and by means of the lovely 'auld brig of Boquhan' entered the eastern end of Kippen parish. It followed the line of the lane through the old Glentirran barony to Music Hall, and by the Burnside to Kippen cross. There it passed in front of the first Crown Inn (which then stood by the churchyard gate and by its name advertised to the world the royal and anti-Jacobite sympathies of the community). The road then ran down by way of what is now known as Rennie's Loan to Little Broich. From there, in a course which has now been lost, it struck to the south, passing the site of the present Shirgarton House on its way to the Brig of Broich, whence it led on to Arnprior and Buchlyvie. (The lane from Strewiebank Balloch to Little Broich curiously did not form part of the military road, but rather was originally the Shirgarton peat road, running up from the mosses to the old mansion and farmtoun.)

The rebellion also led to the construction of bridges at the site of the fords at Frew and at Cardross. Francis Buchanan of Arnprior was one of the very few local lairds who had given support to Prince Charles, perhaps because Buchanan had also become a Highland laird, having acquired land in Balquhidder and Strathyre. Because of his participation in the rising he was arrested and subsequently beheaded and Arnprior was one of the properties – including farms, distillery and mill – that were appropriated and for 40 years run by the Commissioners of the Forfeited Estates. (Arnprior was eventually returned to his sister, Jean Buchanan.) The income from the estates was used to fund part of the construction activity, and this included building the two bridges, the one at Cardross in 1774, and the other at the Frews in 1783. The Cardross Bridge, 200 feet in length and with three 41-foot spans, cost £250 sterling, and the Latin inscription giving the date of opening reads: 'Traveller may you cross safely. Be mindful of the Royal Benefaction.'[6]

The Brig of Frew was first proposed in the 1760s, but funds were diverted to the more expensive Drip Cobble Bridge closer to Stirling. However, work on the project was finally commenced in 1779, partly in response to the fact that a road was being constructed south from Callander and it was intended to be the mail link with Glasgow. The Brig of Frew did not prove easy to construct. At one point the cooms, or arch supports, sank into the clay bottom of the river, causing the central arch to 'key itself'. Then a flood swept away the main and north arches, so that essentially the whole bridge had to be rebuilt. Nevertheless, it was finally opened for traffic in1783 with the help of a £200 grant from the Forfeited Estates.[7] (The old Brig of Frew was an attractive structure, but it was sometimes claimed that it was poorly sited, being close to the point where the Boquhan Burn enters the Forth. As a consequence, it was often held to be responsible for the flooding of adjacent fields and was therefore largely demolished when a new bridge was built in the 1950s.)

In his *Statistical Account* of 1799 Mr Campbell was in no doubt that the opening of the roads had resulted in a considerable increase in arable farming activity in the district, since the farmers were now able to transfer their produce to the growing urban markets. In addition, the improved communications probably also stimulated domestic manufacturing, since Campbell also notes that a number of businessmen from Glasgow were travelling round the area placing spinning, weaving and other manufacturing work with the cottagers.

The union of the Scottish and English parliaments in 1707 did not immediately improve the maintenance of law and order along the fringes between the Highlands and Lowlands of Scotland. On the contrary, at first Scottish internal problems were given very little priority and, as noted above, the British parliament was reluctant to pay for a standing army of sufficient strength to keep the peace. As a result, people in the Vale of Menteith were still occasionally disturbed by the activities of their northern neighbours. The truth was, of course, that the growing population of the Highlands was constantly tending to outstrip the economic resources of the region, so that in years of poor harvests – frequent occurrences between 1690 and 1710 – theft of one kind or another was almost inevitable. To restrain this activity, lairds often felt bound to pay what would today be described as protection money to the more dangerous of the potential thieves.

Rob Roy Macgregor came to specialise in this nasty trade, exacting payments of 'Black Mail' in return for 'protecting' the lands and tenants of the lairds in question. One tale from the period, if true, illustrates his technique. On this occasion in 1710, Stirling of Garden returned home with his wife to find himself locked out of his old moated tower house. In his absence Macgregor had occupied the building and he would not allow the laird entry until he agreed to pay 'Black Mail' money. Mr Stirling spiritedly refused to give way to such bullying, whereupon Rob Roy brought one of the Stirling children from the nursery and dangled the infant out of an upstairs window. With his wife's 'entreaties' ringing in his ears, Stirling had little choice but to give way and stump up.[8]

'Forcible marriage' was another of the more unpleasant features of the old Highland society and it was not uncommon for clansmen to kidnap or steal women, both from other parts of the Highlands as well as from Lowland communities. Very often the real object was to compel a marriage which would lead eventually to rights of ownership to a significant property. The most notorious incident of this kind occurred in 1696 when Simon Fraser of Beaufort kidnapped his cousin, Lady Amelia, widow of the previous Lord Lovat. With Fraser's bagpipers playing outside to drown her cries, the widow was raped and forcibly married, in the belief that the shame would prevent her from repudiating the marriage at a later date and so give Simon access to her estate.[9]

A very similar incident occurred near Kippen in December 1750, and the perpetrators on this occasion were four of Rob Roy's sons. In 1744 Mr John Kay of Edinbellie (a property on the edge of Kippen Muir not far from Lernock, but in the parish of Balfron) died, leaving his considerable wealth to his only daughter, Jean, then just 11 years old. As the years passed Jean Kay naturally grew to be a girl of considerable interest to the surrounding district and soon she had many suitors. When she was 18 she married John Wright, son of the laird of Easter Glinns, part of which then extended into what is now known as Wright Park. Tragically, within a year of the marriage, in October 1750, John Wright suddenly died, leaving his young widow as the possessor of a sizeable fortune.

Robin (or Robert) Oig Macgregor, was outlawed in 1736, accused of having committed a murder. To avoid trial, he had fled to Europe and had apparently soldiered for a time, being wounded at the Battle of Fontenoy in 1745, before returning penniless to Scotland. As he was a widower, when he learned of Jean Kay, the death of her young husband and the fortune that she had inherited, he decided that she would make him an ideal wife. There is no evidence that there had been any previous contact between Robin and Jean, or that he had made any attempt to win her by legitimate means. The first approach apparently was a message sent up to Wright Park from the Black Bull Inn at Kippen demanding that Macgregor be allowed to meet the young woman, and this suggests that the start of the whole affair may have been a spontaneous reaction to idle pub gossip. (The Black Bull, built in 1729 and recently renovated, is now a beautiful private house in Rennie's Loan.)

The request for an interview was promptly rejected, and although it was less than two months since John Wright's death, Robin immediately decided to take the law into his own hands. When his note had arrived, Jean's mother Janet, who was fully aware of the reputation of the Macgregors, had urged her daughter to retire at once to Glasgow for safety, but instead she had merely moved with her household to her childhood home at Edinbellie. Robin, together with his brothers James, Ronald and Duncan Macgregor (or Drummond) and five other men, now came down from Balquhidder and, with two Gartmore whisky smugglers to guide them, descended on Edinbellie late in the evening of 8th December, 1750. The Highlanders, 'armed with guns, swords, durks, pistols, or other warlike weapons' surrounded the house in order to prevent any escape, and then Robin and two of his brothers burst through the door. They found only Jean's mother and aunt and a number of servants, but threatened 'to murder every person in the family, or to burn the house and every person in it alive' unless Jean was produced. The girl had been hiding in a closet, but the terrified women were quickly frightened into revealing her whereabouts. She was then seized and, with wrists and arms bound, laid across the saddle of the horse of one of the kidnappers and carried off, screaming and crying for help all the while. For a time a guard was left on the house to prevent the alarm being raised and, according to the subsequent indictment, before the gangsters left they threatened 'immediately to murder any person who should offer to give the said Jean Kay the least assistance'. Meanwhile the kidnappers fled through the night to the house of a John Leckie at Buchanan near Loch Lomondside, and while they were stopped there Jean was seen to be still in great distress. At Rowardennan the party took one or more boats and made good their escape up the loch and, for the moment, out of the immediate reach of the law.

For the next three months or so Jean was taken from place to place in order to obstruct any rescue attempt, and at some stage during this period a forcible or pretended marriage was conducted between the young woman and Robin Macgregor 'without the free consent and against the will of the said Jean Kay'. However, in view of the likely course of events, and to protect her property, her friends had acted to have her estate sequestrated and to have warrants issued for the arrest of the offenders. It was just as well that they did, for, as the following old rhyme illustrates, no one was in much doubt as to the motive behind her kidnapping.

Rob Roy is frae the Hielands come
Down to the Lowland border
And he has stolen that lady away
To haud his house in order.

With her inheritance!

The legal intervention prevented the Macgregors from obtaining any access to Jean's wealth and an attempt to negotiate her release also broke down. However, in the spring of 1751 Robin's brother James brought her to Edinburgh in an effort to prove to the authorities that she had now given her consent to the marriage and to ask the court to lift the suspension order on her estate. In cases of this kind establishing the truth was sometimes very difficult because the victim was faced with a dreadful dilemma in trying to decide where her best interests had come to lie. Grossly unfairly, whatever decision she took, she was likely to have become a subject of notoriety and prurient curiosity and, in the climate of the time, may have felt that she carried a burden of shame. By this stage she may even have developed genuine feelings towards her abuser and, of course, might also have become pregnant. In these circumstances, provided the husband who had been forced on her was not unbearable, many women in this position tended to acknowledge the legitimacy of the marriage.

This, of course, was precisely the reaction that the kidnappers were hoping for.

In Edinburgh Jean was interviewed by a judge, Henry Home, later Lord Kames, who offered to protect her if she would speak the truth. She agreed that she had been forcibly abducted, but said that she had now become reconciled to Robin and had come to love him. The judge, however, was not satisfied with her answers, 'finding that she embarrassed herself, and could not make her story consistent'. The young woman was therefore, taken into protection, and James Macgregor was instructed to return home. With James removed, Jean now completely changed her story, and in a statement of 20th May, 1751 agreed that she had been kidnapped from her home, raped and forced into a marriage against her will. She was given protection, sent to join her family in Glasgow, and eventually warrants were issued for the arrest of Robin, James and the seven other men involved in the incident.

James Macgregor was captured and imprisoned in Edinburgh Castle pending trial and when questioned he admitted that the forced wedding had taken place at Rowardennan, which means that it may indeed have occurred within hours of the abduction. Almost unbelievably, a year later James managed to break free from the castle disguised as a cobbler, and he escaped justice by fleeing abroad. Following a court martial, as a punishment for allowing this to happen, two lieutenants were discharged from the army, a sergeant was reduced to the ranks and the gatekeeper was flogged.

The younger brother, Duncan Macgregor, was also arrested and tried for his part in the affair, but he pled that he had been unaware of his older brothers' intentions and that he had not meant to be party to anything criminal. As a result he was discharged.

Robin Oig Macgregor eluded capture for several months. However, in May 1753 some soldiers from the fort at Inversnaid trapped him in Gartmore village. He was taken to Edinburgh, charged with the old Scots' offence of 'hamesuckin' – assaulting someone in his/her own house – 'violent abduction', and forcing Jean Kay into a marriage against her will. He was duly convicted and publicly executed in the Grassmarket of Edinburgh on 16th February, 1754. On the scaffold, where 'he was very genteely dressed', he admitted his guilt of the crime against Jean Kay. Sadly, by that time the poor girl was no longer alive, for in October 1751, while staying with relatives in Glasgow she had died after contracting smallpox. She is buried in Kippen's old churchyard.[10]

Interestingly, it was in the year 1750 or 1751 that building of the three-storey, neo-Palladian Georgian country house of Wright Park was commenced, and its splendid structure indicates something of the wealth which she had possessed. It is not known whether it was begun under her direction, or while John Wright was still alive or possibly immediately after her death, but it is a magnificent house which, perhaps because of its isolated and tree-sheltered location, receives rather less attention than it deserves. It remains virtually complete in its original form, which makes it a genuine architectural treasure.

The events surrounding Jean Kay's abduction demonstrate how dangerous and uncertain life could still be around the fringes of the Highlands in the mid-18th century. However, the fact that her kidnappers were eventually brought to court also shows that, particularly after the '45, the criminal law was gradually extending public safety even into relatively inaccessible Highland communities.

In the earlier period the local baron courts were responsible for the administration of petty justice and the Kippen baronies were no exception. Some of the records of Garden's baron court have survived and an example of one case of 1703 is as follows: 'Charles McFeat, drinking with others in the house of William Carrick at Middle Mye, had words with William Kilpatrick, servant to William Carrick. McFeat took up his staff and beat Kilpatrick to the effusion of blood . . . Janet MacAllastair, spouse to William Carrick, being redding [trying to rescue] also got struck, to the effusion of her blood.'

McFeat pled guilty to striking Kilpatrick, but did not remember inflicting on Janet the 'redder's stroke' (the blow received by someone attempting to separate those who were fighting). The laird fined him £100 Scots (£8 6s 8d sterling), a fairly hefty punishment at the time.[11]

The legal function of the baron courts was ended in the 1730s by the 20th Act of Parliament of the reign of George II. Its termination was a response to the gradual development of a modern judicial system of criminal law as well as recognition that arbitrary justice dependent more or less on the whims of individual lairds was no longer acceptable. From that point the baronies began to decline in significance and in many cases began to break up in the face of agricultural development. However, up until the early years of the 20th century some lairds continued to play a critical part in the progress of the Kippen district.

Henry, 3rd Lord Cardross, did not long survive the first Jacobite war, dying in 1693 'from the effects of the hardships he had undergone'. Nor did his title, Earl of Cardross, continue for many years after his death, since his son, David, who had served with the dragoons, soon came to adopt the style of the senior title which he had inherited, namely the Earl of Buchan. Consequently the Cardross estate passed to a junior branch of the Erskine family. Nevertheless, for many decades the Erskines of Cardross remained the most influential land-owning family of the Kingdom of Kippen and, for example, provided the chief patron of the Kirk.

The impoverished Lord Graham of Menteith, who died in 1694, also effectively terminated his ancient earldom, since he had no direct legitimate heir and his estate, more a matter of debts rather than wealth, passed to his nephew, Sir John Graham of Gartmore. He and his descendants were also major heritors in Kippen. The great Gartmore House which, from its commanding location towards the western end of the Vale, seemed to oversee the whole district, was built at the beginning of the 18th century and extensively enlarged about 1780. The radical politician, Robert Graham of Gartmore, who was admired by the Rev. John Campbell, author of the Kippen section of the *First Statistical Account*, owned much of the land in and around Kippen village and it is probable that it was in his honour that Graham Street was named. The little lane originally led from the military road up through a series of feu plots, and existed before the Fore Road was created. In 1796, a year before his death, Robert adopted the style Cunninghame Graham. He had inherited from his mother the Finlaystoun estate of her brother, the last Earl of Glencairn and, in a practice that was quite common at the time in such circumstances, he added his mother's maiden name to his own to form the double-barreled style subsequently used by his descendants.

The Stirlings, of course, continued to provide the lairds of Garden and to exercise a significant influence. For example, John Campbell drew attention to the improving activities of the laird of Garden of his time. In order to provide incentives, the latter apparently repaid his tenants the cost of draining their land through the construction of deep stone-filled ditches which were then covered with a layer of soil three feet in depth, thus permitting the fields to be tilled without damage to ploughs.[12] Similarly the next laird of the period 1816–1842 was particularly notable for his tree-planting activities as well as for keeping meticulous day-by-day diary records of weather conditions.

Broich, Shirgarton, Dasher and Glentirran were all broken up during the process of farm enclosure in the period around 1800, probably partly as a result of successful tenants acquiring ownership of the land and partly through lairds simply selling off their properties. No doubt some lairds sold out to pay debts, but others, such as James Ure, the lawyer son of the Covenanter, may have become absentee landlords while establishing alternative careers in the rapidly growing cities. Shirgarton barony seems to have been sold off in parcels from about 1760, some of it being originally bought and owned for a time by the Earl of Craufurd (presumably the origin of the farm name, Crawfordston). The lands south of Shirgarton farm and at Strewiebank, however, were obtained by the Harvies, long established local tenant farmers. The Ure family did continue in the area for many decades, but in the form of a female succession from Mary Ure, the Covenanter's granddaughter, to the Galbraiths of Blackhouse and Littlecarse (both farms reclaimed from the carse at this time). The Galbraiths were originally lairds of Hill of Balgair and Mary's brother-in-law was forebear to what became a distinguished Scottish political family, which is represented in the current generation by Lord Strathclyde, leader of the Conservative Party in the House of Lords.

In 1753 the Edmonstones moved to the estate of Duntreath (near Blanefield) and Broich was sold to the Leckie Ewings. This family, which was later responsible for the building of the mansion at Arngomery, produced a notable succession of soldiers.

The other key improving lairds were, of course, the Fletcher-Campbells of Boquhan. Although Boquhan was not in Kippen parish, the Campbell lands spread into Kippen and it appears that at different times the family obtained ownership of parts of both Glentirran and Dasher. A succession of Campbell lairds, notably General John Fletcher-Campbell and his son, Henry, led the way in their own estates by propagating modern ideas of drainage and crop rotation and by encouraging the introduction of new and alternative crop strains. They were also influential in initiating from 1794 district ploughing matches to stimulate improved breeds of plough horse, standards of plough design and the workmanship of the ploughmen. In that first competition £12 was distributed among the seven best contestants and subsequently Kippen farmers competed in the events organised by the ploughing or farming societies of Gargunnock and Buchlyvie.

However, an even more influential landowner, in terms of his impact on the Vale of Menteith as a whole, was the judge, Lord Kames. The Home estates were located in Berwickshire, but Kames inherited his wife's Blair Drummond properties and it was there that he chose to live and where he began to put into practice the ideas that were to transform the area. Kames had an immense enthusiasm for agricultural improvement and he used to hurry back from his work in the court in Edinburgh to push and cajole his men in his attempt to drain the mosses of his lands adjacent to the River Teith. At first his efforts were a source of amusement to neighbouring lairds, but the latter were soon forced to change their minds. Kames cut great ditches through the peat-bog and made his men dig through and break up the surface peat. He then got the engineer, Mr Meikle of Alloa to construct a huge 28-foot diameter water wheel that was positioned by the Teith at the Mill of Tor. An aqueduct was then laid for more than half a mile and when the water wheel was set going it forced water from the Teith along the aqueduct, which then washed over the ridge of land and into the Forth, gradually taking with it the loosened peat. Thereafter, chopped-up peat was thrown into the ditches from where water driven by the great wheel flushed it into the rivers and out into the estuary.

To engage the necessary labour and to farm the good clay soil that was being recovered, Kames looked to recruit migrants from the Highlands. He offered low wages, and supplies of meal and the timber with which to construct a dwelling, but he did provide tools, including wooden spades to dig the moss. Most importantly, he gave each man a 38-year lease on eight to ten acres of moss land, rent free for the first eight years, and no more than a peppercorn level for the next eleven. Even when full rents became due, only 2s 6d was to be charged annually for each acre still covered with peat.

Kames' plan was obviously designed to secure the supply of cheap labour required to accomplish the huge task of drainage which he had in mind, but given the poverty existing in so much of the Highlands he clearly offered many families the prospect of creating a better future for themselves. The first 'colonists' were settled to the task in 1767 and by 1774 13 tenants had uncovered 104 acres of the low moss between Stirling and Doune. The 'moss lairds' were initially objects of scorn to the surrounding community, but in time their progress became a matter of envy, and recruits soon had to be limited because of the scarcity of water to carry away the waste peat. Other carse landlords, seeing what was being accomplished had quickly moved to follow the example being set, but their lands were typically in positions where forced water was not available. Nevertheless, they encouraged peat clearance, retrieved the ancient forest remains and cleared the water courses. The fall of the Forth from Gartmore to Stirling was estimated to average only about one foot per mile, so that the flow of the water towards the estuary was inevitably fairly sluggish and it was, of course, tidal. However, considerable improvements were made to the river by removing tree trunks and other debris from the main channel. In addition, various lairds reached agreements with neighbours to concentrate the flow of burns coming down from the hills so as to promote drainage of the uplands south of the carse as well as on the carse itself.

The main Kames project came to an end formally in 1865 when the floating of peat down river was declared to be a public nuisance. It had resulted in the creation of a filthy pulp which floated on the surface of the lower river, and was held to be responsible for the destruction of the oyster beds as well as ruining salmon stocks. Long before then, however, many of the original leases had expired and the cheap rents had generally been discontinued because the value of the improved land had risen rapidly. Inevitably, many of the smallholders had difficulty meeting high rentals and found it hard to resist the temptation to sell, but it is believed that many of the families did at least enjoy a good profit on the ultimate sale of their leases. Altogether it was reckoned that Lord Kames effectively created up to 1000 livelihoods through his reclamation project.[13]

The 'moss lairds' of the carse as far to the west as Kippen were less able to dispose of the moss and peat by casting it into the river, although a pump located at Middle Kerse did replicate something of Kames' technique on a smaller scale. However, most families in the district continued to use some peat as domestic fuel through the first half of the 19th century, hence a little of the better material was consumed in this useful way as the local lairds encouraged clearance as a means of adding to the value of their properties. By the 1790s Rev. John Campbell noted that labour to remove the moss could be bought for about £5–£6 sterling per acre and when the task was done the annual earning value of an acre would have risen to about 15s–20s. This means that the cost of improvement could be recovered in approximately six–nine years. For lairds who could afford the outlay it made good sense, but Campbell also noted that tenants with a typical 19-year lease required more of an incentive before they regarded it as worth making the effort. In the Kippen neighbourhood moss clearance tended to involve using the winter months to scrape off the lighter surface material, ploughing up the main layer and then burning the loosened peat in the drier months of May and June. Sometimes it was necessary to repeat the process more than once. Finally, the ashes could be mixed up with manure, and perhaps also with some of the deep peat and surface clay to produce a good soil. In any event, it was a laborious process, in many cases accomplished with fairly inefficient ploughs or sometimes with no more than spades. For example, this last was the main basic means deployed by members of the McGibbon family in the clearance of the farms of Faraway and Easter Garden.[14]

The strip of land closest to the banks of the Forth was identified as the most naturally fertile of the recovered carse land and it was described as the 'haugh' or 'holm'. But the flat clay soil as a whole was good and was soon being used to produce 'rich crops of every kind of grain common in this country; particularly wheat, beans and peas, and oats'.[15] Naturally, of course, some of the land remained prone to flooding and a wet season could be a sore trial to the farmers concerned.

As noted, the leaders of the local effort were the Fletcher-Campbells of Boquhan and in 1845 it was written of their estate:

> Less than a century ago the lands lay almost in a state of nature, unprofitable to the landlord and repulsive to the agricultural operators; bad roads, the want of enclosures, the stiffness of the soil and ignorance of that species of farming which was not suitable to the District. But headed by the proprietor of the estate of Boquhan and stimulated by his energetic and skilful examples all the heritors in the Carse of Stirling united or rather vied in effort such as draining, ditching, hedging, planting and other improving operations, and speedily achieved a complete and delightful change of both their aspects and their character. [By 1800] only about two acres on the property of Boquhan remained in a mossy condition.[16]

In 1841 Rev. William Anderson calculated that the parish of Kippen contained 5238 acres of cultivated land, 3431 of which were on the dry-field or rising ground and 1807 on recovered carse land. In addition there were a further 4256 acres of moor, just under half described as high pasture, the remainder being unrecovered moss, 300 acres of which Anderson believed could readily be improved to a useful state. Two hundred acres of the pasture were unenclosed common land; there was natural woodland extending to 62 acres and there were 500 acres of planted woods.[17]

In Mr Campbell's time oats, barley and bear (coarse barley) were the main arable crops, with large quantities being sold to Glasgow and the West Highlands for food. However, much of the barley grown in the parish was purchased by local whisky distillers and maltmen, and about half of both the barley and the malt was sold on to Highland distillers. Much less wheat was grown because it was believed that the relatively damp climate was unsuitable and it was very easy to lose a wheat crop in a wet year. Smaller amounts of peas and beans were grown and flax, potatoes and turnips were all produced for local consumption rather than for market.[18] Mr Anderson's report 48 years later indicates that about 12 per cent of the value of the arable crops grown in the parish was being produced from the cultivation and sale of hay, so it was probably in this period that the excellence of the carse land for growing hay for fodder and seed was realised.[19] In addition, the numbers of livestock being retained through the winter months were increasing, so that the market for winter feed was also growing.

If drainage and moss clearance were the primary farming advances of the latter part of the 18th century, the other agricultural activity that blossomed at that time was the Balgair associated trade in cattle. The gradual improvement in security, the ending of the most serious incidents of cattle theft and above all, the mushrooming demand from the growing cities of central Scotland and England, led to the expansion of trade with Highland drovers. In the Kippen parish itself Campbell reckoned that about 1600 head of cattle were being grazed at any one time and 200 or so were bought or sold each year. Forty years on and Mr Anderson was also enthusing about cattle. He pointed out that the main local herds were made up of Ayrshire cows and that great efforts were being made by local farmers to improve the quality of the stock. However, since much of the Balgair business was in black beef cattle, this suggests that Kippen's involvement dealt much more with a through trade rather than direct production for meat. Dairy products for sale to Stirling and Glasgow would seem to have been the main output of the local cattle farmers and there were several flourishing creameries in the district. Curiously, Mr Campbell notes that whereas most tenants traditionally had kept a few sheep mainly for their wool, enclosure of the land had considerably reduced this activity and he believed that at his time the parish contained a total flock of no more than 200 head.

In the 1790s Campbell was meticulous in his listing of the stocks kept by local farmers. For instance, he noted that they possessed about 360 horses, 165 ploughs and 285 carts. He also mentioned that there were three two-wheeled chaises, which presumably did not include the carriages of the gentry.[20]

As the prosperity of the landed community increased it is not surprising that fine buildings soon began to appear at the heart of the main properties. The 18th-century Boquhan mansion has gone, but The Steading (1817), with its pedimented entrance pend, and copper-domed octagonal clock tower, remains as a splendid example of a grand stable courtyard of the period. In 1824 Garden was also completely reconstructed as a classic mansion and another especially fine house of the time is the nearby Arnprior Farm. It is a lovely and entirely unspoilt late 18th-century small mansion, two storeys at the front and three at the back, and its beautiful rooms have some exquisite interior wood and plaster finishes.

The 19th century was, of course, the heyday of horse-drawn farming and the infrastructure needed to support this developed strongly, with many blacksmiths flourishing, not only to shoe the horses, but also to make and repair their implements. Breeding bigger and stronger horses became an extremely important activity, and by the end of the century Kippen district had become particularly notable for producing magnificent Clydesdales of the highest quality. With their powerful physique and generally gentle temperament these horses were the ideal farmer's friend and there was great competition among breeders.

An underlying feature of Scotland through the period in question was the growth in the population, which is believed to have roughly doubled in the course of the 18th century, and doubled again in the first 40 or so years after 1800. It was this population explosion which provided the basis for the expansion of the developing cities. In a rural parish like Kippen pressure of mouths to feed probably meant that many households lived close to the margins of subsistence and that even small changes in the economy of the district could produce significant migrations. For example, in the 1790s John Campbell noted that the enclosure of farmlands was tending to displace some of the cottagers, but also that the development of manufacturing in the neighbouring parish of Balfron in the preceding decade meant that 'many families as well as individuals have removed to that village'.[21] The historians Tom Devine and Rosalind Mitchison suggested that 'two thirds of the families listed for the village of Kippen in Stirlingshire in 1789 were not there in 1793',[22] and probably based that calculation on the contents of a notebook in which the local ministers had maintained precise details of every family in the community. They concluded that the population of central Scotland at the time had become highly mobile. Unfortunately this valuable little book seems now to have been mislaid, but almost certainly the migration noted was simply a local adjustment to take advantage of the weaving jobs being created in that decade in Balfron. Interestingly, however, despite this movement, in the *Statistical Account* Campbell recorded the population of Kippen parish in 1793 as being 1777 persons and estimated that to be only 163 fewer than were counted ten years earlier, but 327 more than were recorded in 1764. Of the 1777 residents, 343 were

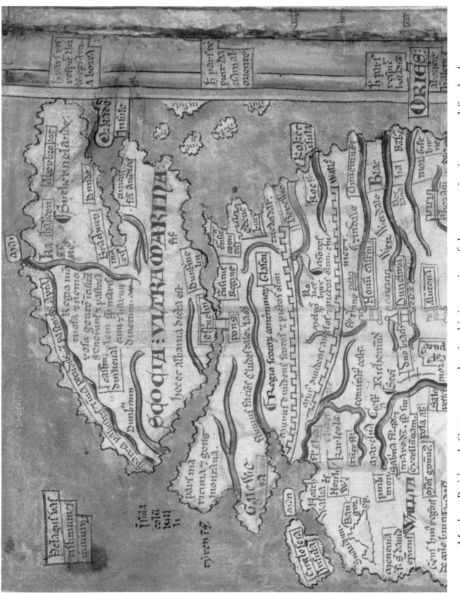

Matthew Paris's 12th-Century map showing his impression of the seas cutting into central Scotland. (By permission of the British Library – Cott. Claud. DVI, F12 V.)

A cast of the Kirkmadrine stone. (By permission of the National Museum of Scotland – X.1B.90.)

A high altitude photograph of Kippen village and its immediate surroundings. (By permision of the Royal Commission on the Ancient and Historic Monuments of Scotland.) To the north (facing the foot of the page) the Forth meanders through the carse. In some ways the most interesting feature is that from this height the shadowy rectangular outline of the Roman camp is clearly visible immediately below the central part of the village (see inset). The ramped approach climbs through the dark line of trees on the left side of the front of the fort before entering at the central drive. The remains of the ancient British church are among the wooded area on the left of the fort, while the mediaeval church is marked by a shadow on the right side.

David Erskine, 3rd Lord Cardross, from a painting attributed to L. Schuneman. (By permission of the Scottish National Portrait Gallery.)

The Battle of Bothwell Brig, by the contemporary artist Jan Wyck. (By permission of the Earl of Rosebery.) Although the river was somewhat wider than it appears here, the essential view of the battle seems accurate. The well-armed defenders of the Brig are on the right side while the Royal army is on the left. The tall toll gate is illustrated and the bulk of the Covenanting army is shown watching from the distance.

The Hole of Sneath waterfall in winter. This shot was taken in December 1995 by Colin Clark and Ninian Clark is standing on the ice.

Traditional Scottish long-horn cattle of John Menteath's herd grazing on Wright Park land early in the 20th century. Quite different from 'Highland' cattle, these animals were probably very similar to the type 'stolen' by Rob Roy in 1691.

Kippen Kirk's ancient pewter communion cups. The flagon and cup on the right date from the early 18th century. The age of the older cup in front is uncertain, but may be from at least 1691.

The old Bridge of Frew, completed in 1783 with the help of a grant from the 'Forfeited Estates'.

Wright Park House.

Burnside towards the end of the 19th century. The man in the centre is believed to be Rev. Patrick Muirhead, the Free Church Minister.

The main street about 1900. With the exception of the cottage on the extreme right, all of the roofs are now slated. The man wearing the straw boater is Willie Dougall, grandfather of the present shopkeeper of the same name, and one of the early street lamps can be seen on the wall of his house. The original Crown Inn is in the centre by the graveyard gate.

Dasher farm servants photographed in 1900.

Kippen railway station about the time of the First World War.

Children from the Oxhill school assembled outside Thimble Row, probably about 1870.

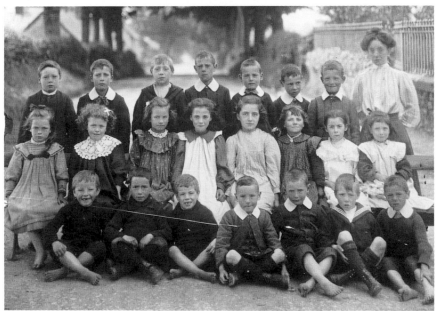

Arnprior junior children arranged across the road about 1900. The pupil teacher may be Miss McGibbon.

The family of John and Elizabeth More of Fordhead farm photographed about 1900. Most of the sons went on to run their own farms throughout the district.

Junior children at Kippen in 1920.

This view to the west from the church tower shows the Fore Road Public School before it was reconstructed as the village hall and the headmaster's villa at the centre right. The 18th-century Shirgarton House is visible through the trees in the middle distance.

A remarkable photograph taken about 1932 of six generations of superb Clydesdales belonging to Mr William More of Fourmerk farm. The mare on the left (held by John More) is the great, great, great grandmother of the foal on the right (held by young William). The foal's grandmother (third from the right) is Fourmerk Princess, a mare that won many show championships in the 1930s.

Selby Buchanan's daughter Suzanne shows off some of the superb grapes.

Harvesting grapes in 1935. Selby Buchanan is on the left and his brother Alex is on the ladder.

Personalities at a Highland games *c.*1930. Standing from the left are Viscount Younger of Leckie, Dr Macdiarmid and the Rev. John M. Younie. Seated are John Menteath of Wright Park (Chieftain of the games), Col. Crawford of Auchenuoig, Sir D.Y. Cameron and Col. Archibald Stirling of Garden.

The bronze figure of the Virgin Mary by Sir Alfred Gilbert.

Miss Eliza Harvie Anderson stands at the door of Shirgarton House *c*.1910. This lady was an aunt of Betty Harvie Anderson, the first woman to occupy the Speaker's Chair in the House of Commons.

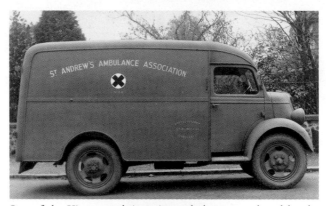

One of the Kippen and Arnprior ambulances purchased by the War Work Party during the Second World War.

Flt. Lt. John Younie, DFC & Bar.

Mr Bennett, Miss Paterson, Miss Buchanan and the Kippen school children in 1949.

Geordie, Jean, Billy and Bertie Davidson, who jointly ran R. Davidson and Sons until the firm was wound up in 1992.

Champions again, 1965.

The last of a long line. Andrew Rennie with some examples of his workmanship.

The new pupils at Kippen School, August 1999, with their teacher, Mrs Jacqueline Gordon. Standing (l to r) are Charlie Branagh, Alastair Lennon, Christopher Shanks, Elliot Quinn and Murray Crawford. The girls are Rebecca Thomson, Annika Little, Ailidh Rutherford and Amy McPherson.

children under the age of ten and, equally interestingly, no fewer than 67 were aged between 70 and 90 years, which suggests a reasonably healthy lifestyle.

Campbell also pointed to the good health of the people and particularly gave as an example a family of blacksmiths (almost certainly the Rennie family) where 'an old man, his son and grandson' all continued to live in the house where they were born and to work together in the same smiddy. He ascribed the health of the community to a favourable if rather wet and windy climate and commented that outbreaks of epidemic disease were uncommon. Nevertheless 'pleuretic fevers' (presumably something like influenza) had occurred in the late 1780s and there were occasional outbreaks of smallpox and measles, which took their toll particularly of the young and the elderly.

The venerable parish doctor, Dr William Leckie, had diligently maintained a record of the weather, but could identify nothing of significance in its capricious patterns. Dr Leckie was an interesting individual who had maintained an extensive practice in the West Indies before returning to Kippen. Over a period of 40 years he had been inoculating about 20 local people per year with smallpox, and he believed that only two of the patients treated had subsequently died (one within 24 hours and the other in three days). Inoculation of smallpox was in fact a fairly effective method of abating the force of the illness since the resulting infection was typically mild, but it did carry a significant risk of spreading the disease and of transmitting other lethal ailments. However, since the alternative and much improved method of vaccination with cowpox virus was not widely accepted until well into the 19th century, the Kippen people of Leckie's time would appear to have been fairly fortunate in their doctor.[23]

Campbell listed the jobs of the local people in 1792–93. There were six 'professionals' – 2 ministers (one established church and the other a nonconformist preacher), 1 physician, 1 writer and 2 schoolmasters. Not surprisingly, farming was the biggest employer, accounting for 100 farmers and 80 male farm servants. There were 8 millers, presumably mainly operating meal mills, but there was also at least one linen mill. Connected to the whisky trade there were 6 maltmen, 4 licensed distillers and 1 excise officer. There were 10 merchants (shopkeepers), and 36 self-employed handloom weavers, 5 employed weavers, and 14 apprentice weavers were noted, but the material that they used was not stated. Presumably they were mainly dealing with work sent out by town-based businessmen, and in addition to the traditional wool they would have been weaving linen and cotton blended fabrics. (Kippen church still possesses a linen communion table frontal that was manufactured in the village about 1800.) There was also 1 stocking weaver. Eight self-employed wrights or carpenters were recorded, and the latter employed a further 3 journeymen and 6 apprentices. There were 2 wheelwrights and 4 hecklers. (The latter name is sometimes applied to a wool-spinning trade, but the position of the hecklers in Mr Campbell's list suggests that he used the word to mean a type of cartwright, who made or altered farm carts.) Six stone masons and one apprentice are listed. There were 19 leather workers – 10 self-employed shoemakers, with 2 journeymen and 2 apprentices, 1 saddler with an employee, and 3 tanners. There were 4 coopers, making barrels; and 18 tailors, including 2 employed men and 2 apprentices. Eight blacksmiths with two apprentices were noted; and there was 1 dyer, 1 baker, and 2 butchers. Eight men ran public houses of one kind or another; and there were 7 carters. Forty-seven day labourers hired themselves for casual work; and finally, there were 4 sheriff-officers (policemen or jailers).[24]

Unfortunately Campbell did not set out the occupations of adult females, although he does mention that 25–30 young village girls under the charge of a mistress were employed to work for a Glasgow manufacturer 'in tambouring muslin' (embroidering fine cotton fabrics), in some cases using locally woven material. Other girls also worked in a tannery at Buchlyvie where 16–20 pools were used to tan cattle hides. But presumably most unmarried women were employed either as domestic servants or as seasonal workers. This is suggested by annual labouring wages that are recorded as £7–£9 for men and £2 10s–£3 10s for women, typically with board and lodging. Harvest workers were employed by the season, with the rate being £1 10s for men and £1 for women. In 1793 the day rate for tailors and casual labourers was 10d plus a meal; by contrast the rate for a carpenter or a mason was 1s 2d. Campbell also noted that whereas blacksmiths had previously been paid by farmers at least partly in produce, they were now being paid in cash at fixed rates for the piece of work, and this demonstrates the gradual development of a more extensive cash-based economy.[25]

Whisky distilling had flourished in the parish in the period up to the 1790s with four distilleries operating under the advantageous tax régime by which Kippen was regarded as being north of a notional Highland line. Under an Act of 1793, however, the formal Highland boundary was repositioned so that Kippen was regarded as Lowland

and therefore, excluded from the tax relief. Only one distillery – probably at Arnprior Farm – was large enough to survive the change and later in the 19th century it was apparently submitting about £17,000 annually to the Excise.[26] But some smaller distilleries did continue to operate from time to time and their locations have been noted as the site of Craigiebarns, Gateside, Ladylands, Laraben, Claylands and Cloney. Proximity to the whisky Highland line meant, inevitably, that illicit distilling and smuggling were problems in the district and apparently at least one excise officer, a Mr Dougal, was murdered by a smuggler. Exactly when this crime was committed is not clear, but Dougal's body was found at Muirend in a ravine at Boquhan Glen. No one was convicted for the killing, but 'well grounded suspicion soon fell upon [a] man who had openly threatened to murder Dougal, and he was afterwards totally shunned by his former companions, and died a wandering outcast'.[27] (The location where Dougal's mutilated remains were discovered gave rise to the suggestion that this was responsible for the naming of the nearby 'Dougal's Tower', but the tradition that it was a look-out point during the Covenanting period seems more probable.)

The pictures created by the ministers in their contributions to the first two Statistical Accounts convey an impression of a diverse and vigorous rural economy. They also show that the villages were becoming more significant both in economic terms and as places of residence. In 1793 Kippen village had approximately 342 residents and Buchlyvie, probably because of the tanning industry, had had its population boosted to about 460. By 1831 the parish contained 2085 people and Kippen had once again become the larger village, with 600 as compared to Buchlyvie's 400 inhabitants.[28] It is thus easy to understand some of Mr Campbell's pride as he surveyed what seemed to him to be a prosperous and steadily developing community.

In the 18th and 19th centuries the key parish institution was undoubtedly the church, for it was not only the place of community worship, of baptisms, marriages and funerals, but it was the essential unit for the organisation and delivery of the welfare system. It brought together the principal patrons and heritors to look after not just the church properties, but the wellbeing of the parish as a whole. The ministers, for good or ill, were therefore important leaders of the community and some were interesting characters.

Michael Potter, minister from 1700 to 1740 and who eventually left Kippen to become Professor of Divinity at the University of Glasgow, was probably responsible for the construction of the manse (Glebe House) in about 1706 (it was greatly extended in 1814). He must have imprinted himself on the folk memory of the district because two tales about him have survived, and one of these concerns his strong disapproval of the practice of playing football on the Sabbath. At that time the players apparently held their games in a field on the flat land at Crawfordston, and one Sunday Mr Potter appeared and demanded to be allowed to join in the game. Reluctantly the astonished men acquiesced, whereupon the minister insisted that they should first start the proceedings with a prayer and a blessing for the ball. Again, the men had no choice but to accept, but their feelings can be imagined when they discovered that the prayer had no end until the last of them had trooped off the field.

Nevertheless, someone, perhaps one of the football players, had their revenge. For all his piety, Mr Potter was very careless with the care of his pigs and gave offence to the community by allowing them to run around at will and particularly to root about in the graveyard. To punish him for this, one dark night one or more of the villagers seized one of his black pigs and smeared it all over with tar. As can be seen from the surviving church gable, at that time the bell was rung by means of a rope which hung down on the outside of the building. The pranksters therefore tied the unfortunate pig to the rope and then set it on fire. As can be imagined the flaming, squealing creature and the wildly clanging bell roused the whole village to cries that the devil was loose in the churchyard. Evidently Mr Potter took rather more care of his pigs thereafter.

The other outstanding minister was, of course, John Campbell, who in 1804 was called to the Tolbooth Church of Edinburgh and eventually became Moderator of the General Assembly. While in Kippen he was evidently greatly loved by the young people of the parish and his vitality and interest in the community emerge strongly from his writing. One of the interesting events of his ministry was the presentation to the church by his friend Robert Graham of Gartmore of two beautiful silver communion cups. These were gifted in 1790 and are inscribed as being donated by Mr Graham 'in testimony of his veneration for the religion of his country, of his respect for the present minister and of his regard for the inhabitants of the Parish'. These chalices are still used.

The 1691 church was substantially reconstructed in 1737 and again in 1779. The ruined remains give the impression of a fairly small building, although it is not known how many people it could have seated. By the latter year the accommodation had certainly become somewhat crowded and this was indicated by at least one fight over scarce seating. The old church had a gallery and in

September 1778 it was there that a struggle broke out between Andrew Lockhart of the Parks and George Lenny, a tenant farmer of Garden. Lenny claimed that he had struck Lockhart because the latter had pushed his mother-in-law, but Lockhart responded that he had had no choice but to do so because the lady concerned, objecting to him sitting in what she considered to be her seat, had stuck her hat-pin into his backside. Understandably the Kirk Session took a dim view of such brawling and fined Lenny two guineas 'for the relief of the poor'.[29] Perhaps it was this incident that persuaded the heritors that some modernisation to the building was necessary. In any event, after the improvements John Campbell thought it had become 'a very decent and commodious place of worship'.

Nevertheless, by the 1820s further population growth meant that a new, larger building was essential. This was constructed in 1825 and ten years later a new church was also erected in Buchlyvie. The new Kippen church, designed by two well-known architects from Dunblane and Falkirk, both named William Stirling, was initially 'a plain, rectangular building, with galleries around three walls and a pulpit in the centre of the south wall' and it was constructed at a cost of £1593.[30] Remarkably it had a capacity to hold about 800 people and in its early years most of the seats were in the gift of heritors. The latter were allocated pews for their families and tenants in accordance with the amounts of money they were assessed as being liable to contribute in support of the parish, and Mr Anderson, writing only a decade or so after the building was opened, noted that only four or five of the pews were available for free use.

In 1845 the annual assessment of the Kippen heritors was listed as follows.[31]

James Stirling of Garden	£66	16s	11d
H.F. Campbell of Boquhan	£38	3s	10d
David Erskine of Cardross	£23	0s	10d
W. Leckie Ewing of Arngomery	£16	18s	1d
William Kay Esq of Wright Park	£9	18s	10d
Andrew Forrester of Arngibbon	£7	0s	6d
William Galbraith of Blackhouse	£6	5s	11d
Andrew Milne Esq	£4	8s	4d
John Graham Esq	£4	5s	
Harvie Brown Esq	£4	2s	7d
Forsyth Esq	£1	3s	1d
John Fisher Esq	£1	1s	2d
Thomas Graham	£1	5s	10d
Messrs Galbraith, Wright & Co		18s	6d

Because parts of the estates of Mr Campbell and Mr Erskine were in the neighbouring parishes, no doubt they were also required to contribute to the churches of Gargunnock and Port of Menteith respectively.

From the late 17th century a key function of the Church was to provide for the poor, and particularly for the elderly or infirm. The income for this purpose derived from a number of sources, including the annual levy on heritors, the weekly collections, occasional donations or legacies, marriage dues, occasional fines imposed on 'delinquents' and the hire of what were called 'mortcloths'. These latter were winding sheets in which those who had died were wrapped prior to burial, and typically Kippen church had two such cloths, one of good quality and one which seems constantly to have threatened to disintegrate. No doubt the normal process of wear and tear and replacement meant that the 'best mortcloth' was the one most recently purchased. In any event, it could typically be hired for 4s or 5s, while use of the 'second' or 'common' mortcloth cost 2s.

Collections at the church rarely brought in more than a few shillings although donations at the harvest communion – by far the best supported service – could realise as much as £40. Given the extensive geographic area of the parish at this time and the diffi-culties of travel for most people it is not perhaps surprising that in the second half of the 18th century the Kirk Session also used a tent during the summer months. This was erected at Cauldhame for peri-odic evening services, and it was also taken to more remote parts of the parish to give everyone the opportunity to attend public worship.

The reputation of the Church of Scotland for hypocritical repression and interference in the personal lives of men and women (particularly as immortalised in the poetry of Robert Burns) stemmed largely from its disciplinary activities in respect of sexual relations and marriage. What has, however, to be remembered when considering this subject is that at the time the population was increasing rapidly, there were no effective forms of contraception and the system for the support of the children of unmarried women was at best rudimentary. The whole point of the Kirk's practices in this regard was concerned with the attempt to ensure that there was provision for children and that adults accepted responsibility for their actions.

Income from 'marriage dues' came in two ways. First when a couple announced their intention to get married and asked to have this declared to the community by having their banns called from the pulpit on three Sundays, they had to submit a marriage 'pawn' which typically amounted to one or two shillings. If subsequently they decided not to go ahead with the marriage, then the pawn was forfeited. Second, at the actual wedding a collection was held, the contents going into the poor box.

The Church tended to enforce strict rules about marriage. Occasionally couples simply decided to live together or to go through an 'irregular' marriage, perhaps making declarations before some friends and exchanging letters, but this was not acceptable to the Church because, if the relationship subsequently broke up, there was little financial protection for the woman or her children. Those who participated in an irregular marriage therefore, were liable to a fine and could be required to go through the formal procedure. If they decided to ignore such an instruction, they risked being denied any support from the parish funds if subsequently they fell into poverty, perhaps through injury, ill health or temporary unemployment. The Kippen kirk records contain regular examples of this form of disciplinary process. To give one illustration at random, in February 1785 Alexander McInnes and Annabella Cassels were fined 10s 6d for participating in an irregular marriage and were also obliged to provide a pawn of 1s 8d ahead of a normal marriage ceremony. However, fines for this kind of behaviour were not automatic, particularly if it was a question of conduct that was a result of ignorance or perhaps undue discretion. For instance, in May 1797 Patrick Campbell, a weaver, and Janet Drummond, a widow, were merely 'rebuked and absolved' for having been 'clandestinely married' – i.e. not having had their banns properly proclaimed.

'Delinquents' were almost all accused of sexual liaisons outside marriage, and very typical was the case in January 1777 of Amy Johnston who, when she was 'found to be with child', alleged that the father was John McArthur. He was accordingly instructed to appear before the session and when he did so he immediately admitted his responsibility and agreed to marry Amy and the elders reacted by deciding to take no further action. A rather different case of that year involved Mary McArthur who had given birth to a child which she claimed had been fathered by Archibald Miller, a farm servant at Arnprior. When both appeared before the session Millar repeatedly disclaimed any involvement, at which Mary 'seemed so grieved and astonished at his denial that she could not properly recollect herself'. Nevertheless the session persisted, recalling them both, and at the third hearing Miller finally admitted that he could have been the father and he agreed to marry Mary.

Occasionally a couple that were unmarried were accused of 'fornication' and sometimes they were really living together and obviously fell into the same category as those who had gone through an irregular marriage. If so, they were normally dealt with in precisely the same way, receiving a fine and being obliged to go through the formal process. From time to time, however, a man would refuse to marry, particularly if he had been involved in no more than a casual liaison. If such a man was found guilty, he would be fined, as happened to Robert Morrison in 1780, when his penalty for being convicted of fornication was 7s 1d.

The interesting thing is that hearings on this kind of matter were conducted in privacy and that the session's obvious objective was basically to insist that both parents of children accepted responsibility for their upbringing through a formal marriage. No doubt at times the conduct of inquiries may have been heavy handed, but in the Kippen records there is no evidence of prurience or of any cruelty in the form of deliberate public humiliation. Rather the picture that emerges from the Kirk Session minutes is one of kindly country people doing their best to resolve the social and economic consequences of very human predicaments.

Another source of funds for care of the poor was from the interest on accumulated savings and from other banking activities. Typically the kirk had a reserve of between £300 and £400 and, in the absence of modern banking facilities, most of this money would be lent to one or more men of good standing in return for a bond and with an agreed interest being paid twice a year. Similarly, individuals in need of a smaller loan for some purpose might borrow from the Church by issuing a bill and paying interest. These activities, of course, were not without risks, although defaults were rare. On one occasion, however, money lent to a minister, Mr Turnbull, was lost when he died unexpectedly and when the lawyer winding up his affairs failed to clear the debt. A week or so later the incoming minister, Mr Campbell replaced the lost money out of his own pocket. Occasionally the parish funds were augmented by gifts from individuals and by legacies left in wills, such as in 1803 when £100 was bequeathed from the estate of Dr Leckie.

Most of the money paid out was in the form of regular pensions to necessitous individuals. Because of the size of the parish it was broken into three districts and money was allocated to a number of pensioners in each. For example, in 1803 at the Easter quarter 'ordinary pensioners' were noted as follows: *Kippen*: 8 females 2 males; *Middle*: 3 females 4 males; *Buchlyvie*: 12 females 2 males. Total 31 persons.

In addition to the regular pensioners paid in that month occasional payments were made to a further 14 women and 7 men. These were very typical numbers for the period from the 1770s to the 1840s, although by the latter years the occasional awards being made each month were to as many as 40 or so individuals, perhaps reflecting at a local level the national economic difficulties of the 'hungry forties'.

The monthly pension payments were inevitably very small and appear to have depended on the circumstances of the recipient – whether they were elderly or an invalid, or perhaps a younger, but poor widow with children. For example, in January 1780 the payments made to the 16 Kippen pensioners ranged from the 4s 6d paid to Katherine Wright to 1s given to Christian Livingston. The latter amount was exceptionally small and most pensions were 2s 6d or 3s per month, so presumably Christian was receiving some family assistance while Katherine may have been on her own with at least one child to support.

The occasional payments make interesting and touching reading and a random handful of examples are as follows:

December 1776
To an orphan for shoes   2s
To John Young for poor scholars   11s

November 1779
To John McDonald in distress   5s 6d
To Alexander King to buy shoes   2s

January 1780
To John McDonald's funeral and coffin   10s
To Malcolm Macgregor's widow   2s 6d
To John Lockhart in distress   5s
To Malcolm Macgregor's coffin   5s
To Jean Parlane to redeem a gown kept by the weaver for   1s 10d
working it

December 1781
To a slater for mending the little house at the Church gate   1s
(This was where the poor would shelter while waiting for help.)
To school wages of two poor girls at Arnprior   2s 6d

April 1782
To David Graham and his wife in distress at Falkirk   14s

October 1805
To advancing money to Militia and Reserve men's wives
    Elizabeth Bachop   £4 10s
    Ann Risk   8s 9d

(This, of course, was during the Napoleonic War with France and such advances to support the wives of men who had been called up in a national emergency were normally recovered by the parish from the Government, although sometimes not for several years.)

December 1843
By Janet Blair – extra ill   4s
By widow Brown, a pauper   2s

March 1845
To widow Graham for a fatuous child   2s 6d
To Mrs MacIntyre for keeping an old woman   5s
To a stranger and child   1s 6d

And so the record goes on month by month, year by year. Sometimes a very elderly person would not be able to carry on subsisting independently and in these circumstances the kirk would take over responsibility. For instance, in December 1807 it was recorded that 'Jean Ure in Kippen gave up her effects to the Session and was taken entirely into their care in December 1806 and died in July 1807. She received in the meantime the monthly allowance of 3s from the Session which they expended for her in part payment of necessaries.'

After her death, as was normal in such circumstances, her effects were sold at a public roup and in this case they yielded a pathetic £1 14s 8d, which was paid into the poor fund.

As the population gradually became more mobile kirk sessions became very cautious about accepting responsibility for poor strangers. Such individuals travelling from one area to another had to have passes so that any costs would fall on their home parish. This was very difficult to operate in practice, but again, glimpses of what happened emerge from the records.

March 1784
By lodging for two vagrant women one night   2s
By Alexander Hay for attending the two vagrant women . . .
. . . and taking them out of the parish   2s 6d

1841
By a poor man and a woman on a pass   2s 6d
By extra expense of removing Dugald McDougal from Glasgow
Infirmary to Dunbar   15s 1d

1843
By expense of carting an infirm man through the parish on a
Pass from Stirling to Dumbarton   2s 6d
By a tradesman on a pass to Dundee   6d
By two men on a pass to Greenock from Aberdeen   1s
A man and 2 children on a pass from Stirling to Greenock   4s
By a poor man and a child for lodgings   1s 6d

(No doubt those heading for Greenock were planning emigration to North America.) Interestingly in December of 1843 the session decided to purchase coal for 14 of its pensioners.[32]

It is clear from the above account that, however imperfect it may have been, as exemplified by Kippen Kirk, the Church operated a vital social welfare system which was invaluable to the community. Mr Campbell concluded that 'on the whole, it is believed that no better plan can be devised for taking care of the poor, than that which is generally practised throughout Scotland'.[33] No doubt he was much too bold in his claim, yet given the limits of the available resources and the extent of the problem, the main impressions conveyed by the minutes and accounts are essentially of a record of kindness and of a community doing its best within impossibly sparse means.

Private individuals, of course, also augmented the Kirk's activities. For example, Helen Forrester of Poldar endowed a private trust for the assistance of the poor. The top end of Fore Road was opened from the Cross about 1800 and a year or two later Helensfield was built for her, perhaps becoming the first house to face the new road. An unmarried lady, she had acquired or inherited a number of properties and feus around the centre of the village and when she died in 1835 her will established a trust for the relief of poor Kippenites. (The Helensfield Trust continues to operate today, and although it is now less important than in the 19th century, it provides some useful benefits to a number of villagers in most years.) Similarly, in 1839 a small poor fund was established in the name of John Buchanan. (Helen Forrester had obtained some of her land from Buchanan and it seems probable that these two friends had collaborated in opening up Fore Road.)

Funerals were one of the great fascinations of 19th-century society and a real fear for a poor person was that there might not be sufficient resources to enable their burial to be conducted in a suitable manner. One of the oldest of the village organisations, therefore, was the Parish Hearse Society. First suggested in 1810, this institution took no less than 26 years to raise the cash to acquire a hearse with which to convey parishioners to their last resting place. However, the vehicle, which was made in Stirling at a cost of £50, was in use from 1836 and it was hired out to members of the Society who paid an annual subscription of 2s 6d and a charge of 5s for the hire. If the hearse was taken beyond the parish boundary the charge became a fearsome 1s per mile and a further 10s 6d if it was away overnight. At the discretion of the Society's management committee, however, poor people were often granted the use of the hearse without charge. Apparently it was a handsome if cumbersome vehicle and some of the more prosperous individuals ensured that they possessed at least one suitable dark horse to draw it if it was being used by a member of their family.

As an institution the Church was, of course, not free from dissension and division in these years. Indeed a religious tradition that was founded on a belief in the direct personal relationship between the individual and God and a form of organisation that required decision-making through debate and argument, was almost bound to invite secessions. Moreover, given the Covenanting history of the community, it would have been surprising if people of the district had not been involved in some of the disputes. In this part of the country minor secessions did occur in the 18th century. However, William Anderson's report in 1841 ironically showed an extra-ordinary degree of apparent conformity within the community. By his time Buchlyvie had its own church, but he indicated that in Kippen, with the exception of six Episcopalians and three Roman Catholics, the entire community adhered to the Church of Scotland.

Just two years later the great Disruption occurred in the Kirk with about one third of the membership splitting off to form the Free Church. This was partly as a result of an objection to the on-going system of patronage in the appointment of ministers, but it was also a response to frustration at the failure of the Church to act with sufficient vigour in addressing the problems of the burgeoning city populations. Mr Anderson led a large part of the Kippen congregation into the Free Church, and their first temporary place of worship was at Douglas Place at Burnside in a building that has now been demolished. The second Free Church was opened in the main street in 1878 and it was largely funded out of the pocket of Mr Anderson's successor, Mr Patrick Muirhead.

No doubt in the 18th and 19th centuries the people of Kippen were as liable to give way to traditional rural superstitions as people elsewhere in Scotland. No example has been found of 'witches' being persecuted in the district. However, one tale of this kind of problem has survived, and it concerned a farmer, James Macfarlane, who, about 1840, built Hawthorn Cottage in the Fore Road, from where he maintained a small croft and a dairy. For a time his wife and daughter seemed unable to churn the cream properly into butter and the Macfarlanes came to believe that the problem stemmed from their cows having been bewitched by one Sandy Risk, who was reputed to be a warlock. On one occasion Risk had asked Macfarlane for the loan of a horse and when the farmer, who was very busy at the time, refused on the grounds that the animals were all needed, Risk had cursed him with the threat that it would 'no be lang afore ye hae as few horses as me'. As luck would have it that night one of the horses fell ill and died, and Macfarlane thereafter ascribed all his misfortune to the malevolent Risk. Firmly convinced that a spell had been cast on his cattle so that they produced only watery milk, the farmer sent one of his daughters with an urgent appeal for help to Campsie to the home of another warlock known as John Rankine. At a charge of a guinea Rankine supplied the girl with a 'witch bottle', and instructed her to return to Kippen by a different route and to speak to no one on the way. Once she was home, in the presence of the whole family she was to bury the bottle under the stone step of the entrance to the byre, and these instructions were carefully followed with the apparent result that from that evening the churning produced only the most beautiful butter.

Subsequently Hawthorn Cottage was bought by Dr Macdonald who was the respected village doctor for many years in the second half of the century, and one day, when some alterations were being made to his property, he discovered the bottle which he thereafter kept on display as a curiosity for the interest of the patients in his waiting room.

Some of the sports and pastimes of the villagers at this period were still fairly rough and cock fights and badger baiting contests were apparently still attracting large numbers of local spectators in the early part of the 19th century. In the latter events a trapped badger was placed in a ten-foot-long box and terriers were put in to see which of them could draw the badger out, with bets being placed on the outcome. Inevitably some of the consequences were bloody and gradually the cruelty of the spectacle brought the practice to an end, but one wonders whether or not 'Badger's Hollow' in Graham Street was the arena for such encounters.

Although the military roads brought an enormous improvement to communications, the one through Kippen did not have a long period as the main link with the outside world. The years around 1800 were the period when the Turnpike Trusts were constructing macadamised roadways. In 1828 such a road was constructed along the carse and a loop was brought up to Kippen by means of what is now known as the Station Brae. As mentioned above, Fore Road had been opened a little earlier (enabling the new church to be built in 1825) and this now linked back into the turnpike at Arngomery/ Broich. A smooth road along the level must have been a great boon to horses and passengers alike and it dramatically reduced journey times to and from Stirling.

In the 1840s a daily post-chaise ran between Kippen and Stirling and another also came out to Buchlyvie, but curiously only on six days in the week. In addition, a stage-coach ran three days a week on the turnpike from Kippen Cross to Glasgow by Fintry and Campsie and about 1850 the adult single fair was 4s 6d. Every Friday a four-in-hand coach also ran between Balfron and Stirling and it called at Kippen to collect passengers. Finally, the main route between Callander and Glasgow came through Kippen parish by means of Cardross Bridge and passengers could join the Callander coach at Arnprior.[34]

However, even public carriages were strictly for those who could afford the fares and the reality for many people faced with a journey was that they were obliged to walk most of the way to their destination. Today the methods by which people had to make their way to and from Kippen may seem strange. For example, in the mid-19th century a woman travelling from Edinburgh to Kippen in order to take up a position in the household of Miss Menteith (whose residence was on the site of the present Menteith Crescent), sailed by boat up the Forth from Leith to Stirling and then walked the ten miles to the village. (This lady eventually married Mr Welsh, one of the local joiners.)[35] Similarly, it was quite normal for people to walk from Kippen to Glasgow and, indeed, some of the poorer people even carried their precious shoes most of the way to avoid subjecting them to undue wear.

At this time newspapers were a considerable luxury and the Glasgow paper which arrived on the coach cost seven pence to purchase. Groups of villagers used to share the expense and pass the paper around the subscribers.

The revolutionary transport change of the 19th century was, of course, the development of the railway network. This reached Kippen in 1856 when the line connecting Stirling, Balloch, Dumbarton and Glasgow was opened. To begin with there were just three trains daily in each direction and the cost of a return ticket to Stirling was 1s 6d. In most cases stations were positioned at suitable locations between villages, hence Kippen station was intended also to serve Thornhill and, since this meant that people had to walk the half mile or so to the station, an enterprising tailor, Mr Gilchrist of Aros House, acquired a pony and trap which he used as a taxi to carry people up and down the hill. Within a few years rail traffic had built up considerably, so that by 1900 there were 17 passenger trains a day and the price of a return from Kippen to Stirling had fallen to just 10d. By this stage there was also fierce competition for local traffic to and from the station with the waggonettes of John Duncanson, Charles Hay and Robert Davidson vying determinedly for the trade.[36]

In one sense the railway brought increased employment in the form of station attendants, line maintenance men and so on and indirectly to local carriers of the kind mentioned above. However, steam power also devastated much of the local rural economy in ways that may not be instantly obvious.

The railways were constructed to connect the main centres of population and this enabled industry to be centralised more effectively. Large-scale factory production was stimulated, particularly with the related application of steam power to drive machinery. This process boosted industrial cities and encouraged further migration of the labour force, but simultaneously the growth of the factories and the flow of cheaper mass-produced goods crushed many of the small craft industries that had been at the heart of village economies earlier in the century. For example, the last handloom weaver in the Kingdom was James Lennie of the Clachan of Loaningfoot at Ladylands and his retirement in 1870 ended the last flicker of the previously thriving cottage textile activity so proudly described 80 years earlier by Mr Campbell.[37] The cottage workers were simply unable to compete with the power looms of the major manufacturers. Similarly local producers of almost every type of product increasingly found themselves having to contend with goods brought from the main urban markets or purchased in town with no more additional cost than a cheap return ticket for the train.

The farmers did enjoy great benefits from the coming of the railway, particularly in the early years, because of the ease with which their output could now be transferred to large centralised markets. However, this development effectively sounded the death knell for Balgair and the other drove trysts. The improvement of farming conditions through the 1850s and 1860s was particularly noticeable and many of the farmhouses and outbuildings still to be seen in the district appear to date from this period. But later in the century the inflow of inexpensive produce from North America began to push prices downwards and UK farming generally went into a period of long-run depression. In keeping with what happened in other parts of Britain, farm rents in the Kippen area fell from about £2 per acre to just 25s, reflecting the falling product prices at market. This recession caused an acceleration in the introduction of improved farm machinery and, to save wage costs, a reduction in the size of the permanent agricultural labour force. From the 1880s an

increase in seasonal short-term agricultural employment was evident, but it was at the cost of longer-term local jobs. For a time,
therefore, workers increasingly spent the winter and spring months
in Glasgow, returning to Kippen only for the harvest months.

It is probably the case that at this time carse farming really came
into its own through the production of hay for horse and cattle
fodder. 'Timothy' hay became the crop for which the area became
particularly renowned and this may have enabled local farmers to go
through the difficult late 19th-century years without undue distress.
Timothy was a heavy-cropping variety imported from America and
it has been suggested that it was introduced to the district by Mr
Martin of Middle Kerse about 1890. Within a very few years the
crop was being sown by farmers all over the carse, which was understandable since it evidently yielded three to three-and-a-half tons per
acre in comparison to the equivalent two tons produced from traditional rye-grass. Fourteen pounds of timothy seed sown on an acre of
carse land would give as many as six to eight years of crops and
would provide a harvest of both bulk fodder and seed.

The hay grown in the district was typically bought by dealers
based in Stirling and then carted directly to the main market in
Glasgow to provide for the city's huge horse population. The railways, however, created a requirement for hay to be made available in
a form that was more suitable for transport and storage and this
explains the introduction of baling at this time. At first the bales
were made by hand-operated machines and two men could apparently bale three to four tons in a day. However, within a few years
steam-powered balers were enabling the two men to prepare five or
six times as much.

The huge demand for powerful heavy horses also further stimulated
the interest of local breeders and the Clydesdales of the area were
especially admired. Some of the prize-winning animals were household
names. For example, 'Royal Gartley', 'Royal Favourite' and 'Gartley's
Heir' were great championship-winning stallions bred by the Dewar
family at Arnprior Farm. The most famous of all, of course, was the
great 'Baron of Buchlyvie', bred by William MacKeich at Woodend
and born in 1903. When it was eventually sold, the price was bid up
to an astonishing £9500 and, after its death, its skeleton was
obtained for display purposes by Glasgow Art galleries.[38] But this
was really the tip of an iceberg, for by 1900 almost any farm in the
area could have shown a number of superb Clydesdales. For instance,
the Boquhan estate, by this time in the hands of Steven Mitchell (a
notable benefactor to the Kippen community), specialised in short-

horn cattle, but also bred magnificent draft-horses.

Although remaining generally prosperous, farming in the area obviously changed significantly. However, it will be clear from the foregoing discussion that the economies of Kippen and the neighbouring villages suffered many problems in the second half of the 19th century and local jobs for young people were not always readily available. Migration tended to be the alternative, usually simply to Glasgow, but sometimes overseas. More often than not this was purely a matter of individual choice, but in the early 1890s two young men were given some sharp encouragement from their father. The carter and dairyman, James Hay, had four sons. The youngest, Charles and George were not yet ready to leave home, but after one piece of particular boisterousness the two oldest boys, James and Sandy, were given the options of joining the army or a few pounds in their pockets to assist them with emigration to America. Not surprisingly, they chose Wisconsin in the USA and married their sweethearts on the way out. Sadly one brother was soon murdered in the relatively lawless Klondike gold-field of the Yukon in Canada, but the other, soon joined by a sister, settled down and did well.

Most people, of course, went willingly, looking to the future, but almost always with some sadness. It was at this period, when families and friends were frequently being split up by the emigration of loved ones, particularly to North America, that the poems 'Oot O' The World And Into Kippen' were written by Stewart A. Robertson of Stirling High School. The supposed context of the poems is of a husband and wife who had emigrated many years earlier and who were then living in New York. The husband writes the following for his wife:

'Oot o' the world and into Kippen,'
Eh! Jean, d'ye mind the braes
That rise sae bonnie frae the carse?
D'ye mind the summer days
When you and I were bairnies there,
And never thocht we'd be
Sae far frae hame in this far land
Across the saut, saut sea?

'Oot o' the world and into Kippen,'
The folks wad laugh and say,
Losh keep me! Lass, hoo things come back,
It seems but yesterday
Since you and I forsook the braes
And owre the waters came,
To settle in this weary land,
Sae far, sae far frae hame.

'Oot o' the world and into Kippen,'
Eh! Jean, that that could be?
There isna ocht I hae on earth
But I wad gladly gie
If only we could tread again
The paths where ance we ran,
Where the heather grows on Kippen Muir
And the braes abune Boquhan.

Oot o' this world o' noisy streets
Into that place o' calm,
Where to the hills men lift their eyes,
D'ye mind they sang that psalm
The Sabbath we were kirkit there?
Aye, fifty years are gone,
But ye were then the bonniest bride
'Tween Kippen and Balfron.

Oot o' this world o' unkent things,
Oh! That we baith could win!
And hear the pee-weep on the hills,
And see the yellow whin,
And see the bonnie gowans smile
As if they kent us a',
And welcomed us to oor ain land,
The best land o' them a'.

'Oot o' the world and into Kippen,'
Jean, lass, it ne'er will be,
The burnie's waters ne'er run back,
Nor buds the uprooted tree.
The fecht o' life for us is past
Forfochen wi' the fray,
Oot o' the world and into – rest,
Ere lang we baith shall gae.

In Robertson's imagining the poem was sent to friends in Kippen and one of them penned the following reply:

Thy voice across the saut, saut sea
Has reached the 'Kingdom' high,
And draws from kindly Kippen folks
The tribute of a sigh.

That a warm, human heart should long,
In New York's surging city,
For breath o' auld warld Kippen air
Fills all our souls with pity.

Though times are changed sin' ye left here,
And auld folks passed away,

Mayhap as kindly hearts beat now
As flourished in your day.

Whatever changes come to pass
'Mangst men and their affairs,
Still winds the Forth through fair Menteith,
Still blows heaven's balmy airs

O'er Kippen Muir, through garden bower,
Round many a humble dwelling,
Or doun the glen, by Dougal's tower,
The same brown spate is swelling.

The rushing waters o' Boquhan
Falls o'er the 'Hole of Sneath',
And rest awhile, from their turmoil,
In the deep, dark linn beneath,

Then onward through the red rock bowls
The 'Devil's Cauldron' boiling,
And round and round, with deaf'ning sound,
The angry waters toiling.

Anon, through 'Belly o' the Whale',
Where brown trout dart and quiver,
And laddies throw the baited hook
Today – the same as ever.

Still the shy dipper lays white eggs
In Cuthbertson's shady glen,
And the grey wagtail rears her brood
Where truant schoolboys ken.

Still slips the burn o'er rocky bed,
O'er 'Leckie's Loup' it dashes,
Round the Keir Knowe, to join the Forth,
Through marigolds and rashes.

Athwart Ben Ledi – Hill of God –
Falls the weird morning light,
And heralds each returning day
Born of the silent night.

The varied gleams of fairy light
Still dance on Flanders Moss,
And glory bathes the ancient oaks
And mansion of Cardross.

Still Glenny and Mondouie's slopes
Look on the 'sharp steel sheen'
That girds the holy island which
Once sheltered Scotland's Queen.

O, Hill of God, that doth abide
While generations pass,
I to thy heights will lift mine eyes,
Will sing my morning mass.

The parson from the manse still views
The mountains, plain, and skies,
Still, for men's sins he cannot cure,
He supplicates and sighs.

'Oot o' the world and into Kippen,'
Far from the rough world's din,
May your spirit come o'er the saut, saut sea
To rest with your kith and kin.

Despite the romantic nostalgia and pathos of the poems, the truth is
that life in Kippen towards the end of the 19th century was not
always idyllic and sometimes could be fairly dangerous. Epidemic
diseases such as influenza, diphtheria, measles, whooping cough and
so on visited the community from time to time and usually took their
toll, especially of the young. Indeed in the second half of the century
Kippen seems to have suffered particularly from occasional occurrences of typhoid or, as it was sometimes then known, enteric fever.
By far the most severe outbreak occurred in the winter of 1893–1894
and it was first notified in the Castlehill school log book as follows:

Dec 8th
> Received notice from John C. McVail, Medical Officer of Health
> for the County Council of Stirling that Typhoid Fever exists in the
> houses of
>
> Archibald Macdiarmid, Kippen
> Robert Dougall, Post Office, Kippen
> Andrew Dunn, Crown Hotel, Kippen
> James Kerr, Surfaceman, Kippen
> James McCallum, Old Free Church, Kippen
> Mr Buchanan, Cross Keys Hotel, Kippen
>
> No children from the above families are to be admitted to school
> until a medical certificate is received by the teacher that they are
> free from infection.[39]

The outbreak became very serious and, as the above entry
illustrates, attracted the attention of the recently appointed County
Medical Officer of Health, Dr John McVail, who described it in a
section of his subsequent Annual Report. He also provided an interesting glimpse of contemporary living conditions. At the time it
appears that the population of the village (as distinct from the
parish) had declined to about 310 inhabitants who lived in 78

houses, most of which were cottages. 'Much of the house accommo-dation is bad, the prevailing defect being damp,' and in many cases the dwellings were certainly grossly overcrowded by modern stan-dards. Most of the houses were connected to a central water supply that involved gathering water which drained naturally from the moor above the village into a cement-lined covered tank located in the Black Brae wood, and then distributing it to the houses via pipes and pillar wells. This system had been constructed about 1860. However, about 20 of the houses were still dependent on the older traditional water supply of open 'dip' wells, the water being carried to the dwellings in wooden buckets or 'stoups'. Drainage within the village was still primitive and drains were formed from a mixture of clay pipes and rubble-filled channels, with, in one case, an open 'foul ditch leading down the hillside from the village' and into which at least two water closets drained. Most of the houses had no more than an ash-pit for the disposal of human sewage, although some of the waste was also used as manure.

From the foregoing discussion it will seen that the opportunities for the spread of infection were numerous, if not quite on the scale of the conditions in some of the contemporary cities. However, Dr McVail concluded that the typhoid epidemic of 1893 originated in James Hay's dairy at Burnside. A few years previously the land (at what is now known as Broadlees) had been sub-let by the tenant farmer to Hay, who had established a small dairy without registering his premises or having them examined by the council's dairy inspec-tor. (It was a very small-scale business based on just three cows.) The first to become infected was the dairyman's daughter, although the village doctor, Dr McDiarmid did not at first distinguish the disease from influenza which was also present at the time. Within a few days, however, typhoid fever was clearly established and over the next few weeks 40 cases occurred, being concentrated mainly on 11 families, nine or ten of which obtained their milk from the dairy.

As McVail's report makes clear, it was a nightmare for the village, but in fact the health services were now slowly becoming able to respond to this type of crisis. The district 'infectious disease' hospital at Bannockburn was only in course of erection, and some of the cases were so severe as to make removal to Falkirk Hospital impracticable. In these circumstances, the Public Health Committee sanctioned the obtaining of trained nurses from the Glasgow Nurses' Home to reside in the village and to take charge of the patients.[40] (In 1887, to cele-brate the 50th anniversary of Queen Victoria's accession to the throne, an organisation had been set up to recruit and train nurses to assist particularly poor women in caring for the sick in their own homes. Queen Victoria's Jubilee Nurses were the forerunners of the modern district nurses, and in Scotland they were centred on two training homes located in Glasgow and Edinburgh. It was the good fortune of the Kippen people to be among the very early beneficiaries of their services.)

The report continues

> The house accommodation was . . . in some cases so very bad, and the overcrowding so great, that proper treatment of the patients and the stamping out of the disease were alike impossible. Then the trustees of the Public Hall [The Gillespie Memorial Hall] offered to place it at the disposal of the Committee as a temporary hospital, and this offer the Committee gladly accepted. Bedding, furniture, cooking utensils, and all the necessary equipment of a hospital, were obtained with the least possible delay, the hall was sub-divided into two wards, a room attached to it was established as a store and kitchen, and Dr McDiarmid and the nurses already in the village were put in charge. The hall made an exceedingly comfortable and satisfactory hospital. No doubt it was overcrowded, but not nearly so much as had been the houses of most of the patients, and medical attendance and nursing being concentrated in one building, were carried on to much greater advantage than when the cases were scattered all over the village. The outbreak was of a severe type. In the forty cases three deaths occurred, but the severity is not to be measured by the fatalities alone, for many of those who recovered did so only after a long struggle. Intestinal haemorrhage complicated four cases, and nearly one half had relapses.

One patient was under treatment for more than 100 days and a few others for more than two months, but Dr McDiarmid and the nurses toiled heroically, and indeed the nurse in charge herself had the misfortune to contract the disease. However, of the 33 patients nursed in the temporary hospital, none died and all recovered in due course. The three deaths were all among people who had been infected in the early part of the outbreak and who had consequently been cared for at home. Two were young girls aged 14 and 16 years and one was a young man.

While it was readily demonstrated that contaminated milk had spread the infection throughout the dairyman's customers, Dr McVail also speculated as to the real origins of the problem. He noted that Kippen had experienced occasional incidences of typhoid fever before, although not on such a scale. But he then pointed out that at the time diseases of this kind were much more likely to be found in the teeming city communities where families lived in densely packed tenements and where many had to share hopelessly inadequate privy toilets and ash-pits. He explained that sometimes the accumulated human sewage was sold to farmers, brought out from Glasgow to the country by rail and then spread on the fields as manure. At the end of September a load of such waste had been delivered to Kippen station and used on a field close to the main road and below the village, and the stench had given rise to loud complaints by a number of villagers. It was impossible to prove with absolute certainty that the infection could be traced back to this manure, but it certainly seems probable. The farmer developed what was originally diagnosed as influenza, but several other members of his household were all confirmed as having contracted typhoid, although they did not obtain their milk from the Burnside dairy. Moreover, the dairyman, James Hay, had assisted in carting the manure to the field for several days after its arrival at the station. The likelihood therefore appears to be that, via its rail link, Kippen had inadvertently imported one of Glasgow's classic 19th-century afflictions.[41] (Hay did not live for long after this outbreak, but his widow continued to run the dairy for many years.)

If the railway was something of a mixed blessing it did, nevertheless, point in some ways to the future of the village. Because of the scarcity of jobs as a result of the destruction of domestic production and the increased mechanisation of farming, and through migration of one kind or another, the population of the parish had plummeted from 2085 in 1831 to just 1036 by 1891. A report a few years later indicated that in the latter year the village had presented a poor appearance 'with its old houses in ruins and others in a tottering condition'.[40] However, slow recovery was also discernible over the next decade or so. Around the turn of the century something of an outbreak of building occurred with more than 20 large villas being constructed on Fore Road and on the main street up towards Cauldhame, while older cottages were also being modernised and a terrace of new houses for rent was built at Forthview by the Wright Park landowner, John Monteath. Houses which date from this period include Oakbank, Ambruach, Arndarroch, Dundaff and Strathview. Above the Station Brae Glentirran House was built and was followed by Dun Eaglais, with work commencing on the latter in 1902. Dun Eaglais was built as a residence and workplace for the artist, Sir D.Y. Cameron, but essentially the building activity marked the beginning of commuting to and from the village and there were two sources behind the demand for the up-market houses. Some were completed for Stirling businessmen while others were holiday or summer residences for well-to-do families from Glasgow. Many of the new dwellings were built by Thomas Syme who combined farming Shirgarton with his construction activities.

As this development gradually became a trend so pressure built up for a greatly improved standard of water supply since, of course, all of the new houses were equipped with modern bathrooms and toilet facilities. In order to comply with the Public Health Act in 1901 the County Council therefore purchased the Kippen Water Company and sunk a 90-foot-deep bore in a field above Cauldhame with a capacity to supply the village with over 17,000 gallons per day. While providing an adequate source of water this innovation did not, of course, immediately result in piped supplies being led into the older houses, hence at first a number of cast-iron stand-pipes were strategically located throughout the village. These featured lions' heads and the water gushed from their mouths. It was not a perfect solution, but it is difficult to imagine a more appropriate way for the community to have greeted the 20th century.

Less immediately successful were the early efforts to provide the village with some street lighting. The first attempt was promoted in 1898 by William McQueen, and six paraffin lamps were located in strategic positions about the centre of the village. Not surprisingly, they did not prove very effective. However, about 1912 William Dougall and William Dewar collected enough money from villagers to provide six more lamps and to pay a lamplighter 5s per week throughout the winter months, and this made for a modest improvement. An example of the brackets used to hold the lamps can still be seen on the wall of Aros House at the top of Fore Road. As this episode suggests, gas was never generally available in the village, although a small private gas plant was built on land above the Crown Hotel, and its output served the requirements of the dwellings and workshops of Mr Welsh, the joiner, and his neighbour, Mr Rennie, the blacksmith.

Another public health venture occurred in 1898 when it was accepted that the old churchyard had simply become packed to capacity and that it was time to replace it with a modern cemetery. This was duly opened on land purchased at Drum, about a mile west of the village.

A positive private development of the period was the establishment of the Forth Vineyards Company by the cousins Duncan and William Buchanan. At this time, before the extensive use of refrigeration and cold storage, UK producers of fresh fruit and vegetables had a considerable trading advantage and there was a great extension in market gardening in suitable parts of the country with the produce being delivered by rail to the city markets. Duncan Buchanan in particular was well placed to develop in this area for he had learned his trade in the great gardens at Lambton Castle in the north of England and at Culzean Castle in Ayrshire, and he had an excellent grounding in the mysteries of fruit cultivation under glass. In 1890, therefore, the cousins leased some land at Cauldhame from an uncle and by the turn of the century they had already built up a successful fruit and flower-growing business. William then moved on to become head gardener to the Earl of Marr and Kellie at Alloa, but Duncan continued to work on in the gardens at Kippen. 'He could scarcely have predicted, however, that one of his young vines would grow so rapidly that, within the space of his own lifetime, it would develop into one of the most productive and valuable single plants in the world'; or that this vine would put Kippen on the map in a quite remarkable way.[42]

A SCHOOL HISTORY OF KIPPEN

It is impossible to say when formal education first reached the parish of Kippen. As has been explained, the pre-Reformation Church had extensive lands and properties in the district and it may well be the case that the Augustinian monks of Inchmahome Priory did provide some education of a general nature. However, the fact is that there is no real evidence of any such activity either in Kippen, or elsewhere in the area.

On the other hand, George Buchanan, the 16th-century scholar, who was brought up in humble circumstances by a widowed mother, wrote that he had been educated in 'the schools of his native country' before being sent by an uncle at the age of 14 to study at university in Paris. Since Buchanan was born in Killearn in 1506 and almost certainly spent the first part of his childhood there and, from the age of seven, at Cardross, the inference must be that he did attend schools, if not in Kippen, certainly in nearby parishes.[1] In that case there is a fair possibility that the communities in and around the Vale of Menteith had some organised schools by the early 1500s.

At the Reformation the reformers placed great stress on the importance of education as being necessary for the inculcation of godly conduct 'and gude maneris' and to safeguard the long-term future of the reformed Church.[2] The basic unit on which the education system was to be constructed was the parish, and every Kirk was required to make local provision for all children, including those of poor parents. An Act of the Privy Council of December 1616 laid down 'that in everie parroche of this kingdome, whair convenient meanes may be had for interteyning a schoole, that a schoole sal be establisheit, and a fit person appointit to teache the same, upoun the expensis of the parrochinnaris according to the quantitie and qualitie of the parroch'. The Act required the schools to educate children in 'civility, godliness, knowledge and learning' and it emphasised the importance of reading, writing and religious instruction. Responsibility for enforcing the system varied throughout the course of the disputes of the 17th century, but the consolidating Act of 1696 confirmed that it was the duty of kirk sessions to organise a suitable school and teacher, that heritors were essentially responsible for ensuring that there was sufficient funding, and that presbyteries were to carry out inspections and if necessary require compliance with the law. In fact, of course, this latter task proved almost impossible where parishes were poor or where heritors declined to make adequate resources available, hence, despite the best intentions of the kirk, educational provision remained patchy in many parts of the country.

Kippen certainly had a school by the time of the 1696 Act. In that year an inspection by a delegation from the Presbytery of Stirling found that the schoolmaster was satisfactory and diligent in his conduct.[3] However, the probability must be that many years earlier some sort of school was functioning. James Ure the Covenanter seems to have been brought up in the parish and his standard of literacy was excellent. There is, of course, no guarantee that he was educated in Kippen or that his father did not employ a resident tutor. But also worth noting is the fact that ordinary troopers in Cardross's Dragoons, such as Thomas Turnbull, were able to write fluent and informative letters to the Earl. Again, Turnbull may or may not have been educated in a parish school in Kippen, but the indications do seem to suggest that at least by the mid-17th century a reasonable level of education was available to young men in the district.

In the *First Statistical Account* John Campbell reported that the school was formerly held within the church building. This was not uncommon in the early 18th century and emphasised the responsibility of the Church for education. In Kippen this arrangement operated until the refurbishment of the building in 1779, which suggests that the changes to the structure made it no longer suitable for teaching children, possibly as a result of the installation of fixed pews.

The legal obligations placed on the Kirk and the heritors appear to have been based on the assumption that a single school would be sufficient for any parish, but the sheer geographic size of Kippen made such an arrangement fairly impractical, particularly for young children, so that from an early date it was found necessary to have additional schools located in the west. The need for several schools created severe financial problems, because heritors were often very reluctant either to provide the extra funds themselves or to pass the burden on by a levy on their tenants. Moreover, if the normal school fees to parents had been increased to any great extent it would simply have resulted in the withdrawal of many children because, of course, attendance at school was not a legal obligation. As a consequence head teachers were often severely squeezed. For example, the master appointed at Kippen in 1752 was required to provide out of his own endowed salary of £100 Scots, two additional teachers, one to teach 'at Buchlyvie, the other at the burn at Arnprior, for six months in the year'. If he was unable to provide this support, a sum of fifty merks (£33 Scots) was to be deducted from his salary by the parish authorities, presumably to go towards the cost of paying the required two teachers.[4]

Such an arrangement was fairly hopeless because it would have been impossible for the various teachers to have survived with such pitifully small assistance, and it seems unlikely that the session was able to recruit competent teachers in such circumstances. As a consequence, in 1763 it was decided to have two schools, one in Kippen village and the second at Claymires, midway between Buchlyvie and Arnprior. To provide payment for both teachers the Kippen master's basic endowed salary was reduced to £75 while £40 was awarded to his colleague. In 1782 a purpose-built 'tolerably commodious' school building and house was completed at Claymires and it was soon well attended. However, in one sense the project failed because the school at Arnprior still proved to be necessary and it therefore continued to function over the winter and spring months.

When the Kippen school was removed from the church it was relocated by taking out a long lease on a house in the village which thereafter doubled up as a dwelling for the master. The position of this school is somewhat uncertain. The 1790s feu map shows a school on Burnside, but one local tradition places the old parish school on the site of the present Cross Keys Hotel. By the end of the 18th century there was a Cross Keys Inn in the village, but it was then located in the house at the cross directly beside the war memorial, where a small general store operated until very recently. In the winter of 1793 the numbers of pupils in regular attendance at the three schools were noted as 60 at Kippen, 36 at Arnprior and 64 at Claymires.

An edition of the *Glasgow Courier* of January 1810 carried the following advertisement.

> A schoolmaster is wanted for the Parish of Kippen. Candidates must produce ample testimonials of good character, and must be qualified to teach English grammatically, Latin, Writing, Arithmetic and Book-keeping – The election to take place on the 28th February. The salary is 300 merks. The Schoolmaster's house is capable of accommodating a few boarders. The yearly income of a well-qualified teacher is computed to be upwards of £100. For particulars, apply to the Rev Mr MacFarlan, Kippen.

The appointed teacher was Mr James Auld, and we know rather more about this man and his times because he kept a diary. Sadly, the whereabouts of this day-by-day account of Mr Auld's dealings is not known, but some notes made from it have survived. Apparently the diary did not contain much descriptive narrative, being rather more a record of his financial transactions. However, some of the information is useful and interesting. For example, Auld served as the village's schoolmaster from 1810 until he died in harness in 1864 when he was aged 85, presumably hanging on to the end because without a pension he simply could not afford to retire. Indeed, towards the end of his time, following an inspection, a report to the Presbytery of Dunblane of 1856 complained of his age and infirmity and his obvious dependence on his assistant.

Auld was a graduate of Divinity Hall, Glasgow University, and he was what used to be known as a 'stickit minister' – i.e. one who was unable to secure a church of his own. In an age when the legal patron's voice was technically still decisive over church appointments it was not unusual for able individuals to find difficulty in obtaining a charge, and many men such as Mr Auld had to settle for the alternative of a teaching position.

The main income to the school obviously came from the endowment from the parish church and the fees of parents who could afford to pay. But despite having the school house Mr Auld could not hope to live on his salary and he had also to work as clerk to the heritors from whom he received a small additional payment. Unfortunately many of the heritors (and parents) seem to have been habitually late payers and he appears always to have been owed money. Other jobs from which he received some remuneration included keeping the accounts of the local militia company, taking the census, acting as the local surveyor, teaching pauper children at a flat rate and providing private tuition to backward children. However, despite all these various efforts, he never managed to lift his income to the promised £100 per year.

It is not known if he took boarders as suggested in the original advertisement. Certainly had he done so, this would not have been unusual, because it was quite common for better-off parents who lived at a distance from a parish school to board their children for part of the year. However, if the school was on the site of the present Cross Keys, the two buildings shown in the position on the 1790s feu map of the village appear very small and the presbytery report of 1856 mentioned above claimed that the school was so small that it failed to meet the legal requirement.[5] Since Mr Auld had a substantial family to support, it may be that he simply came to need most of the accommodation as his own dwelling.

Not surprisingly Mr Auld was forced to turn his hand to many things. For example, he kept his own cow, and sold surplus milk from time to time. He sometimes regretted having to buy hay for the animal, but was pleased if it fetched a decent price when it came to be sold. In August 1813, for example, he was happy to sell a cow for £7 19s, and in April 1861 he noted that he had obtained his first 1d worth of milk from a new animal. He personally made the ink for his scholars and on one occasion he noted that the cost of materials to manufacture a sufficient supply was 2s 2d. He also had to buy books, paper and quill pens. His school house was, of course, thatched and he evidently purchased 20 stone of thatching material for 7d, which suggests that he intended to carry out the repairs himself.[6]

William Anderson reported that in about 1840 there were seven schools in the parish. Two of these were the parochial schools in Kippen village and at Claymires, four were entirely unendowed 'adventure' schools, one in Kippen, one at Arnprior, and two at Buchlyvie, and one was a school for females.

The adventure schools were so called because they were commercial businesses and the teachers were completely dependent on the income that they could obtain from parents' fees. Parish authorities tended to tolerate such schools, particularly where the official facilities were lacking and where there was a clear need for additional provision. This was obviously the case in Buchlyvie and Arnprior, but the existence of the additional Kippen school suggests an awareness that the building operated by Mr Auld had insufficient capacity, and the fact is that allowing a commercial business would certainly have been cheaper from the point of view of the heritors than providing a larger parish school. The Kippen adventure school probably attracted its pupils by charging a slightly lower fee, although this competition may have been intensely irritating to Mr Auld. The adventure school seems to have been located at Oxhill in Fore Road and this is shown in a village map of 1862. An old photograph shows the children gathered next door at 'Thimble Row', a cottage which may have been constructed about 1830 or perhaps slightly earlier, around the same time as the present church was built. Judging from its traditional name, Thimble Row may have begun life as the place where the mistress and her girls tamboured the muslin, and there may have been some connection with the school. It is possible that the needlework lessons were given there.

According to Mr Anderson the teacher of the 'female school'

apparently received 'from subscriptions by respectable individuals around £20 yearly, besides half of the school fees'[7]. In other words, wealthier individuals in the community made donations of about £20 per annum to subsidise education for girls, but the school was only able to charge fees at half the rate typically applied to boys. The reason was quite simply that in these days many families were unwilling or unable to accept the costs of education, and when it came to a choice, scarce resources normally went to provide for the sons who would one day have to support their own families. The educational needs of girls, therefore, tended to be neglected or to depend on the type of sympathetic support outlined here. The subjects studied in the girls' school would have been similar to those provided by Mr Auld, but by this stage would also have included needlework. Where this school was located has not been discovered, but it could have been at 'Thimble Row'.

By the time of Anderson's report the endowed part of Mr Auld's salary had risen to 500 merks Scots (£27 15s 6d Sterling) while the teacher at Claymires now received a mere 100 merks (£5 11s 1d). The official fees paid by parents per quarter were related to the subjects taught and were 2s 6d for reading, 4s for writing, 5s for arithmetic and book-keeping, and 7s 6d for Latin. The parents of a pupil studying all of the standard subjects could therefore expect to pay the master 19s per quarter.[8]

The Arnprior school appears to have operated in one of the cottages in or close to what was known as 'the Street'. It was very small, but it may also have been fairly effective. In August 1850 the *Stirling Observer* reported that

> the school at Arnprior in the parish of Kippen was examined on Wednesday last, in the presence of the minister of the parish and others interested in the cause of education. The scholars acquitted themselves in a manner most creditable to their teacher and to themselves, and we feel confident that under the superintendence of Mr Ferguson the youth of the district will make rapid progress in all the branches of a useful education.[9]

Ferguson was followed at Arnprior by a teacher known to the community as 'Dominie' Miller. Interestingly, his daughter Jean, who was lame, may have been one of Scotland's first postwomen. Apparently each day she collected the mail from Port of Menteith Station and delivered the letters and packages round the farms and cottages, and on a Friday she also brought copies of the *Stirling Journal* at a cost of 1d.

After the 1843 Disruption, the new Free Church lost no time in launching a remarkable programme of building schools, for the children of its members. Within seven years it claimed to be subsidising no fewer than 657 schools, providing an education for 75,000 children. Among the communities to benefit from this activity was Kippen and the new Free Church school was opened at Castlehill in the original part of the present-day village primary school. Perhaps inevitably the existing parish church authorities responded, opening another new school in Fore Road in the front of what is now the village hall. The map of the village of 1862 shows both of these schools.

The most significant change in education in the 19th century followed the passing of the 1872 Education (Scotland) Act which laid the foundation on which modern Scottish primary education is grounded. In the years 1864 to 1867 a Royal Commission chaired by the 8th Duke of Argyll had investigated the education system, and this enquiry had been provoked by two factors: first, the rapid growth of urban communities (especially in the greater Glasgow area) had progressively overwhelmed the ancient parochial schools, and second, the provision of elementary education had become hopelessly fragmented and in many places was largely in the hands of a variety of charitable and religious organisations as well as independent adventure schools of the kind that had appeared in Kippen parish. As we have seen, the failure to come to terms with the collapse of the urban parish structure had been one of the factors in the Disruption, but despite the huge voluntary effort of the new Free Church, there was a growing awareness that the education system was inadequate and that it was not keeping pace with the needs of the developing population.

When the various reports of the Argyll Commission were published the conclusion was offered that of the 500,000 Scottish children then requiring basic education, 200,000 received it under reasonable and effective conditions, 200,000 were enrolled in uninspected schools of questionable merit, and 90,000 or so were attending no school at all. The worst situation was in Glasgow where the enquirers concluded that less than half of the children were on a school roll. In passing, true attendance levels were probably often poor with many girls, in particular, being required to look after younger children or to otherwise 'help their mothers'.

From the evidence collected for the Argyll Commission it can be seen that Scottish education in the mid-19th century was less than adequate, but it is also interesting to note that there appear to have been significantly more Scottish than English children receiving elementary education and that, for the time, Scotland had a comparatively low rate of adult illiteracy.[10]

Following the report, the 1872 Act was passed. It was to prove a major point of departure and a considerably more powerful measure than the equivalent English Act of 1870. Under its terms a national and unified system of elementary education was established as the schools of the Presbyterian churches were taken over by secular authority in the form of a network of locally elected school boards. Compulsory attendance for all children between 5 and 13 years became possible almost at once, and over the next three decades Scotland was provided with an excellent system of elementary education as many fine schools were created. Only the Episcopal and Catholic schools stood out of the system and continued to be funded by voluntary means.

The Scotch Education Department was also created in 1872, but its location in London fostered some allegations of the 'Anglicising' of Scottish education, and the education system certainly became somewhat centralised. However, the thousand or so school boards which were created in cities, towns and parishes across Scotland ensured an important degree of local influence. The churches and other vested interests tended to dominate the boards, but they were often particularly important to women who, for the first time, were permitted not only to vote but to compete for public office in an electoral contest. It is sad to note that the Kippen women do not seem to have made any early impact and the school board that was set up for the parish did not include any females at any stage in its history.

The new system introduced by the 1872 Act was not universally popular because, of course, some of the old parish schools (particularly in rural areas) had been very good indeed. In 1903, William Chrystal of Kippen concluded that the former system had great advantages, 'the pupils under the old régime having been well grounded in a few subjects, instead of being washed with a dozen'. Interestingly Chrystal also assured his readers that 'for ages the parish has been productive of sons and daughters who have acquired high scholarly attainments'.[11]

The first election to the school board of Kippen parish took place at the old Arnprior School on Saturday, 29th March, 1873, and those elected included Henry Campbell of Boquhan (chairman), Daniel Fisher of Ballamenoch, Rev. P.T. Muirhead of Kippen Free Church, George McFarlane of Buchlyvie station and James Stirling of Garden. Shortly afterwards the Rev. William Wilson of Kippen parish church, joined the board in place of Mr Campbell, and James Stirling became chairman, a position that he maintained for 30 years. The board was subject to triennial elections.

The Kippen school board was at first responsible for four schools – Kippen Public School (the old parish school), Kippen Castlehill School (the former Free Church school), and the schools at Arnprior and Buchlyvie. The last named was actually jointly run with approximately two-thirds of the liability falling on Kippen and the remainder on Drymen school board, presumably reflecting the catchment area which cut across the boundaries of the administrative parishes.

Initial thoughts of the board may have been immediately to merge the two Kippen schools in one common building, but that proposal for a new school was rejected by the Education Department in London.[12] As a result, for the next couple of decades the Castlehill school took the younger children, while from the fourth year on the children attended the school in Fore Road. In 1877 the rolls of the Kippen parish schools were recorded as follows:[13] Kippen Public School – 72 pupils; Kippen Castlehill School – 85 pupils; Arnprior Primary School – 76 pupils.

At the time, of course, despite the economic problems of the district, family sizes were large – hence the remarkable number of children. Moreover, the chances of survival of children in country communities were beginning to improve, although infant mortality rates were still very high by modern standards. (In 1879 a severe outbreak of scarlet fever forced the Kippen schools to close their doors for six weeks and deaths of children during such epidemics were sadly common at that time.)

As has been explained, the two Kippen school buildings were fairly new at this stage, but the cottage at Arnprior was hopelessly inadequate, which is not surprising given the figures quoted above. The parish minister, Mr Wilson, said that 'the school accommodation there for a long time had been extremely defective', and in the mid-1860s he had attempted to obtain new premises.[14] However, in 1875 the board addressed the problem by acquiring from Mr Stirling land by the roadside at Kepp and building a new school. This was formally opened in October 1876 and its first head teacher was James Hunter.

Under the new régime school income was now derived from three sources – school fees for which parents were liable (although some 'pauper' children had their fees met by various charitable trust funds), an end-of-year deficit subsidy from the parochial board, and a grant payable by the Scotch Education Department after annual examination of the children. This meant that part of the head teacher's income was directly linked to the performance and attendance of the children under inspection.

Mr Hunter's basic salary was £85 per year, but as a general rule he was able to earn about another £35 as reward for the good results achieved by his pupils. Curiously, this typically outstripped the earnings at the Kippen village schools where, in 1879 for example, the grant payments to heads were £25 and £20. The probable explanation is that the two Kippen schools were effectively being managed as a single school with two buildings, and the grant was probably simply being split between Mr Williamson at Fore Road and Miss Trench at Castlehill. At this time the Castlehill staff were all female and it was therefore sometimes referred to as a Dames' school.

Archibald Williamson was an interesting man who served in Kippen up to September 1893. He apparently had an artificial limb, a 'peg leg' that was made for him by one of the village joiners. At Arnprior the new school had a small cottage attached for Mr Hunter's use from 1877 and about this time a substantial detached villa was also built for the Kippen head teacher at the rear of the Fore Road school.

One of the subjects that greatly concerned the new Scotch Education Department was the level of illness among schoolchildren and the ease with which infections tended to spread. Part of the problem was the poor quality of school toilet facilities and school inspectors frequently addressed this issue in their reports. For example, the report of 1876 complained that the Fore Road school toilets were entirely unsatisfactory. 'They are placed in a corner of the small play-ground attached to the school and have not even separate approaches'. The inspector advocated an additional playground with toilets for the girls being separated from those for the boys, and this issue was mentioned in several following years with the threat of grant being withheld unless suitable provision was made.[15]

Even the new school at Arnprior had similar problems; neither the school nor the house was connected to an adequate water-supply and the toilet facilities were initially 'ill ventilated' closets and an ash-pit. Mr Hunter repeatedly protested to the board and in 1879 it instructed that the school be provided with water without delay. This was eventually done in April, the water being taken from a field opposite the school. However, it seems that the farmer was less than pleased to have the school draw off his spring water, and this was the cause not only of delay, but of long-running difficulty. Even although the piped water brought about an improvement, the board chairman 'could not say that it was quite satisfactory'. Indeed it was far from satisfactory and an erratic and poor-quality water supply remained a problem for the school for many years, the closets and cess-pit continuing in use far into the 20th century.

At the Fore Road school and at Arnprior, pupil teachers were typically appointed to assist the qualified head. Normally an older scholar who wished to continue his or her education would be recruited on probation as 'temporary monitor' and, if satisfactory, would then be appointed pupil teacher a few months later. Effectively this system meant that 13-year-old children became apprentice school teachers, although not all of the youngsters so appointed attempted later to follow careers in teaching. In fact the scheme was the most obvious method through which a gifted lad or lass 'of pairts', whose parents were relatively poor could make their way through to a career for which a higher education was necessary. Their contracts with school boards lasted for anything from one to five years, during which time, in addition to undertaking teaching duties, the individuals concerned prepared for professional examinations, sat the examinations of the Society of Science and Art and/or attempted to obtain entrance to university or to one of the teaching colleges. While acting as pupil teachers they received a salary of £10 per year (reaching £20 from their 18th birthday) for which an education department grant might or might not be partly available, depending on their progress in exams. The pupil teachers also usually attempted to obtain a bursary or scholarship to fund their future studies. In retrospect it was a gruelling entrance into higher education and, not surprisingly, many failed to complete the course.

A notable example of a pupil teacher was Charles S. Dougall of Kippen, who taught and studied at Arnprior school under Mr Hunter from 1884 to 1887, at the end of which time he sat the entrance exam at the Glasgow Church of Scotland Training College. He secured first-class passes in all his exams, finishing fourth on the published list and, as a result, was offered immediate entry to Glasgow University.[16] There he took an MA in mathematics and natural philosophy and obtained a distinction in classics. He was awarded the Eglinton Fellowship in 1890 and was Cunningham Gold Medalist in 1892. Given such glittering academic progress, it is not surprising that Dougall was one of those who did stay in education, eventually becoming 'an outstanding' rector of Dollar Academy 1902–1922.

Among the pupil teachers who served in one or another of the schools in the period were William and John Armstrong, sons of the Arnprior blacksmith. John successfully completed the Customs House entrance examinations in 1891. Others included James Short, Andrew Trotter, Robert Dougall, Andrew Edmonston, Lizzie Welsh (daughter of the village joiner who had made Mr Williamson's leg), Nellie Robertson, Jessie Dougall and George Motion. The last named was the son of the clerk to the school board, and he was part of a family that emigrated together in 1884 to start a new life in Canada.[17] Lizzie Welsh and Nellie Robertson were pupil teachers who went on to complete their apprenticeships in Kippen and undertook their examinations with no more assistance than the normal instruction provided by Mr Hunter, who, by this stage had moved to become head at Kippen. They were awarded their professional qualifications in 1897 and 1898 respectively and, without any additional training, in 1899 Miss Welsh was appointed head teacher of Great Elm School in Somerset.[18] Small wonder that when her successful qualification was intimated by the HMI, whose annual report also indicated the award of a grant to the school of £174, the board wrote to Mr Hunter expressing its 'entire satisfaction with the Report and the Grant earned in your school'.[19]

The activities of the pupil teachers illustrate the fact that in the last quarter of the 19th century, although the schools of the parish were classed simply as public elementary schools, their range of work was extensive. The basic programme was to prepare children to be examined at seven different 'standards', the content of each standard being set out in the 'Scotch Codes' provided by the Scotch Education Department.[20] The subject matter was essentially the 'three Rs' – reading, writing and arithmetic, but, in addition, music and drawing were taught, and needlework instruction was given to the girls. Her Majesty's Inspectors visited the schools each year to test the children to ensure that at every stage they met the required standard. Basic religious instruction was also compulsory, but this subject was tested simply by the local clergy.

However, as explained, the pupil teachers were deemed to be serving as apprentice teachers and the 'master' was obliged to give them and other older children of appropriate ability, training up to university entrance level. It will be evident, therefore, that Mr Williamson and Mr Hunter taught over the full range of school education and, for example, in addition to the basic subjects, senior pupils were given instruction in Latin, Greek, French and Science.

The two heads at this time seem to have been first-class teachers and school reports are generally full of praise. For instance, in 1890 the inspector, Mr Waddell, wrote of Kippen:

This little school makes, as usual, an excellent appearance. All the branches of the Standard work are most meritorious, but particularly writing, spelling and composition. The Class subjects also have been most carefully mastered, with the partial exception of Map-drawing, which might improve a little. The Specific Subjects (taught to meet the needs of individual children) and the industrial (needle) work are quite satisfactory; and the tone and order are all that could be wished.[21]

Similarly, two years later, the HMI reported that Arnprior was 'an admirably conducted school. The younger classes reach the highest level in every branch . . . The class subjects have been taught with the utmost success; for intelligence, eagerness and widely diffused information the answering could hardly be surpassed'.[22]

As mentioned above, needlework was taught to the female pupils. The mid-Victorian age was, of course, a time of considerable poverty, of few labour-saving household devices, of only limited forms of mass produced clothing, and when most food processing and storing was still done within the home. Inevitably, therefore, the domestic burden on women was heavy in many working-class households. From the early 1850s a group of wealthy women led by Louisa Hope of Edinburgh had campaigned vigorously to have practical domestic education introduced into elementary schools. Their objectives were fundamentally to improve the quality of the lives of females by giving them better household skills in the hope that this would make for better family life and do something to improve the health of children. Little progress was made at this time with respect to cookery, but nevertheless the campaign was moderately successful, and in 1861 an Act was passed providing grants for schools which employed a woman to teach needlework skills to girl pupils. By the time of the 1872 Act 70 per cent of Scottish schools had needlework teachers and Kippen school board continued to obtain funding for this purpose. Jane Taylor, Miss Hunter, Miss Lamont and Miss Skinner were some of the needlework teachers who worked in one or another of the Kippen schools.

The campaign for cookery instruction developed during the mid 1870s when the Society of Arts in London initiated a drive for improved food preparation and better hygiene both in domestic and commercial kitchens. This led to the establishment of specialised cookery schools in Edinburgh and Glasgow to train suitable teachers, but school boards were typically reluctant to spend the money required to equip ordinary schools with cooking facilities, and they were also unwilling to accept responsibility for buying the raw materials to enable pupils to practise the necessary skills. In the following decades, therefore, travelling teachers came out from the city cookery schools into communities and held day and evening classes for a fortnight at a time for women of all ages. To begin with these were held in front of huge audiences in the main population centres, but as the numbers of instructresses increased so the classes spread out to rural communities.[23] The campaign reached Kippen in 1893 when in May the Fore Road school was entirely given over to cookery classes for two weeks.[24]

Two problems which troubled the Kippen school board in its early days were parents falling into arrears with fees and poor attendance. As far as fees were concerned, in the context of legally enforceable compulsory attendance, these must have been something of a nightmare to poor families, particularly where there were a number of children of school age in the household. It must have been a great relief to many when fees were abandoned from 1st October, 1889.[25]

As was to be expected in country schools, attendance varied considerably from season to season. Although the school board employed a 'compulsory officer', Mr McAlpine, to enforce attendance, in fact it was generally understood that older boys from farms would be expected to stay away from school when essential seasonal work required the use of every available hand. The system was known as 'half time' where such boys were broadly exempt from April to September, but the reality was that the harvesting period often extended late into the autumn.

In the 1870s and 1880s the school year was organised to take account of the annual round of farming activities. The main holiday period extended from August to the beginning of October and was obviously intended to enable children to assist in bringing in the crops. However, the problem was that harvesting methods were still fairly slow, with the result that in a year of poor weather it could be November before the process was complete. (In passing, in the 19th century there was no Christmas holiday, but the schools did close for a few days around New Year.)

In 1891 the school summer holiday was moved to the more familiar Scottish period from the end of June to mid-August.[26] Quite why this change was made is unclear, although it may be related to the fact that grain harvesting was becoming more mechanised and less labour intensive or that an increasing proportion of Scottish children were living in an urban environment where the farming calendar would have been irrelevant. However, for the next 30 years Kippen teachers were bedevilled by poor attendance of some pupils in October/November, during the potato gathering season, and this problem seems only to have been partially resolved during the First World War, when it was finally decided to grant a short autumn holiday for the purpose.

Other episodes related to the farming year could also create attendance problems. Typically day holidays were granted on the days of the main cattle fairs. Although the June Balgair fair by now only cast a shadow of its former significance, up to about 1900 pupils usually were given the day off to attend, and the same was true with respect to the December Kippen cattle fair. However, the June Stirling fair was also important, and if a holiday was not granted on such occasions the attendance at school typically slumped. Sometimes on other specific occasions, heads and board members again simply bowed to the inevitable, as in September 1899, when it was decided to close the Kippen school for the day because the great Barnum and Baillie Show was visiting Stirling.[27] Similarly, if a mobile steam-driven threshing machine was operating on local farms every available hand, including those of children was required to ensure that it worked flat out and then moved on without delay, and the heads could only resign themselves to the consequent empty desks. Finally, in the pre-First World War era there were many seasonal farm workers who came out from Glasgow for the summer and autumn, and returned to the city in winter. The children of the people concerned, therefore, attended the schools only during the months from August to December.

Illness was another problem that affected not just the attendance of the sick children, but also often of older girls. For example, in 1890 the Kippen head noted the presence of influenza in the village and complained of the low level of attendance of female pupils for several weeks in January and February. He commented that at one point as many as 50 per cent of the older girls were off, and the inference is that in many cases they were being kept at home to nurse other members of their families.[28] The head's concern in this instance was probably not unrelated to the fact that he was trying to prepare his pupils for the annual inspection by the HMI, which was scheduled for the end of February. However, as a general rule, girls over the age of twelve were permitted to stay at home if justified by family circumstances.

Causes of absence were critically important to the schools and the board, since part of the grant paid by the Scotch Education Department was strictly linked to the total number of attendances recorded for pupils each year. Keeping an accurate register was an important task because a visiting inspector who suspected that the roll was being falsified might cut or withhold the grant. Inspectors occasionally descended on the schools without prior warning in order to test the accuracy of records, and for this reason board members not infrequently also made unannounced visits to check that the children in attendance tallied with the names ticked off on the register. The real root problem was that at this time enforcing compulsory attendance was extremely difficult because hard-pressed families were often desperately eager to get older children out to work. But equally if children legally obliged to attend failed to do so, the school and the board lost grant money and had a struggle to meet bills. Head teachers, therefore, were frequently caught in the middle of a fierce battle of wills between families and the school board.

As mentioned above, illness was a key influence on attendance levels, and this was particularly the case with the regular outbreaks of epidemics of one kind or another. These could occasionally be so severe that one or another of the schools might be forced to close for several weeks at a time. For example, in 1879 an outbreak of scarlet fever forced closure of the Kippen schools for six weeks, and influenza, diphtheria, whooping cough, and measles also produced closures from time to time. Interestingly, however, the typhoid fever outbreak of 1893 did not actually result in the shutting of the school, although the New Year holiday was extended for a few days.

The other factor that could also adversely affect school attendance was, of course, bad weather. In these days children walked to the Kippen schools over distances extending up to more than two miles – sometimes without shoes, and often on roads that were little more than badly maintained cart-tracks. For instance, in 1884 Mr Hunter at Arnprior reported 'very stormy weather, and children are cold and sometimes wet – attendance very good considering the long miry roads many of them have to walk over'.[29] Perhaps more typical was Mr Williamson's terse note of 7th January, 1887 – 'Attendance very low on account of the stormy weather and state of the roads'.[30] As a response to the winter difficulties and, in particular, to the lack of daylight, school hours were adjusted to run from 9.30 in the morning until 3.30 p.m., with just a half-hour break between 1 and 1.30 for lunch. Even so, some disruption was inevitable in most years.

A glance through the available registers and school prize lists indicates that many of the pupils attending the schools in the period 1876 to the First World War came from families of long-standing in the district, whose names are often still familiar a hundred years on. Surnames such as Allan, Armstrong, Buchanan, Chrystal, Crawford, Davidson, Dewar, Dougall, Dow, Duncanson, Ferguson, Forrester, Gray, Hay, Keir, Leckie, McCallum, McDiarmid, McCowan, McGibbon, McKay, McGregor, McLaren, McQueen, Mills, Morton, Muirhead, Rennie, Risk, Syme, Welsh, Wright, Yule and many others catch the eye. (Interestingly, the immigration into the district through the 18th and 19th centuries of families with Highland origins is clearly indicated by contrasting many of the above surnames with those from earlier periods.)

Comparatively little is indicated about the employment destinations of the Kippen children on leaving school at the age of 13, but in a few cases the details for the Arnprior children are noted. Not surprisingly 'farm service' appears for boys and 'at home' or 'gone into service' is the occasional comment by a girl's name. Sometimes there is something more specific: for example, in 1887 Willie Dow left to become 'an ironmonger with Graham and Morton'; Agnes Graham was 'gone to be a dressmaker'; and George Paterson was appointed 'Clerk at Fairfields' shipyard. A good number, however, 'gained a bursary' to continue their education. For example, in June 1896 it was announced to a gathering of pupils, parents and board members at Kippen that John Allan and Katie Fisher had 'at the recent competition in Glasgow, been successful in gaining Marshall bursaries of the annual value of £10 per year, tenable for five years conditional on their attending Stirling High School'.[31] 'Kay Trust' bursaries were also available and awarded after competitive examination, but typically for shorter periods.

Departures to new lives overseas were also noted quite frequently. In a laconic comment in the school log for 28th May, 1909 the head recorded 'four boys and three girls left this week. Four went to Falkirk, two to New Zealand and one left for farm work'.[32] Two years later 'two pupils left today for British Columbia' and shortly after a highly-regarded infant mistress, Margaret Erskine, left to be married and to settle with her new husband in Queensland, Australia.[33] This pattern of outward migration characterised the period and perhaps reached its peak in Kippen in 1925 when it was noted that 'seven children left today. They sail for Canada tomorrow'.[34]

During the years around 1890 the numbers of junior pupils in Kippen continued to increase and in 1891 the Castlehill school roll reached 112. To address the resulting overcrowding, following Mr Williamson's retirement in 1893 it was decided to extend that school building and finally to bring the two Kippen schools together under the one roof. To lead the unified school Mr Hunter was transferred from Arnprior and awarded a salary of £100, plus half of the annual SED grant and, of course, use of the fine school house. Mr Williamson, relinquishing his position on the grounds of ill health, was treated well by the board, being awarded an annual pension of £110, and his work at Kippen received a glowing acknowledgement in the board minutes. Interestingly, the vacancy created at Arnprior attracted no fewer than 126 applicants, the successful candidate being Mr Gardner.[35]

The extended building at Castlehill was opened formally on 16th December, 1895 and in the log book it was recorded that 'the children of the senior division marched up in fours from the old building to the new – the bells of the Established Church and Free Church ringing merry peals. At the new building a large company of ratepayers, parents and others had assembled' together with the members of the school board and one of Her Majesty's Inspectors.[36] By 1898 there were 193 pupils on the register of the unified school and the average daily attendance was about 170.[37]

William Hay was taught by Mr Hunter at Kippen during the years 1908 to 1916, and looking back 80 years later remembered him as

> a grand teacher. He was hard, but honest. If you would learn, you got every chance; and if you wouldn't learn, he belted it into you. But he was a decent, good man for all that. I often think of him and of these days. He wanted me to stay at school, but because of the war I was called to work on the Inch farm when I was thirteen. I was ploughing with two horses when the church bells rang on armistice day so I suppose I learned something else.[38]

The children who attended the Kippen and Arnprior schools were no doubt typical Scottish children of their own generations. The games that they played were presumably much the same as would have been enjoyed by their peers in any similar country school.

In the early period, games did not normally involve a direct contribution from the teachers and the choice of pursuit was a matter for the children themselves. There were morning and afternoon play breaks of 15 minutes. Typically the playgrounds were divided so that boys and girls were confined to separate areas, and William Hay recalled that at the Castlehill school Mr Hunter rigorously enforced the segregated playgrounds with any boy straying into the girls' zone being liable to be walloped.

In the years before the First World War football seems to have been the preferred game for the boys, and whenever possible matches of the kick and rush, 'all in' variety would develop, if necessary in a field near the school, although usually these took place out of school hours. Mr Hunter evidently regarded all games as a diversion from the real business of the school, and he particularly disapproved of football. Far from providing a football via school funds, if he found one being used during intervals, he would confiscate it and hack it to bits with his pen-knife.

In the general course of things, suitable footballs were in short supply and tennis-type balls were commonly pressed into service, but from time to time a generous father would buy the real thing, which was thereafter literally kicked until it disintegrated. By the early 1900s occasional matches were being organised between Arnprior and Kippen schools, and these took place on a Saturday morning with the boys walking between the villages to take part.

'King' was the other favourite boys' game and this was a form of tig, where the king boy would attempt to defend the space between two marked areas. In the autumn 'conkers' was played for weeks, with the many chestnut trees in the district providing a rich harvest of ammunition. 'Bools' (marbles) was also a favourite pastime with 'muggie' being the preferred local variation. Again, out of school hours in summer, rounders and cricket were played by the boys, especially when the sons of seasonal workers from Glasgow were available to take part.

As a general rule girls seem not to have been allowed to join in such activities – presumably because of the attitude of adults such as Mr Hunter. 'Peever' (hopscotch) and skipping, sometimes with five or six girls simultaneously under the one rope, and taking turns to enter or leave to a variety of chanted rhymes, were the favourite girls' games.[39]

In the years around the turn of the century the children were occasionally given some instruction in military drill (marching etc.) by the head teacher, and in March of 1901 the board responded to a departmental circular by asking its heads to provide such training.[40] This was a very early response by the leaders of the state education system to the ominous fitness problems being revealed by the South African War (1899–1902), when many of the young men volunteering for service, particularly from urban communities, were shown to be in a wretched physical condition. In some areas as many as 40 per cent of the men were rejected by the examining doctors as being unfit to serve, while many others dropped out because they could not physically cope with their basic training. In addition, the infant mortality rate in Scotland still stood as high as 124 child deaths per 1000 births. (Interestingly, the infant death rate in Kippen about this time was just over 70 per 1000, which emphasises how much better the chances of survival were for country children when contrasted with their urban contemporaries.) Not surprisingly, therefore, informed medical opinion became increasingly concerned about the fitness of children and about how problems of poor child health might be addressed by schools.

In 1902 a Royal Commission was established to report on physical training in Scottish schools and on its instructions a major investigation was conducted into the health of children. This was carried out by two similar studies in Aberdeen and Edinburgh, the latter being conducted by the medical inspector at the Scottish Office, Dr W. Leslie Mackenzie and his wife Helen, a schoolteacher before her marriage. They demonstrated that urban working-class children were smaller, lighter and obviously less well nourished than children from middle-class and rural districts. Moreover, they illustrated that, in poor areas, astonishingly high proportions of children suffered from at least one significant medical defect. They followed this up in 1904 by presenting further persuasive information to an inter-departmental Royal Commission on Physical Deterioration and argued that the root causes of the problem were poor housing, overcrowding, lack of adequate nutrition and ignorance of food, health, hygiene and child care among mothers.[41]

As a result of these and other investigations the seminal 1908 Education (Scotland) Act was passed and this instructed school boards to organise the regular medical inspection of schoolchildren, to take action against parents whose children were verminous or unclean and to provide lunch for the children of the poor. In addition, organised physical exercise was to be provided and instruction in domestic science was to be fully introduced in larger schools or made available through supplementary classes. These efforts were very successful, halving infant mortality rates within two decades and, for example, reducing the incidence of rickets among Scottish children from 9 per cent in 1910–1914 to just 1.5 per cent by 1937.[42]

Physical training was introduced in the Kippen schools about this time, and by 1910 the children were performing 'Swedish' drill (involving much arm swinging, trunk turning, bending and stretching) on two periods per week.

The other big change in the delivery of education had been introduced from 1902 when the school leaving age was increased to 14 years of age. This was at first addressed by providing a final year 'supplementary course' for those children who were not attempting to progress into secondary education. The deliberate intention was to make the instruction as practical and useful to the children as possible, and in the case of the boys this was done by laying on courses in woodwork, technical drawing and agriculture or gardening. For the girls, it was at first rather more difficult, partly because of the lack of cooking equipment, and at least one HMI strongly criticised the fact that while the boys in Kippen were being taught useful skills the girls were spending their extra year on difficult Shakespearian tragedies or advanced geometry.[43]

The addition of the extra year and the nature of the subjects made Kippen school impossibly overcrowded, and the technical classes were therefore at first held in the Gillespie Hall on a Saturday morning, while classes in household economy and 'artistic needlework' were subsequently organised for the girls and held in the Public Hall (the former Fore Road school). For a time this remained the situation, although the school was modernised and further divided internally in 1907. By 1909 there were 196 pupils on the ordinary school roll, while 49 older children were attending the supplementary classes, so it is easy to understand the problem. Moreover, the situation was to some degree compounded by the fact that Arnprior school simply did not have the capacity to provide for supplementary pupils, and the experiment of attempting a cookery class had caused so much noise and disruption to the rest of the pupils that it had been ruled out as a regular activity. As a result, older Arnprior children were required to join the extra classes either at Kippen or Buchlyvie. Since this inevitably involved a long walk, absence rates were high among the children concerned.

By 1909 cookery instruction had become obligatory. Facilities had to be provided and the first regular classes were operated from April 1909. Interestingly, within a few days a cookery class was overseen by Miss J.G. Crawford, the first female inspector at the Scottish Education Department and a distinguished pioneer of this type of work. She reported:

> Cookery is taught to the pupils of this school on Saturday mornings. It is observed that at least four pupils are being deprived of the lessons on account of distance or home duties. The lesson was quite successfully carried through; and the tidy smart appearance of the pupils was a credit to the school. The continuance of the class on Saturday is recommended for this session, but in future, the work should be done on a school day when every pupil could attend. The equipment is fairly good, though the introduction of a sink would be a great improvement and advantage.[44]

Within a few months the senior girls were undertaking a programme which included cookery, infant health and care, and home nursing, and this type of activity in Scottish schools was clearly a major factor in the improvement in child health which is so noticeable over the next two or three decades. The school did not have the ability to provide meals, but at least a hot drink was made available at lunch time.

The other key development following the 1908 Act was, of course, the regular medical inspection of all children. The first school medical inspector was Dr A. Josephine Gardner of Stirling and she visited the schools of the area from 1909 until 1916 when she departed to take on war duties. In the pre-war period female doctors found it very difficult to break down some of the barriers of professional prejudice and to obtain positions in some of the more prestigious medical activities or well remunerated practices. Very unfairly, they often found it necessary to seek employment in what were then perceived to be low-status areas in which their male colleagues were less interested, and it is therefore not surprising that many of the first generation of school doctors were women. However, they soon made an impact. Under the new system children were routinely examined at the ages of 7 and 13, and by the outbreak of the war in 1914 almost every child attending a Scottish school was being properly examined on at least two occasions. Where necessary individual children were seen and given treatment or had their school training adjusted. For example, in 1912 after one typical inspection at Kippen, Dr Gardner identified no fewer than three girls with heart problems and instructed that they were not to be required to take drill.[45] In addition, head teachers now had a duty to report to Dr Gardner whenever an infectious disease such as diphtheria, whooping cough, chicken pox or mumps broke out, and children from the infected family were immediately sent home whether or not they were ill. If necessary, the doctor would require the school to be closed for a few days in order to curb the spread of an infection.

Kippen school had its share of such outbreaks. For example, in 1911 the school was closed because of an outbreak of whooping cough and the following winter it was measles that forced closure for three weeks.[46] Arnprior school, however, seems at this time to have been especially unhealthy, for there epidemics disrupted activity very frequently. In 1898 one pupil, Agnes Spowart, died of typhoid fever and a number of other children were extremely unwell, and then in many of the years leading up to the war the school was interrupted by epidemics of one kind or another. In this case part of the problem was undoubtedly the inadequate toilet facilities. HMIs often complained that 'the offices smelled badly and should be regularly deodorised' and in both 1907 and 1909 concern at the problem forced the board to have the school thoroughly disinfected. Nevertheless the disgusting closets and ash-pit remained a frequent cause of complaint. The real source of the problem was almost certainly a combination of poor conduct and an inadequate water-supply, and this was revealed when, in 1910, the water pipes were finally opened up. It was then discovered that the school supply had simply been obtained from a field drain rather than the nearby spring. Whether this was done originally or was the result of later intervention is unclear, but it would appear that someone had at some stage redirected the spring water. However, after samples were analysed by the doctor it was realised that, even with the pipes properly connected, a new supply was essential.[47] This was demonstrated vividly in 1911 when the school and school house were without any water at all from May until November, during which time water had to be carried by hand from a local well. Not surprisingly under the conditions prevailing for much of the time infections spread rapidly among the children, and in 1913 Dr Gardner again insisted that the school be closed because of an outbreak of measles. (The water supply at Arnprior was at last significantly improved when Mr Stirling of Garden had a new fresh-water system installed that was designed to deliver 100 gallons per day to the school at an annual charge of £5, a fee that the school board accepted with unbelievably grudging ill grace. This new supply permitted a w.c., bath and wash-hand basin to be fitted to the school house for the first time.)[48]

A severe epidemic occurred in 1918–1919 when the vicious influenza outbreak, which caused enormous loss of life all over Europe, struck the parish. Kippen school closed for three weeks in October, Arnprior for five, ostensibly to allow potato harvesting, but latterly because of the illness, with two attempts by the head teacher to re-open being defeated when only eight or nine children were fit to turn up. Influenza remained a serious problem well into the following spring.

The schools, of course, lost their share of children during such epidemics and, for example, there was sadness at Arnprior in September 1920 when one child, John Macgregor, died of scarlet fever. Luckily his brother Peter, who had also been extremely ill, recovered. Sometimes, however, tragedy was mixed with what can now be seen as significant progress. In March of 1911 it was noted that James Inglis returned to school 'after a long absence having undergone an operation for appendicitis'. This pupil must have been one of the first to have successfully gone through such an operation at Stirling Royal Infirmary. That, in the absence of the means to control infection, it was still a dangerous procedure was illustrated in the following year when two girls, Katie Hastie and Marion Groves, both died after unsuccessful appendix operations.[49] In passing, by this stage children suffering from serious infections such as diphtheria were being cared for in the infectious disease hospital at Bannockburn.

From the foregoing discussion it will be clear that the medical inspection of children became at this time a crucial part of the school system, and in addition to Dr Gardner and her successors, nurses and dentists became regular and frequent visitors to the schools. Teeth and eye defects were common, and the dentists were soon treating large numbers of children every year. Scabies, impetigo, ring-worm and nits were the typical problems confronting school nurses and, for example, in 1923 little girls were taken home from Kippen school because they were severely verminous and dirty and the parents almost certainly threatened with legal action.[50]

Given the probable poverty and living conditions of the family, prosecution may not have followed. However, what is clear from the Kippen school records is that the various measures introduced by the 1908 Act and at other points during this period were unquestionably successful in bringing about a major improvement in the health of rural children. The most obvious evidence for this is that by the 1930s schools were almost never being forced to close because of epidemic diseases, and it was increasingly rare for attendance figures to fall significantly for more than a few days because of medical problems. Moreover, the evidence of children receiving regular atten-tion and treatment for minor defects is quite explicit in the continuously recorded visits made to the schools by the various health professionals.

Shortly after 1900 the pupil teacher system was replaced by the appointment of properly trained and salaried assistant teachers. The additional expense involved may have created some problems and the school board sometimes had considerable difficulty in attracting suitable staff. The basic salary for a young assistant had to be increased from £60 to £70 per annum about 1907 in order to obtain a qualified person willing to stay at Arnprior for any length of time and the board had virtually to be ordered by an HMI to recruit an extra teacher for Kippen in 1909.[51]

An interesting group of children attending the Kippen schools around the turn of the century were boarded out 'pauper' children. As far as can be determined from school records these children seem to have been sent to live with country families, mainly by the parish council of Edinburgh, but also occasionally by the Councils of Glasgow and Falkirk. Council inspectors sometimes visited the schools to pay relevant fees and to check on the children's progress. It is impossible to be sure of precise numbers of such children living in the parish at any one time, but in 1910 a group of 13 children funded by the parish of Edinburgh were checked at Kippen school, and three years later at Arnprior 'six boarded out pauper children' were examined by the local government board inspector. As late as October of 1922 Edinburgh children were still being placed with families in Kippen.[52]

As was noted earlier, country children at this time were generally healthier than their city counterparts, hence it was probably good for many of the children concerned to be placed in villages like Kippen. They were apparently quite conspicuous, since they were all provided with standard brown serge clothes, with white aprons for the girls. Most of them were probably decently looked after, with some effectively becoming members of the families with whom they stayed, and maintaining relationships on through adulthood. However, almost by definition they tended to be placed with poorer households where the parish money was a welcome source of income. Inevitably, therefore, some of these children had a pretty tough existence. For example, about the time of the First War three youngsters named Alexander – two girls, Maggie and Alice, and a boy called John – were boarded out in Kippen with an elderly widow who appears to have grudged spending sufficient money to provide them with adequate food. Since they were always close to starvation they took to scavenging for scraps among the village refuse, and the little boy began stealing the contents of the sandwich boxes of some of the other schoolchildren. Moreover, the widow would not allow her charges to wear their gloves except on a Sunday, so that in winter their hands were often blue and swollen with cold. Fortunately some of their classmates and a kindly young teacher sensed their plight and did what they could to help out from their own meagre resources.[53]

Another pauper child at Kippen about the same time was a lad named James Porter. As an infant he had been found wandering the streets of Edinburgh, but his parents were never traced, and in 1914 he was brought to Kippen and boarded out with Mrs Reoch in Graham Street. It was said of him that he was 'well behaved at school and industrious when he went out to work' and that subsequently he often visited his foster family. His life, however, was a short one and the village sadly noted his death in 1941.[54]

Academic inspections of the children were, of course, much more frequent than medical inspections. Mental arithmetic tests took place almost daily and there were monthly tests conducted, particularly to prepare older children for the 'control' and 'qualifying' exams which were usually held in April or May, and which went far to determine their educational futures. Both these examinations were introduced as part of the gradual development of secondary education. The qualifying exams commenced from 1903 and were intended to act as the gateway into high school education, for Kippen children either at Balfron or Stirling. The control exam was undertaken by children who wished to enter the 'advanced' division of their school and so continue with a conventional education rather than just the practical supplementary classes. Advanced divisions were introduced in larger elementary schools from 1923, and were intended to provide what was sometimes known as a junior secondary education for those children not going on to high school. Initially an advanced division was developed at Kippen and the older children at Arnprior were required to travel to Kippen, against the wishes of some of the parents concerned. The purpose of the various exams was essentially to determine the appropriate stream for each child and it is evident that it was based on a three-channel educational system with routes which might be identified as academic, technical and practical.

In addition to the formal examination system, however, the conduct and operation of the schools were frequently checked by visits from HM Inspectors and it can be seen that the system of education which developed from 1900 down to the Second World War was very much geared to monitoring the condition and progress of children.

With so many examinations it is not surprising that the children were given various incentives in the form of prizes for particular success. At the head of the prize list each year was the dux – the most successful senior pupil – and usually the winner received a gift donated by one or another of the wealthier members of the community. For example, in 1907 the Kippen dux was Janet Thomson, who was rewarded with a magnificent 12-volume edition of the works of Shakespeare, presented by Stephen Mitchell, then laird of Boquhan. However, in 1922 the system was formalised when an annual dux medal was endowed in the name of John Leckie. It was provided by Mr Joseph Leckie, then MP for Walsall, and was in memory of his father who was descended from an old Kippen family. The first gold medal winner was Ian Smith. Similarly, from 1912 Arnprior had a dux medal which was provided by John Brown, a former pupil who had gone on to become a prosperous lawyer.

Education Acts of 1918 and 1929 brought an end to the old school board system and schools in country areas passed into the hands of county councils. Kippen school board was wound up in 1919 and its schools were handed on to the western division committee of Stirling County Council. While this brought some loss of local control the new arrangement did permit a greater degree of coherence in the activities of schools. However, one of the results of this reorganisation was that the advanced division at Kippen was wound up in 1931 and the 14-year-old children engaged in technical courses were transferred to Balfron High School. This was at a time of severe economic depression and the Government insisted that local authorities curb their expenditure, and particularly their education budgets, thus producing this kind of rationalisation. The transfer to Balfron was, of course, only possible because an efficient regular motor bus service had now become available. Shortly thereafter Kippen was formally reduced to a three-teacher school.

From the 1890s on falling birth rates resulted in a long-run decline in family sizes all over Scotland. In addition, as we have seen, there was a continuing level of outward migration from the area as workers were displaced from farming and moved either to the shipyards and related industries of Clydeside, or to seek new opportunities abroad. Later another sad factor involved the effects of the First World War when the loss of potential fathers brought about another reduction in numbers of children. These demographic changes were gradually reflected in the rolls of the Kippen schools, with numbers showing a prolonged decline. In the 1890s the Arnprior roll had typically included about 75 children, but throughout the 1920s numbers hovered around just 34 or 35, and by 1932 the roll was down to 22, at which point the school was reduced to a single teacher. At Kippen the falling numbers were at first somewhat masked by the additional provision for 14-year-olds. However, with the transfer of the advanced division, the numbers of children in the school had declined to about 80 by the mid 1930s, which was less than half the number on the register 40 years earlier.

One of the factors in the lives of Scottish school children was, of course, 'the belt'. It is difficult to know how freely this was administered, but it is likely that it was very commonly used both to discipline children and in an attempt to compel the completion of homework and other tasks. For instance, looking back on the years around the First War, William Hay remembered the strapping of children by Mr Hunter and his colleagues as an ordinary everyday feature of school life which excited little comment.[55] Once the county councils became responsible for schools, however, it was only a matter of time before some effort was made properly to regulate the disciplinary system and to prevent abuse. In 1937 Circular 555 advised heads that the 'corporal punishment of any child in the infant department is prohibited'. Similarly, it was stated that corporal punishment should not be administered to older girls. Effectively this restricted the use of the belt in primary schools to older boys and even in their case 'the Head teacher should make it his constant duty to see that the infliction of corporal punishment is reduced to a minimum'.[56] This circular appears to have been simply a guidance note, and the extent to which the strap was used remained largely at the discretion of individual heads. Certainly, and despite the terms of the circular, in addition to their male companions, primary schoolgirls in Kippen were still being subjected to this kind of physical punishment on into the 1950s. Interestingly, only one parent at Kippen ever seems to have objected to excessive beating. This happened in October 1949 when one mother complained that her two children were being strapped too often by the female teacher in charge of the junior classes. The head, then Mr George Bennett, rejected the allegation, and a subsequent investigation by the council's director of education upheld his finding.[57] (Technically, use of the strap or tawse was not prohibited until the 1980s, but it appears to have been rarely used in the Kippen schools after the mid-1960s.)

From 1947 secondary education for all children became available, and for most Kippen children this meant transfer to Balfron High School at the age of 13. A few children went to Stirling High with, for many years, the Boquhan Burn being the dividing line for the respective territorial catchment areas. This change meant that the Kippen and Arnprior schools were now formally known as primary schools. However, by this stage the context within which the local schools were required to operate was again changing, and it is now appropriate to turn to the wider parish community as it developed through the 20th century.

7

THE MAKING OF THE
MODERN KINGDOM

The Edwardian era is sometimes remembered as a kind of golden age before the world was darkened by the catastrophe of the First World War. It is not exactly an accurate memory, of course, because, as the experiences of the lives of the people of Kippen illustrated, living conditions were sometimes cruelly difficult for many individuals, particularly if they were poor enough to be on the edge of subsistence. Nevertheless, the impression has prevailed of an age of relative innocence, and certainly if one had good health and even a fairly modest income, the attractions and opportunities of life in the first decade or so of the 20th century were considerable, and nowhere in Scotland was this more true than in Kippen.

The flavour of the period is memorably captured in a report of the *Stirling Journal* of 7th September 1911, which describes an occasion when the schoolchildren were invited to Wright Park to join in a celebration to mark the impending marriage and departure for India of their hostess, Miss Monteath and her fiancé, Major Galbraith of the Royal Artillery:

> A large number of carts – seventeen in all – were kindly lent by the farmers for the conveyance of the youngsters to their destination. The 'carriages', all in the glory of new paint, and with horses gaily decorated, having each received its complement of youths, set off from the school at 2.15 . . .

> Tea having been served, sports were indulged in, and a delightful afternoon was spent – the kindness and assiduity of the hostess and her friends, the beautiful weather conditions, and the exceeding beauty of the charming spot where the fête was held, all contributing to make the few hours pass quickly, and to make the scene one that can never be forgotten by those who were privileged to be present. After a service of cakes, fruit and confections . . .

Two children, May McQueen and James McDiarmid, presented Miss Monteath with a set of silver napkin-rings and in return were assured by Major Galbraith that when his bride-to-be was in her 'new home in far off India [the rings] would serve to remind her of the happy faces of the young folks of Kippen'.[1] The carts, each one full of singing children, then wound their way back to the village. Remembering this echo of his childhood more than 80 years later, William Hay sadly reflected that a number of the older boys who sang their way home from that outing had not survived the First War.

The bare facts of the contribution that the young men of Kippen made to Britain's armed services during the war were carefully documented in the form of a roll of honour which is located on the wall by the main entrance to the church. This was begun in the early days of the conflict and was written by the artist, Sir David Cameron, but it is clear that he did not initially envisage the demands which the war would impose, because an additional lower part of the chart had to be added, and the later names are squeezed in at the bottom. The list is not entirely accurate, and, for example, a few of the names on the war memorial are not included on the roll of honour. Apparently part of the explanation is that a number of the young 'pauper' lads who were sent out from Edinburgh to Kippen school subsequently obtained employment on local farms, but when as young men they then joined the forces, they had no families to give their names to Cameron and no one else thought to rectify the omission. Similarly, the artist was himself in France for some months during the war and it may be that some departures for the services went unrecorded. Fortunately, in the cases of those who were killed, their absence from the roll was not repeated on the memorial.

The roll indicates that 199 young men went out from Kippen to fight in the war, but perhaps for reasons such as are indicated above the true figure may have been around 220. The largest contingent of 45 men, including Archibald Stirling, the then young laird of Garden, served with the local regiment, the Argyll and Sutherland Highlanders, but Kippen men were found in all the main Scottish regiments as well as with English units or the Royal Engineers or the Royal Artillery. Inevitably, in the first modern technological war, specialist outfits tended to multiply and a number of men entered communications and logistical corps. A few were cavalrymen or, later in the war, were in armoured units and a handful found their way into the Royal Navy, the Royal Naval Air Service and the Royal Flying Corps.

It is extremely interesting to note that included on the roll of honour are the names of seven men who were in regiments sent from different parts of the Empire. They were identified and recorded as serving with troops from Australia, Canada, New Zealand and South Africa.

The war memorial, designed by Cameron and dedicated in 1920, indicates that 44 of the men lost their lives (more than one in five of those who went to war). The worst single year was 1917, when 16 men were killed, perhaps in many cases during the nightmare of Passchendaele. Some families suffered cruelly, and none more so than that of the writer, William Chrystal, whose three sons, Robert, Andrew and William had all lost their lives by the end of 1916, and whose nephew, Alexander Chrystal, was killed in 1918. Two Lennie boys, Alexander and William, died, and it is striking to see engraved on the stone other familiar Kippen names that echo down the centuries – Buchanan, Davidson, Leckie, Syme, Welsh, Kerr, McGibbon, Drummond and so on. Most of the casualties were no doubt sustained in Flanders, but they occurred in almost every theatre; for example, Sergeant William J. Syme was killed during the British advance on Jerusalem at the end of 1916.

One death which impacted heavily on the community actually happened after the war, in December 1919. The gentle parish minister, the Rev. Peter Smith, had joined up, appropriately as chaplain to the Cameronians – the Scottish Rifles (in the event, he had spent much of his service with a Black Watch battalion). He had been pushed beyond endurance, perhaps by what was then known as 'shell shock' or possibly simply by the relentless stress of attempting to sustain and support men through many months of brutal conflict. During a period of duty in Germany just after the war, he finally collapsed and was sent home, where an operation failed to save him, and he died in Kippen manse just a week after the birth of his sixth child, also named Peter.

In his funeral oration it was recognised that he had died 'a soldier's death' and his name was added to the memorial.

At least four men, Alex Davidson, Tom Richardson, Henry MacFarlane and John Welsh, returned home with very serious injuries, and a number of others carried the scars of wounds for the rest of their lives or, like Robert Leckie, struggled on for many years with lungs damaged by gas. Major Archibald Stirling was among those who were badly injured early in the war at Mons and he had spent the next four years as a prisoner of war in Germany.

Seven men and one woman from the community were known to have been decorated for gallantry. Nurse Mary Baird was mentioned in dispatches, Sergeants Syme and Grey each received DCMs,

Captain Gilbert Rennie was awarded an MC and four others, Hugh Thomas, John Buchanan, J. Ferguson and Tom Richardson, gained military medals. On the other side of the coin, one man deserted, and interestingly he seems to have been to some degree shielded by the community. As the war unfolded it became clear that some men could persevere bravely, sometimes for years, but then reached a point where their spirit or nerve simply cracked. Perhaps one of the most famous individuals to whom this sort of thing happened was the poet, Siegfried Sassoon, but whereas a well-known officer might have expected some sympathy from the authorities, an obscure private soldier undergoing such a crisis was at first likely to be treated very harshly. At some point in the winter of 1917–1918 this man decided not to return to France following a spell of leave, and instead he took to the hills. He was then sheltered by a farmer and allowed to work quietly on the farm until an amnesty for such men was announced in 1922, enabling him to return to his home. He seems to have been received with understanding, certainly from the other former soldiers. His name remained in place on the roll of honour and the author vividly recalls as a youngster listening while he and another ancient veteran discussed the terrors of huddling in a trench under a 'creeping' barrage.

One man who had watched the lengthening casualty list with horror was James Hunter, the village headmaster. Almost all the men had been boys under his care and he was gradually crushed under the weight of the long chain of sad news. Even his increasingly terse notes in the school log book in some ways reflect his darkening mood and waning enthusiasm. Nevertheless, the school also made its contribution to the war effort, particularly from 1917 when the mounting loss of ships to submarine warfare led to food scarcity and the eventual introduction of partial food rationing. Local food control committees were established across the country and the schools were urged to lay on classes of 'war cookery' to advise housewives how to get the best out of their meagre supplies. The first of these demonstrations held at Kippen was in May 1917 and was led by a specialist adviser, Miss Swanston, but later in the year two of the school's teachers were given instruction at Stirling prior to running their own classes for local women. The children also participated by assisting in various collection campaigns and, of course, lending a hand on the farms during harvests. In June of 1918, with the pupils standing at attention, Mr Hunter read out a message from the king indicating appreciation of the work performed by the country's schools in connection with the war.[2]

In July 1919, with most of those who had been in the armed services safely home again, the community held a public reception in their honour. Nurse Baird was presented with a gold medal, each man who had been wounded or decorated received a gift of money, and smaller tokens were given to the others. Cash payments were also donated to a number of war widows. These presents were, of course, purely informal marks of gratitude from the people of Kippen.[3]

The most senior First War officer from the Kippen district was Brigadier-General Sir Norman Orr Ewing of Cardross, honorary colonel of the Argylls, and he accompanied the Duke of Montrose at the dedication of the War Memorial in 1920.

On the day after the Armistice of November 1918 the prime minister, David Lloyd George called a general election and repeated his promise to obtain 'habitations fit for the heroes who have won the war'. Undoubtedly housing was a major preoccupation of the governments of the next few years. Housing Acts of 1919, 1923 and 1924 made various attempts to establish a financial basis through which the state could become directly involved in the attempt to improve the housing of lower income groups and essentially ushered in the concept of housing provided by the local authorities. Inevitably, Kippen was not top of the priority list for Stirling County Council, and villagers had to be patient, but during the inter-war years a beginning was at least made in replacing (and providing an alternative to) some of the worst of the old cottages at rentals which were affordable to people with modest incomes. At this period, therefore, six council houses were built at Burnside and nine others just above Point End. In retrospect, housing provided following the 1920s legislation can be seen to be amongst the best and most successful of the houses constructed for Scottish local authorities and the dwellings above seem to reflect that view.[4]

An Act of Parliament that created problems at this time was the Rent Restriction Act of 1915, which was introduced as an emergency measure to prevent landlords from undue profiteering during the war. However, it became politically almost impossible to remove the Act with the return of peace, with the consequence that private landlords became very unwilling to invest in new properties from which they would have been unable to derive any reasonable income. Not surprisingly the private rented sector in Scotland went into long-run decline. Very few new houses were built for private letting and the only ones constructed for this purpose between the wars in Kippen were the four-apartments at Wingate Place which were built in 1933. Interestingly, a little later the landlord of the 1906 terrace of cottages at Forthview, opposite the school, became so disillusioned with his inability to charge rents sufficient to cover the costs of adequate maintenance that he offered the properties for sale to his tenants at very modest prices.

The inter-war years were generally characterised by economic crises and a period of high unemployment, starting in the early 1920s and reaching its climax after the 1929 collapse of the US stock market, which triggered a deep world-wide recession. The time was disastrous for many of the workers in older and heavy industries such as shipbuilding, and the related steel making and coal mining. However, for people in work and with a reasonable income the period saw rising 'real' wages as a result of reduced costs, falling prices and low interest rates on borrowings. Mortgages were particularly cheap and the cost of buying a new house became very low during these years, with a brand new three-bedroom bungalow, for example, typically selling for something in the range £600–£800. Not surprisingly, therefore, in Kippen building for private purchase returned to the pre-war pattern and villas such as Shoreland, St Michaels, Lynwood and Dalveen date from this period. Indeed, when Dalveen was completed about 1930, at the nadir of the recession, it was several months before it was eventually sold for just £500. The fine house of Arnmoulin, on the Back Road at Cauldhame was built in the late 1930s and its design is technically described as 'inter war council with Dutch gables'.[5] Not only is it an exceptionally handsome building set in a spacious garden, but its north-facing windows provide one of the most superb views from the village towards Ben Ledi.

The building surge in Kippen in the 1930s was almost certainly boosted by the arrival of electricity in 1933 and many houses had cabling installed over the next two years. By 1935 the school was wired-up and the village had also been provided with electric street-lighting.

The most famous and architecturally important house constructed near Kippen in this period was Gribloch (1937–1939) located on its commanding position on the moors above the village. It was built for the iron and steel manufacturer, John Colville, and his American-born wife, Helen, shortly after their original house in Lanarkshire was destroyed by fire. Colville had spent much of his childhood at Kippen where his parents were tenants at Arngomery (Broich) and he identified the site for his house on a ridge from which he could look south to the Fintry Hills and then north through a sublime panoramic sweep of the Grampians, extending from Ben Cleuch in the east to Ben Lomond in the west. In terms of outlook, it is hard to believe that any house in the UK can match Gribloch's breathtaking position.

Colville was a governor of the Glasgow School of Art and a member of the organising committee for the 1938 Empire Exhibition. He was deeply interested in modern design and craft-work, while Helen brought an informed American slant to bear, especially on some of the interiors. The real secret of the house, therefore, lies in their joint ability to obtain the assistance of some of the most interesting architects and interior designers of the inter-war period while, at the same time, retaining the self-confidence to impose many of their own ideas and choices. In particular, the contemporary constructional techniques and materials often suggest that their use in this context had their origins in Colville's own engineering background.

The principal architect was the 30-year-old Basil Spence who, after the Second War, was knighted for his work in designing the new Coventry Cathedral, and he was responsible for the fundamental layout and shape of Gribloch and its essential sensitivity to its surroundings. However, the American architect, Perry Duncan, was also brought in to speed some of the work and many of the interior designs were planned by John Hill, working for the decorating firm, Green and Abbott.

> There are no country-house interiors of the period that so perfectly embody 1930s elegance as its entrance hall. Spence was responsible for the painstaking working-out of its oval form, dominated by the great bow window through which the swimming pool sends dancing reflections into the room on even the greyest day. Perhaps this prompted Hill's exquisite decoration, which light-heartedly suggests a Regency marine villa: at cornice level, a plaster rope is looped between plaster shells, all painted white, and the colour scheme of pale blues, turquoise and mauve was set off by Hill's specially woven shell-pattern carpet and the white painted shell chairs.[6]

As the above comment illustrates, many of the furnishings were specifically crafted for the house; in some cases they were created by Betty Joel, one of the most notable British furniture designers of the period, and the house in fact contains the finest collection of her work still retained in a domestic setting. A striking example is Colville's magnificent desk made from Australian walnut. From a modern perspective, perhaps the most exciting point about the house is that the key architectural features and the contemporary furnishings remain virtually intact and in beautiful condition. For example, at Helen Colville's insistence every effort was made to make the domestic arrangements as up-to-date as possible and this included a fitted kitchen on American lines. It was apparently the first of its kind anywhere in Britain and, remarkably, it remains essentially in its original state.[7]

Among the young men to return to Kippen at the end of the Great War and ready to work himself back into civilian life was Petty Officer Duncan Selby Buchanan (generally identified by his second name) who, in 1919, rejoined his father Duncan at what became known as the Kippen Vinery Company. The firm by this stage was specialising in 'table' or dessert grapes and had developed a number of vines of different varieties. Black Hamburgh, Alicante and Muscat of Alexandria were types that had been introduced (indeed as many as 30 varieties were tried at one time or another), but much the most prolific was a Gros Colman vine which extended through an L-shaped system of glass-houses in the lee of a red sandstone wall. As early as 1910 this 'Big Vine' was producing 'over 600 bunches per year – already more than London's famous, and much older, Hampton Court Vine – and it was beginning to attract the attention of other British vine growers'.[8]

Long before the war Duncan had shown himself to have an extraordinary understanding of vine husbandry and he had produced a number of other very large vines as well as developing the general market-gardening business. Vines are not the simplest plants to cultivate under glass. No doubt the shelter of the wall and nature of the soil at Cauldhame helped, but the secret of the Buchanans' success in growing their vines seems to have been their careful attention to soil, heating and ventilation according to the rhythms of the seasons and the meticulous hand thinning of every bunch shortly after the berries had formed. Apparently, the process of hand-thinning a great vine is an extremely satisfying activity for the real enthusiast, and this kind of loving care and patient work resulted in the big Kippen vine yielding a typical annual crop of 2000 bunches.[9] Since, by the inter-war period, there were normally another dozen or so large vines under cultivation in the garden the extent of the gardeners' task will be appreciated.

After the war Selby and his father exhibited at all the major horticultural shows, displaying not only grapes, but other fruit and vegetables as well. But the grapes were the product on which the firm's steadily growing fame was based. Father and son won 'numerous awards, including gold medals from the Royal Horticultural Society in London, and it was not uncommon for them to exhibit magnificent bunches of grapes of between five and ten pounds in weight'. Often the show bunches came from the Great Vine, but other varieties also sometimes won and the greatest delicacy was apparently provided by a Canon Hall Muscat, 'the translucent, golden-yellow berries of which were as large as plums'.[10]

By 1922 the Big Vine was being acknowledged as the largest vine in the world and it was decided to use its fame to attract visitors who could be shown round for a small charge. People were, of course, keen to buy grapes and cuttings from the vine and the opportunity was taken to sell other fruit and vegetable products to a gradually expanding visitor market. In 1935 Selby was invited by the BBC to broadcast on the subject of vines, and he explained to his radio audience that most plants reach their best at about ten years, but that the Kippen vine was still flourishing and in a good season producing almost 3000 bunches. Amazingly, the plant continued to thrive decade after decade, avoiding serious diseases and even surviving a huge storm in 1927 which blew away its greenhouses.

The grapes from Kippen were sold as luxury products at some of the leading shops in Glasgow, Edinburgh and London and they were carefully boxed and sent to individual customers all over the country and even overseas. The bunches were never touched by hand in order to avoid damaging the berries or tarnishing their bloom, and when packed they were laid on fluted cardboard trays on white tissue paper, with a red and gold company seal attached to the stem.

By the later 1930s increasing importation of foreign grapes began to affect the British market and, like similar companies, the firm had to diversify into other products, including tomatoes and pot plants. Gradually many of the other older vineries were forced out of business, a process accelerated during the Second World War when it became illegal to plant new vines. However, the Kippen Company held on, supported by the fame of the great plant and the fact that it had become a significant tourist attraction.

To continue the narrative on this topic to its conclusion, by the 1950s the high cost of heating the greenhouses was steadily squeezing the profitability of grape growing, and it was only the stream of visitors that continued to make the activity commercially viable, particularly through purchases at the garden shop. Apart from the years of the First War, Selby spent his entire working life from the age of 14 in his gardens at Kippen and throughout this period, on a regular basis, the firm provided full-time employment for two or three men and, from each spring to autumn, for another two or three typically female gardeners. In the summer months, 5 or 6 older schoolchildren were employed during their holidays and at weekends, to carry out such tasks as helping to thin plants, potting out, showing visitors round and assisting in the shop. It will be seen, therefore, that over many years the firm made a significant contribution to the village economy.

By the early 1960s Selby himself was becoming old and was in increasingly poor health and he decided, therefore, to sell up. At the time the 'Big Vine' was attracting 20,000 visitors a year with up to 1000 per day at the height of the season. Moreover, as if sensing what was at stake, in 1963 the vine produced a record crop of 3249 bunches which brought its total output since it was first recorded to an amazing 103,243. Despite such buoyant figures, no commercial buyer could be found, probably because potential investors recognised that the business required a high degree of specialised horticultural skills. Sadly, therefore

> on a cold, grey morning early in 1964, Selby Buchanan took a saw and cut through the (55 inches) thick, gnarled trunk of the Big Vine. One can only guess at his emotions as he set about destroying in a few minutes the plant he and his father had tended so assiduously for 73 years. Understandably perhaps, he allowed no-one to help him with the task. Some time later he created a personal souvenir of the Big Vine: a set of chess-pieces carved from the root.[11]

Almost everyone in Kippen shared a little of Selby's distress and there was certainly a genuine sense of shock and loss throughout the community, even among villagers who had rarely ever visited the gardens, because they had all been quietly proud of their vine. Shortly afterwards the land was cleared and sold to enable a housing development to take place. Looking back on this episode from the point of view of an outside observer it is impossible not to regret the waste involved in the destruction of the magnificent plant. Perhaps in 1964 few could have foreseen the huge growth in car-borne tourism that was to occur in the following decades. But it is not difficult to believe that an imaginative buyer would have had an increasingly favourable context within which to develop further a prosperous business. That said, in a sense the vine continues to survive, for cuttings from the amazing mother plant are still to be found flourishing in greenhouses in Kippen and in many other parts of Scotland.

Undoubtedly the most famous and probably most influential individual in Kippen in the first half of the 20th century was Sir David (D.Y.) Cameron and he was to leave a very considerable legacy to the community.

Cameron was born in Glasgow in 1865, and was a son of the

manse, his father being minister of Cambridge Street Church in the
city. As a young man he entered business, but in 1885 he exchanged
part-time classes at the Glasgow School of Art for full-time training
at the Royal Scottish Academy in Edinburgh and he thereafter pursued his career as a painter and etcher. He quickly established himself
as a fine painter and his reputation was carried forward as a member
of the flourishing group of young artists who collectively became
known as the Glasgow School. Although perhaps not the most obviously gifted member of the group, working in oils or in water colours,
Cameron certainly produced some excellent paintings, notably, in his
early period, of rural France and Italy, but increasingly as he grew
older in his favoured form of Scottish landscapes. However, it was as
an etcher or printmaker that he achieved much of his success and his
career flourished at a time when print technology enabled people of
moderate means to look to limited edition prints for their wall
decorations.

Unlike many artists, Cameron achieved a great deal of recognition
as a relatively young man, and interestingly he was perhaps more
highly regarded by his contemporaries, including other artists, than
he has so far been by later generations. Some of his early paintings
were bought for display by various major galleries, including the
Tate in London and the Adelaide Gallery, and honours of all kinds
were heaped upon him. He was knighted in 1924 and a few years
later he was appointed as the King's Painter and Limner in Scotland
and became a trustee of both the National Gallery of Scotland and
the Tate. Despite such public fêting, however, he seems to have
remained extremely modest, and a feature which emerges strongly
from his obituary and other pieces written about him, is that he was
genuinely liked and respected by almost everyone with whom he
came into contact.

On the success of his painting 'The Bride', later bought by the
Adelaide, he decided to move to Kippen in 1898, taking up residence
at Kirkhill and staying there while his large villa at 'Dun Eaglais' was
being constructed above Kiln Park on the opposite side of the Station
Brae. (The use of the name 'Dun Eaglais' on this location is fascinating, for not only does it mean the same as Kirkhill – church hill,
but Eaglais, Eagles, and Eccles place names are often associated with
very early Christian sites. They derive from the Latin word *ecclesia*
which would have been used before the Gaelic word for church
(*cille*) had been developed and, in view of the account set out in the
first chapter of this book, it would have been very appropriate to
have discovered such a name being applied to the hill on which

Mauvais' church was located. However, no evidence has been discovered of Eaglais or Eccles being used in Kippen prior to the building of Cameron's house, and it would seem probable, therefore, that the artist simply borrowed an older variation of the Kirkhill theme. If so it was very much in keeping with his habit of using traditional Christian imagery).

Cameron lived in Kippen for almost 46 years, during which time, together with his wife Jean, he played a significant part in the life of the village. In particular, he supplied the guiding hand behind much of the renovation and reconstruction of the parish church in the inter-war period and succeeded in turning the building into arguably one of the most beautiful of the churches of Scotland.

The decision to reconstruct the church was taken at a meeting of the congregation in January 1924 and it was partly intended to mark the approaching centenary of the building. That meeting had been chaired by the minister, the Rev. John Younie and one of the key ingredients in the course of events was his willingness to work with Cameron and, as far as possible, to give the artist his head. The partnership and understanding between the two men was essential to the final outcome. As must be obvious from what has already been written of Cameron, his personal contacts stretched throughout the many branches of the British artistic community and he used this network to the full in order to obtain contributions from a number of outstandingly talented people.

The architect chosen for the main redesign was Reginald Fairlie of Edinburgh, a Roman Catholic, and there is no doubt that his influence helped to produce a building form which is unusually Latinate for a Scottish church. The main internal changes were that the old three-sided gallery was replaced by a simple rear balcony. The central pulpit was removed and the south wall was pushed out to create a chancel or, more accurately, an apse in which was located the communion table. The ceiling and lower side walls were wood panelled and the central entrance at the north end beneath the clock tower was replaced by a doorway at the side. These first alterations were accomplished by 1926, but in 1929 Sir David and Lady Cameron purchased the adjacent thatched croft, 'The Grove', and presented the building and its land to the congregation. The architect, Eric Bell of Stirling, incorporated 'The Grove' into the church as a church house and connected the two by an entrance hall and staircase, and this resulted in the basic elegant 'L' shape of the complex, a form which perfectly suited the warm red local sandstone of which the building is constructed.

Part of the success of the reconstruction hinged on the way in which the skills of artists of national reputation were combined with those of local craftsmen. All the stone and joinery work was done by local men such as masons John Duncanson and Thomas Syme and the carpenters of J. & N. Miller and Alexander Welsh. Indeed, it has to be noted that while works of ornamentation of one kind or another probably attract most comment, it is the stone masonry and wood panelling to walls and roof that provide the superb interior context.

After the basic reshaping had been accomplished Cameron enthusiastically used his contacts to commission some wonderful interior decorations and furnishings. The church already had a few interesting 19th-century windows, but over the next decade no less than 15 new windows were constructed by the leading stained-glass designer, Herbert Hendrie of Edinburgh. Together these windows comprise perhaps the finest collection of his work in Scotland. Most of the designs were his own, but one or two were from drawings prepared by Cameron, and these windows, together with the warm wood panelling provide the church with its magnificent colouring.

Elsewhere there were bronzes by Henry Wilson and Sir Alfred Hardiman, wood carvings by James Woodford, Thomas Good and Douglas Bliss, and sculptures by Hew Lorimer and Thomas Whalen. Many of the beautiful furnishings were made by the Edinburgh firms of Whytock & Reid and Scott Morton, and a rich-toned pipe organ was custom-made for the church by Norman & Hill Beard of London and Norwich.

The cost of almost everything was met by gifts, and in many cases they were paid for by Sir David and Lady Jean themselves. At first a number of the more traditional Presbyterians in the congregation were less than comfortable with the introduction of statues and other symbolic ornamentation to their church, but others came quickly to appreciate the beauty of what was being created and joined in the process either by donating money or by making their own personal contributions. For example, a 16th-century altar frontal was obtained in Assisi and gifted by Mrs Mather of Kirkhill, and turned into an arresting wall tapestry. Other members of the Women's Guild used their needlework skills to create a magnificent passion flower panel to a design by Cameron's sister, Katherine Cameron Kay.

Perhaps the most remarkable additions were three bronzes by the most famous sculptor of the day, Sir Alfred Gilbert, creator of the figure of Eros in Piccadilly Circus. The first of these is a lovely statue of the Madonna and Child and it is incorporated into the baptistry.

The superb carved housing was made by Morris Maclaurin and contains not only the bronze sculpture, but the original silver baptismal bowl standing on a pedestal and base of Ionian marble. Inevitably, at the time, the inclusion of a statue of Mary was regarded as highly controversial, and to keep the peace among some of the traditionalists she was euphemistically identified as Charity. Similarly, a charming small window by Hendrie on the west wall of the apse on the same subject, also masquerades under the guise of Charity.

The story of the other two Gilbert bronzes is quite astonishing. In January 1892, Edward, Duke of Clarence, son of the then Prince of Wales (later Edward VII) died and Sir Alfred was commissioned to design and make an ornate tomb to be located in St George's Chapel at Windsor Castle. Gilbert duly produced a design which included the figures of a number of saints to be positioned in niches around the sides of the tomb. The main tomb was completed about 1898, but most of the stands for the figures remained empty. According to an article in *The Times* of August that year, the statues had actually been completed, and over the next two decades the positions were filled. However, not all of the Windsor figures were of uniform quality and rumours began to surface that Gilbert had at least used his moulds to manufacture several copies or, worse still, had sold some of the original figures and replaced those on the tomb with some inferior reproductions.

One of the buyers of work from Gilbert was Sir D.Y. Cameron. There is no doubt that Gilbert was in severe financial difficulties in the years around the turn of the century and at some point at that time he sold to Cameron two bronzes, one of St Elizabeth of Hungary and the other of the Virgin Mary. Initially these were described by Cameron as 'trial' bronzes – bronzes that were poured in order to test the mould and the design. The author's father, the late Robert Begg, minister of Kippen (1941–1942 and again from 1956 to 1974), discussed the figures with Cameron in 1941 and later recalled his account of the purchase as follows: Gilbert was desperately in debt and short of money and when Cameron visited him at his studio he pleaded with his guest to purchase something, anything in the studio that took his eye. Cameron spotted the two figures, bought them at an agreed price, and brought them back to Kippen. He eventually gifted them to the Church, causing them to be installed in a little prayer chapel at the rear of the renovated building which was designed especially to house them.

In a book *The Shadow of Eros*, written in 1952 by Gilbert's nephew, Adrian Bury, the suggestion that Gilbert might have sold off two of the original figures from the Duke's tomb and so perhaps cheated King Edward, was indignantly rejected.

> A misfortune that had contributed more than any other to Gilbert's disgrace was the fact that replicas of some of the figures for the Clarence tomb had got into circulation. This was, indeed, a very serious and blameworthy fact, but I am absolutely convinced that it was done without the sculptor's wish and knowledge. However he might delay, however he might fail in fulfilling commissions, he was quite incapable of dealing in his works. It was well-nigh impossible to buy anything from Gilbert. How inconceivable then that he should have attempted to sell what he regarded as the most sacred of all his works!

On the other hand, in 1926 the art critic, Marion Spielmann, had reported claims that Gilbert had removed some of the figures from the tomb against 'the King's wish and then said that they were melted down; these figures were in due time reproduced and offered for sale in Bond Street'. And certainly it is true that a few relatively inferior copies were sold around this time.

The evidence from an examination of the statues at Windsor and a comparison with those at Kippen seems quite conclusive. The figures at the front of the tomb are delightful, being delicately and beautifully finished in detail. In particular, St George, in his suit of armour, seems poised to step out from his position. His face, as with those of his neighbours, is carved from ivory. However, as one moves round the tomb so the majority of the saints can be seen to be plain bronze statues, comparatively dull and obviously more cheaply produced. On the other hand, the two Kippen figures are again quite exquisite, having the ivory faces and all the intricate details of the finest of the Windsor statues. St Elizabeth, as befits her legend, has roses tumbling from her gown and both figures are rich in colour. Despite Mr Bury's belief, it would thus appear quite certain that Cameron was able to purchase two of the originals and that their counterparts at Windsor are replicas. How did this happen?

The truth seems to be that one of the reasons for Gilbert's financial problems was that he had been commissioned to undertake a very expensive piece of work but, for whatever reason, the Palace appears to have been either slow or unwilling to meet the bill. The death of Queen Victoria and then of Edward VII in 1910 may have meant that the affair dragged on with no one being prepared to settle the account, and in desperation Gilbert may have produced and sold a number of copies as well as some originals, including the pair to Cameron. Indeed, if, as Spielmann suggested, he was allowed to remove the figures against the king's will, one has to assume that he had been forced to repossess them for non-payment.

Whether or not Cameron fully realised what he was purchasing is another question. Given that he seems to have been an absolutely honest and deeply religious man it is very unlikely that he would have connived at anything untoward, still less illegal, and it also has to be remembered that he gained a royal appointment as the King's Painter and Limner. It may well be that he genuinely believed the two figures were trial replicas. However, given his artistic expertise that seems very improbable. Much more likely is the notion that he knew exactly what they were, but bought them because he sympathised with Gilbert's predicament and believed that the latter was acting entirely within his rights in recouping his losses by repossessing and discreetly selling off the two figures, while completing the work at Windsor with more simple pieces. Perhaps because of a desire to protect both the sculptor and the reputation of the Palace, Cameron may then have been perfectly content to let it be assumed that his Kippen figures were copies. (Indeed, the possibility also has to be considered that the Palace was well informed at each stage in the transaction and was in fact grateful to Cameron for having come up with a solution which eased Gilbert's financial problems while ensuring that no embarrassment was caused to the royal family.) It is impossible to keep a secret of this kind for ever, of course, and when the statues were borrowed in 1968 for a Fine Art Society exhibition in London their probable authenticity was soon spotted.[12]

The figures themselves lost nothing by finding a place in a Scottish country church rather than in one of the great buildings of England. Indeed the sheer elaboration of the ornate surroundings in St George's Chapel tends to diminish and overwhelm the figures around the Duke's tomb, so that they become somewhat lost. By contrast, in Kippen the simple space of the prayer chapel provides an almost perfect setting. The figures stand on their own plinths and cast their presence over the little room which they share with a third bronze, a Head of Christ by Alfred Hardiman. This peaceful setting has provided a haven for reflection for many a troubled visitor to Kippen church over the years.

The work of decorating the renovated church could not, of course, be completed all at once and, indeed, continued for many years as individuals and members of the community took the opportunity to commemorate loved ones by providing suitable gifts. For example, in 1931 when Jean Cameron died, Sir David commissioned Hendrie to produce the magnificent west windows, by the side of the pulpit, and four years later the equally superb 'Motherhood and Childhood' windows opposite were gifted by Lady McNair Snadden in memory of her mother.

The work of finishing the building was still going on when Cameron himself died suddenly in 1945. As a notable Scottish artist, his memory is certainly preserved in his paintings. However, to many of the Kippen people his real masterpiece is, without question, the church. Although the work of many hands – famous or only remembered by local people – the building as a whole was formed under his inspiration and he is undoubtedly the author of the particular spell that it casts through its almost tangible atmosphere and which leaves few visitors untouched. Over the years since his death many further additions have been made, but perhaps the most important was in 1964 when the yew wood pews of the old St Oswald's Parish Church of Edinburgh were rescued, refurbished and installed in Kippen. On advice left by Cameron the opportunity was taken to arrange the pews in such a way as to produce a broad central aisle with a red carpet which leads the eye naturally down through the church, over the ancient prayer carpet on the apse steps and then up to the great banner of silk rose-damask which is on the back wall above the communion table. In a sense, therefore, some 20 years after his death the pews and centre aisle finally completed Cameron's vision of the interior.[13]

As mentioned previously, the ornamentation and imagery introduced into the building were not without their critics in the early years. However, the villagers soon came to appreciate what had been achieved and in the longer term perhaps became grateful for having been provided with a building which was so ideally suited to the needs of the modern community as a whole. Christians of all denominations or even just occasional visitors now gather there, particularly at the great festivals of Christmas and Easter or for weddings and funerals, and feel entirely at ease while taking pleasure or comfort from their surroundings.

One of the driving forces behind the inter-war renovation of the church was an appreciation by the respective ministers and kirk sessions that the reunification of the parish and United Free congregations was imminent. Locally there had been a great deal of friendly co-operation between the village ministers for many years, and this was especially true during and immediately after the First War when the sharing of important services was common. Nationally the general assemblies were unified from 1929 and union in Kippen was clearly bound to follow the retirement of the United Free Church minister, Henry Hunter, who had faithfully served the community for no less than 54 years, and part of the motive for the basic modernisation was presumably to produce a building capable of meeting the future needs of the united congregation. The local union duly occurred in 1944 and inevitably the restored parish church was the one retained for public worship, with the Free Church building in the main street eventually being sold into its modern use as a garage. This process was painful for some people to accept, since their traditional loyalties were severely challenged, and on the morning of the first service of the newly united congregation, the village black-smith and former Free Church session clerk, Andrew Rennie, chose to indicate his defiance by loudly ringing the bell of his old church. However, the bitterness soon subsided, and indeed over later decades the parish church had no stauncher supporters than Andrew and other members of his family and friends.

A key change to village life of the inter-war period was brought about by the arrival of the motor bus. The first service was opened by an owner/driver, Mr Rankine, who, about 1921, commenced a Thursday service between Balfron and Stirling with the intention of taking people to and from Stirling's weekly market. On its first run the bus apparently provided just one passenger with a return journey between Balfron and Kippen at a fare of 5s. Other firms soon entered the business and competed vigorously until, in the early 1930s, they were all taken over by Alexander & Sons. The introduction of bus traffic had a great influence on the way of life in the area. First of all, it allowed people of very modest means to commute to work in the town and it was a key factor in enabling the county council to pro-mote the centralisation of rural secondary education with older children from Kippen and the other western villages travelling to Balfron High School. It was this kind of activity that provided the commercial basis for the rapid growth of bus services during the period.

As the coaches became more important so, of course, local passenger rail travel declined and the line through the valley rapidly became uneconomical. Part of the problem was that the stations were at a distance from the villages and if it was necessary to take a bus to reach the station it was obviously more convenient and cheaper to stay on board all the way to Stirling. The bus similarly greatly reduced the occasions when it was necessary to walk a half mile or more in wet weather. By 1934 the railway stations at Kippen and Port of Menteith were closed to passenger traffic, although Buchlyvie still continued to enjoy a connection along the Blane Valley to Glasgow. However, this too was terminated in 1950. For a few years thereafter goods trains did provide a low level service, particularly for the farming community, but even this was ended in 1959 because, just as the bus had taken away the passenger demand, so the motor truck was proving more efficient at hauling livestock or bulk commodities like hay directly from farms to market.

Despite the general difficulties of the period, the later years between the wars appear to have been good for Kippen, with renewed vigour returning to the community. The renovation of the church and the house-building activities brought employment and greater purchasing power into the village, and this seems gradually to have made some impact on the quality of people's lives. In addition, many of the local clubs and societies flourished. For example, in 1930 and again in 1932, the village football team reached perhaps the absolute high point of the club's history when it completed double triumphs by winning the Forth and Endrick League Championship and the knock-out trophy, the Cameron Cup. Interestingly these contests among teams from all the villages of west Stirlingshire and southern Perthshire were commenced in 1910 and ever since have taken place in the summer months, to some degree reflecting the pattern of rural seasonal employment in the early years of the century.

Other buoyant organisations at this time included the Women's Rural Institute, founded in 1919, which attracted great support throughout the area; the annual Kippen Flower Show Society, established earlier in 1885, but reaching exceptionally high standards of display between the wars; and a fine mixed-voice choir led and conducted by the Arnprior head teacher, Mrs O'May. From 1898 Kippen also held its own Highland Games, an event which became part of the local circuit for semi-professional athletes, but which also included contests – some serious and some purely for amusement – restricted to youngsters living within 12 miles of Kippen Cross. One of the high points of these games occurred in 1935 when, at a ceremony on Dasher Common, William Chrystal, author of the original *Kingdom of Kippen* (published in 1903) was 'crowned' King of Kippen. Sadly, annual Highland Games were discontinued on the outbreak of the war in 1939 and were not subsequently resumed, although much later, in 1980, an annual Street Fayre was commenced, replicating a little of the spirit of the original celebration.

Kippen seems to have approached the onset of the Second World World War with much the same mixture of sad resignation and quiet determination as was felt elsewhere in the country. The mood was captured by the village poet, Tam Clark of Cauldhame, who, in the guise of 'Auld Sodger', on 14th September, 1939 submitted the following thoughts to the *Stirling Observer*.

Lines to Herr Hitler

Losh, Hitler, ha'e ye a he'rt o' steel,
Yer cruel deeds wad shame the Deil;
Tae freen an' foe ye've pity nane –
No' even tae the helpless wean.

Tae Chamberlain an' men o' peace,
Yer evil thochts, they didna cease;
Yer conscience yet'll haunt ye sair
When Hitler, lad, ye'll be nae mair.

Auld Kippen's sons the warl' oer
Are ready, as in days o' yore,
Tae fecht ye an' yer kith an' kin,
An', by my sang, we mean tae win.

The Second World War was in some ways much less severe on Kippen than was the previous conflict. The war memorial records eight men as having lost their lives and an interesting feature of the list is that, unlike their earlier counterparts, only one of the casualties seems to have been a private infantryman. On this occasion the other seven were officers or senior NCOs and serving in all branches of the forces.

The first impact of the war on the parish was felt in the schools. On 15th September the numbers of children on the Kippen school roll shot up to 161, with no fewer than 85 being evacuated youngsters from Glasgow, and similarly at Arnprior the attendance list doubled with the addition of 20 evacuees. Children from Glasgow were present in the community for most of the war years. To begin with the authorities were very unsure about the risks involved from enemy bombing, hence the immediate dispersal of urban children, but there were few air attacks early in the war, particularly on Scotland, and after a time families from the city began to recall their children. By May 1940, for example, the number placed at Arnprior had dropped to 12 and early that year 33 or 34 of the children originally at Kippen had also returned to their homes. This attitude changed abruptly with the heavy attacks on Clydeside in March and May of 1941 and by April of that year the population of evacuated children living in the community and attending the schools had increased again. Later in the war and as the danger declined the numbers began understandably to fall back once more, but as late as the spring of 1945 four Glasgow children were still on the roll at Arnprior and a few also remained at Kippen.

When the children first came out to the country they brought with them a number of teachers, and some senior students from the teacher-training colleges who were rushed into temporary service. At this time under normal circumstances classes in city schools quite often had as many as 70 pupils crammed into large rooms, so when the children had to be accommodated in the smaller rural buildings there were not nearly enough teachers to go round, and hence the need to call on the students. Initially the teaching team at Kippen was increased to six, with two being young assistants, while an additional student was also found to help the single teacher at Arnprior, Mrs O'May, to enable her to cope with the 40 or so children now spread over the seven years of the primary school. During the war staff numbers tended to fluctuate, since whenever possible the students were withdrawn to complete their own studies.

As well as bringing their teachers the evacuees also produced some improvement to school facilities and, at a basic level, this took the form of dual desks which were brought out from the Glasgow schools in order to fit in all the children. More excitingly, the Ministry of Information's Travelling Film Unit now arrived from time to time, providing both educational and comedy film shows. Presumably the idea was to compensate the city children for not being able easily to attend a cinema.[14]

The dispersal of city children from poor urban communities was a traumatic experience for Scottish society. Children had been instructed to bring with them a fairly straightforward list of ordinary things such as warm clothing, a raincoat, a change of underclothes, house slippers, a toothbrush, comb, towel and soap and a tin cup, but it soon became obvious that such routine items had simply been beyond the resources of many of the parents. Instead children stepped down from the coaches and trains in the only clothes they possessed, and many were dirty and obviously verminous, being infested with fleas and head-lice. Others had contagious diseases and some were so ill that they should have been in hospital. Moreover the standard of conduct and personal behaviour of some of the children – many of whom, for example, had never lived in a house with its own toilet – came as a grave shock to some of those now receiving them into their homes. This was the revelation which confronted, stunned and embarrassed many of Scotland's small-town and rural communities and a report to Stirling Town Council summed the situation up as follows. Evacuation

> has lifted the veil on the lives of thousands of the populace, disclosing such conditions of squalor, disease, dirt and ignorance of the elementary laws of health and decent living that has appalled those of us who have had to cope with it . . . we would all willingly have become evacuees ourselves to escape from the hundreds of frantic householders asking what we were going to do about ridding them of the lice and filth that had invaded their homes.[15]

Even seasoned nurses found the business of delousing parents, children, bedding and so forth almost too much to endure, but most people just rolled up their sleeves and got down to work with soap, hot water, paraffin and steel combs. Some unfortunate children had to have their heads shaved, and they were usually provided with a cap or headscarf to wear to school. Inevitably a few of the incoming boys quickly came into conflict with local children and blows were often exchanged before the schools settled down again.

Kippen seems to have taken most of this in its stride and many of the children who stayed over the longer term settled in and became for the duration virtually members of the families with whom they stayed. In March 1941 an HMI visited the village school and in his subsequent report he somewhat patronisingly noted that 'the 33 evacuees now on the roll of the school are mainly children of good quality who have fitted in easily into the classes and have maintained a satisfactory position there'. What he meant by 'good quality' is not certain, although presumably he was suggesting that the children had not come from the poorest areas of Glasgow. Whether or not that was actually the case, he does make clear that the children had settled down happily, had been accepted properly into the school and were thriving, and that was greatly to the community's credit.[16]

Most of the children were accommodated in homes around the district in the villages and farm houses. However a dozen or so at Arnprior found themselves staying at the mansion of Garden in the home of no less a person than the District Commissioner for Civil Defence, Glasgow, Sir (later Lord) Steven Bilsland. The Bilslands had obtained the tenancy of Garden some years before the war and Lady Bilsland in particular became a friend of the little school over very many years, donating annual prizes, organising outings and so forth. During the war, however, she excelled herself by devoting a great deal of her time and attention to the needs of the evacuated children, not just by opening her own home to some, but also by organising parties and regularly checking the progress of the children through-out the area. She was also a visitor at the large evacuation camp built at Dounan's farm in Aberfoyle which at times housed as many as 150 Glasgow children.

The evacuees undertook the same education as the local children and, when ready, sat the qualifying exam at Balfron High School. What the children concerned thought of their rural experience one can only guess at. No doubt, some often had sore hearts, missed their own families and perhaps were less than lucky in their personal hosts. However, some parents made the effort to come out to the country at prize-giving days and so on, and in July 1943 one father turned up at the end of term gathering at Arnprior and insisted in addressing the company to express his gratitude and to make clear his opinion that life in the country had been of great benefit to the town children.[17] Perhaps one of the most impressive indications of the feelings of some of the youngsters, however, is that when Arnprior school celebrated its centenary in 1975 several of the former evacuees turned up to join the party and endowed a Mrs O'May prize for mathematics in memory of the teacher who had cared for them during the war.[18]

As it happened Kippen children made their own distinguished contribution to the war effort. Apart from harvesting wild fruit from the hedges, heaths and shrubs in order to provide sources of vitamins, local schoolgirls entered nationally organised cookery competitions to demonstrate the most effective ways to use basic commodities such as oatmeal, potatoes and herrings. Farmer's daughter Margaret More was a Scottish finalist presented to the queen in Edinburgh in 1943, and two sisters, Nan and Helen McCowan, were prizewinners in similar contests in the following year.

Kippen was, of course, never under any great direct physical threat during the war although the air raid alert was sounded on 9th January, 1941 and the schoolchildren were under not very impressive cover for the best part of an hour. On that occasion 'the senior pupils assembled in the corridor running north and south while the infants and juniors were taken into the ladies staff room'. Quite what was going to be achieved by that particular deployment is unclear, but no doubt some thought had been given to the most secure part of the building. The school log records that the children spent the hour 'singing and playing games'.[19]

On the nights of the great raids on Clydeside on 13th to 14th March and 5th to 7th May, 1941 many of the German bombers flew along the valley before turning south to attack Clydebank, Glasgow and Greenock. At the time many of the Kippen mothers and children followed the public advice by sheltering under tables which had been dragged into the stairwells. Few of the local people had much more by way of protection and the reinforced bunker in the garden of Ambruach in the Fore Road is believed to have been the only thing of its kind constructed in the district. On these nights Robert Latta and the other members of the local branch of the Observer Corps did good work from their post which still stands close to Claylands farm and provides an unbroken view over the length of the valley. Although the detonations of heavy explosions were clearly audible in the village, no bombs fell within the immediate area. However, as they returned from the raid, many of the German planes ejected their remaining bombs. One landed close to Auldhall and many small incendiary bomblets fell up on the moors and in Boquhan Glen, where they plunged deep into the soft peat and did no damage. In the following weeks, local youths had great if dangerous fun retrieving them and then subjecting them to some fairly lethal experiments, but fortunately no one seems to have been hurt.

In the immediate aftermath of the March raid Kippen found itself thrust into the role of temporary shelter for hundreds of people from Clydebank who had been forced to flee from the bombing. The initial attack had taken place on a Thursday night and over the following weekend local women volunteers rallied round and provided many hot meals for the refugees. By the Sunday, however, the authorities' emergency plans were being implemented and the visitors were being moved on to communities more able to provide for their shelter and support.[20]

On the outbreak of war Parliament had passed the National Service (Armed Forces) Act under which all men aged between 18 and 41 were liable to be called into the fighting services. However, on 7th September the *Stirling Journal* reported that two-thirds of those who tried to enlist were at first turned away, although those who had formerly been regular soldiers or who had particular skills, such as being able to drive motor vehicles, were welcomed at once. Those rejected were given a ticket home and told to wait for further instructions. This was extremely sensible, and avoided a repetition of much of the disruption that had been caused by indiscriminate recruitment at the start of the First World War. It also gave time to consider what the needs of the home labour force were likely to be to enable an effective war effort to be sustained.

Throughout the war a record of the departure to the services of people from Kippen was apparently carefully maintained by a retired officer, Colonel Ballingall of Ambruach. Unfortunately, the list does not appear to have survived, so it is impossible to say exactly how many people from the parish were directly involved. In any event, over the almost six years of world war the population of the area (as with the country as a whole) became unusually mobile, so that it would have been increasingly difficult to have kept an exact account of the movement of individuals throughout the period.

One of the first men to excite the interest and admiration of the community was the merchant seaman, Chief Radio Officer Sydney Patrick of Lynnburn. Early in October 1939, just a month after the outbreak of war, his ship, the *Lochavon*, was torpedoed and sunk in the North Atlantic. The order was passed to abandon ship and it seems that crew and passengers successfully took to the lifeboats. However, realising that the ship was taking rather longer to sink than expected, Patrick bravely returned on board, reactivated his radio and repeated distress transmissions before swimming back to a lifeboat. The result was that within half an hour or so of the *Lochavon* disappearing below the waves British warships appeared on the scene and rescued everyone. When he returned to the village later that month for rest and recuperation Patrick deservedly received a hero's welcome. Sadly, in March 1944 the community was plunged into deep gloom when it was learned that he had been killed as a result of another sinking.[21] (A second merchant seaman from Kippen who was also lost during the war was Chief Officer Ernest Vallance.)

May and June 1940 was, of course, the period of the 'miracle' of Dunkirk, during which much of the British Army was successfully evacuated from northern France. For many Scottish households, however, this was a time when disaster was unfolding further to the west at the little fishing port of St Valery-en-Caux. The 51st Highland Division, made up largely of territorial soldiers, had been detached from the British Expeditionary Force to operate under French command, and in the path of the German onslaught, along with other elements of the French 10th Army, it had been forced back to the coast. Sadly, St Valery proved little more than a trap for the Scots, for, with their allies surrendering and German guns soon dominating the harbour, by 12th June their commander, General Fortune, had little option but to order his men to submit.

If these events were a tragedy for communities all over Scotland, they were a particular nightmare for the Stirling district, for trapped with the division was the local territorial unit, the 7th Battalion of the Argyll and Sutherland Highlanders. Commanded by Colonel E.P. Buchanan, the laird of Touch, the battalion contained many men from Stirling and the surrounding area and for weeks afterwards families did not know whether their men were alive or dead. Only in late August did Red Cross cards begin to trickle through with the news that many of the men had become prisoners of war. In fact, during the retreat to St Valery, on the 1st June the battalion had been given the hopeless task of attempting to defend a wide front close to the River Somme, and in bitter fighting over the next five days it had simply been over-run by overwhelming enemy forces. With ammunition spent and no prospect of relief the survivors were obliged to surrender, with only 100 or so managing eventually to escape from Le Havre.[22]

Fortunately only a handful of Kippen men were caught up in this debacle, but among those captured at this time were the badly wounded 2nd Lieutenant Alan Orr Ewing of Cardross (his brother, Captain Ronald Orr Ewing of the Scots Guards, also became a POW), and Private Thomas Black of Strewiebank (both 7th Argylls), Lt. David Macdiarmid (son of Dr Macdiarmid of Kirkhill), and artilleryman Lance Corporal Thomas Young of Dun Eaglais Lodge. A year later Kippen learned with sorrow that 20-year-old Lieutenant Peter Smith of the HLI, youngest son of the village minister who had given his life at the end of the First War, had been killed in the fighting before St Valery.[23]

No doubt all of the men who went out from the parish to take part in the war would have had a tale to tell, but the records as represented by the reports of the local newspapers indicate that a number were recognised for particular gallantry. For example, in 1943 Scots Guardsman Lance Sergeant Robert Miller of Myreton farm was awarded the Military Medal for his brave conduct in an action in Tunisia, during which he was wounded. Regrettably he was killed a year later during the Italian campaign. Another Scots Guardsman to be killed was tank commander Sergeant Leslie Stewart of Thistle Cottage who died in the fighting in Normandy in August 1944. He was 25 years old, was one of the first villagers to volunteer, and before the war had worked as a plasterer during the building of Gribloch House. Also killed in Normandy was Royal Marine Commando Jack Murray of Taylor's Building. He was an older man who, before the war, had been a well-known football player with Greenock Morton.

Alex Chisholm of Glentirranmuir, a veteran of the First War, sent four of his sons to the war. The eldest, Donald, a sergeant air gunner, was killed on a bombing raid in 1943, and the third brother, Robert, also an airman, was shot down in the same year, but survived as a prisoner of war. Sergeant Air Gunner John Miller, a member of the family of village joiners, was also killed at about this time.

One of the most decorated of the Kippen men was the minister's oldest son, Flight Lieutenant John D. Younie who was awarded a DFC and Bar for his activities as a pilot flying Spitfires with a fighter/reconnaissance squadron in North Africa and Italy. John Younie had been educated at Stirling High School and Fettes and had won a major scholarship to Cambridge when the war intervened, and he was aged just 24 at the time of his second decoration. On that occasion, the citation referred to his 'gallantry and devotion to duty' in the exercise of a series of difficult air operations. In 'adverse weather and over difficult terrain' he had 'consistently pressed home his attacks with accuracy and determination' and had 'set a fine example' to his colleagues.[24] Fortunately John Younie survived, as did his younger brother Edward, (currently the Kippen Kirk session clerk) who flew with the Fleet Air Arm in the closing months of the war.

One of the senior army officers from Kippen was the professional soldier Lieutenant Colonel Roderick Leckie Ewing of Arngomery who commanded a battalion of the Highland Light Infantry. His absence for much of the war coincidentally gave Kippen a particular connection with the Royal Navy. During 1940 the houses around a number of the historic naval bases in the south of England were heavily damaged by enemy bombing, so that it became necessary to find alternative homes for some of the families and Arngomery House was therefore leased for the purpose for the duration of the war. Among those accommodated at Arngomery was the family of Commander (later Vice-Admiral Sir) W. Geoffrey Robson, DSO and Bar, DSC, in whose career the village thereafter took great interest.

In 1939–1941 Commander Robson captained the destroyer HMS *Kandahar* which was part of the famous Fifth Destroyer Flotilla commanded by Lord Louis Mountbatten in the *Kelly* (subject of the Noel Coward film *In Which We Serve*). In May 1940 the *Kelly* was torpedoed and badly damaged in an action with German E boats in the North Sea, and Robson first came to prominence for the skilful way in which, in rough weather, he used the *Kandahar* to take off wounded crewmen and then to shield *Kelly* for four days, enabling her to be towed safely back to the River Tyne for repair.[25]

Robson and his family (his wife was Sylvia Forrester) must have become very popular in Kippen because the whole community seems to have held its breath when *Kandahar* was reported to be lost in the Mediterranean on 18th December, 1941. While attempting to locate an enemy convoy part of a British squadron became trapped in a minefield and the cruisers *Neptune* and *Aurora* were disabled. *Aurora* was towed clear, but *Neptune* detonated further mines which resulted in her capsizing with the loss of all but one of her company. As this tragedy was unfolding, in a desperate but gallant effort to rescue the crew of the stricken *Neptune*, Robson took *Kandahar* into the minefield where yet another explosion blew her stern off, leaving her helpless. The rest of the squadron now withdrew to escort the *Aurora* back to Malta, but two days later another destroyer sent to search the area found the *Kandahar* which was just still afloat, having drifted clear of the mines. Most of her company were rescued and Robson's safe recovery was duly intimated from the pulpit to a relieved Kippen congregation.[26]

Three years later Robson, by now commanding an escort group guarding an Arctic convoy, again survived the loss of his ship, this time HMS *Hardy*.

With the invasion of France in May 1940, the Government took the decision to recruit a local defence volunteer force which, a few months later, was referred to by Winston Churchill as the Home Guard, a name that stuck and which perfectly captured the spirit of the initiative. Kippen soon had its own Home Guard platoon (part of the 1st Stirlingshire Battalion) made up in some cases from veterans of the Great War and even of earlier conflicts, since the upper age limit was 65, but also of younger men waiting for their call-up papers. The hard core, however, were men who had been just too young in 1918, but who, 22 years on, were at the back of the queue of those capable of being drafted for full-time service. Among those who flocked to enlist was William Hay, who much later loved to watch the television programme *Dad's Army*, which he maintained bore an uncanny resemblance to the experiences of the Kippen company. For example, he claimed that the kind of petty jealousies and pretensions of Captain Mainwaring and his sergeant were a fairly accurate reflection of some of the sentiments of the members of the guard who could never quite shake clear of their civilian identities.

However, despite the nonsense, the seriousness of their purpose was never in doubt and night after night the men came out after long hours at their day jobs (which often involved vital work) and took on the role of soldiers. They trained hard and sometimes in company and competition with front-line troops, and within a year or two they had become reasonably armed and believed that they would have been well able to have given a good account of themselves should the need have arisen. Occasionally indeed they took over real local guard duties. At different stages in the war munition dumps were created on the moor above the village and down by the Lake of Menteith, and from time to time the Home Guard companies were used to relieve the resident troops in maintaining security at the dumps.

While the significance of their contribution should never be undervalued, the truth is that the farcical element was also never far from the surface, and some of William Hay's stories were hilarious, especially when told in his own quiet way and accompanied by mischievously twinkling eyes. Three of the tales are as follows. To begin with, the platoon had few weapons and had to improvise, but being countrymen many of the farmers (and local poachers) had their own shotguns which were duly pressed into service. One

autumn evening early in the war they were training at Arnprior farm
with some of the local men attempting to attack a Kippen group
positioned further up the hill towards Cloney. Some sentries were
sent out to give warning of the 'enemy's' approach and one of the
fitter men shinned up a tree and lay on a branch from where he
watched one of the Arnprior men wriggling slowly on his tummy up
the line of the hedge until he was directly underneath and almost
within touching distance. Not knowing how else to warn his company the Kippen man fired his shotgun into the air, whereupon the
would-be attacker simply 'levitated', his whole body coming off the
ground with his hair standing straight up, and when he touched the
earth again he was already running so that he was back down the hill
and out of sight in seconds. The poor man got a tremendous fright,
but no one would reveal the identity of the fellow who had discharged the gun above him. As it happened, the pair lived on into old
age and were latterly great friends, spending many hours in each
other's company, but so deeply offended had the victim been that the
Kippen man never quite had the courage to confess his guilt.

On the first night of the bombing raid of May 1941, the Kippen
platoon was at Balfron, training with their colleagues there. The bus
service was soon shut down and there was no option for the men but
to march back to Kippen. As they crossed the moor they realised that
some of the enemy planes were flying low above their heads and occasionally seeming to come within range of rifle fire. They therefore
stopped and checked on the state of their ammunition. Because they
had been firing earlier in the evening there were only enough bullets
to give each man one, but they decided that with the spread of a single
volley one or two rounds might just find the target, so they shared out
the bullets and marched on, while looking and listening in awe to the
flashes and din of the attack going on south of the hills. Soon a plane
was heard approaching and in a scene straight out of *Dad's Army*,
rifles were raised – 'up, two, three; aim, two, three' – but with a roar
the aircraft was already past and disappearing into the gloom, the
men still spinning round trying to get a decent sight for a shot while
avoiding harming each other. One or two did manage to get a shot
off, but with no evident effect, and to their bitter regret, no other
plane came close enough to give the others a second chance.

The most absurd prank followed a visit to the Cross Keys Inn by a
number of the men. On this occasion they had only recently been
issued with some venerable American carbines, part of the consign-
ment of weapons which Churchill was able to obtain from the
United States under the 1940 Lend-Lease agreement and which

enabled some of the most urgent shortages of equipment to be addressed. The small rifles were obviously fairly ancient and many of the men had little confidence in them and this provoked a dispute about their accuracy. After a drop too much to drink several of the men sallied out of the pub, determined to put the matter to the test, with wagers being laid by various members. Eventually a shot rang out and a hole appeared directly under the eleven on the east face of the clock on the church tower. Satisfied that, if not quite spot on, the rifle was capable of doing damage, the company fled, but for the next 46 years or so, a long rusty red tear disfigured the clock face and reminded the community of their antics.

Ironically, the greatest danger to the local community may have occurred shortly after the war, although little seems to have been said about the subject at the time. As was mentioned above, some armaments were stored in 'Nissen' huts and on dugout sites on the moor, and although it is impossible to be precise about the nature of the contents, locally it was believed that the material included chemical bombs or shells which fortunately were never used, but which were manufactured so as to be available in the event of the enemy having had resort to similar types of weapon. With the ending of hostilities the authorities had to confront the dire problem of how best to dispose of the munitions, and it appears to have been decided that they were too unpleasant to shift and that the best thing was to destroy them on site by burning. Looking back from over 50 years, this procedure sounds almost unbelievably casual, but presumably in the aftermath of such a dreadful war attitudes towards such matters were rather more stoical than would now be the case. Inevitably there must have been a problem about how to generate sufficient heat to ensure that dangerous material was not released. However, all that seems to have been done was to wait for a day when the wind was blowing from the south so that the smoke would be carried north and away from the centres of population. In due course, in 'the late autumn' of 1945 the fires were started, but unfortunately the wind dropped so that a thick pall of noxious, yellow-brown smoke rolled gently down the hill and lay over the carse for many hours. A number of the farmers and their families apparently suffered from stinging eyes and sore throats for days afterwards, but mercifully there was no loss of human life. However, some cattle were reported to have died and farmers in due course lodged claims for compensation. Perhaps a more serious disaster was averted because the harvest had already been gathered. In the following autumn samples of crops grown in the affected fields were fed by government scientists to animals under test conditions, but according to the Secretary of State for Scotland, no significant consequences were discovered.[27]

One of the saddest events of the war years for Kippen was the death in a car accident of the popular Dr Fletcher of Strathview. The accident happened in October 1942 and (like many others at the time) was caused primarily by the inadequacy of the masked car headlights enforced by the wartime 'blackout' regulations, the doctor's car colliding with a stationary vehicle on the road near Arnprior. Charles Fletcher, who had served the parish for 12 years, had been fully involved in the life of the community as amateur 'actor, scout-master, chorister, Home Guardsman, sportsman, and in many other roles, all of which he filled with zest and efficiency'. It was said of him that 'his was a happy, graceful friendship. His character was frank and generous, and his temperament optimistic and gay. His entry into a house of sickness was not a solemn professional event . . . and he always brought and left real help and a lightening of the spirit'. His untimely death 'in the prime of his life and work' caused great distress, but to express their feelings and as a memorial the community raised the funds to establish a library in the nurses' residence at Stirling Royal Infirmary.

As happened in various parts of the country, many of the Kippen women devoted themselves to the activities of the 'War Work Party'. Under the leadership of Mrs Scott of Benview and Mrs M.A. Patrick, between 1939 and 1946 the ladies of the district knitted some 6800 garments which were distributed to the Red Cross, to the Argyll & Sutherland Highlanders' Comforts unit, and to a similar unit of the Royal Signals. Gifts were also sent to local men in the forces and particularly to those men from the area that were being held as prisoners of war. In addition, the Kippen and Arnprior party adopted a minesweeper, the *Queen Empress*, and her crew was kept well supplied. Moreover the women raised £1514 from general campaigning and used this money to purchase two ambulances and a mobile canteen, that were then gifted to the Red Cross. Finally they organised a 'penny-a-week' savings scheme over a period of 52 weeks, collecting £1018, and organised numerous dances, fêtes and so on to gather money in support of the 'Welcome Home Fund' that was intended to give some tangible mark of gratitude to the returning service personnel.

On this occasion, because the war in the Far East continued for several months after the end of hostilities in Europe, and because national service was carried on into the post-war period, it proved impossible to organise a reception for everyone who had 'done their bit'. Nevertheless, in November 1946 'a large party of those who served' were entertained to dinner in the public hall and 86 men received monetary gifts as a token of thanks. In the case of Sapper Alex Davidson the presentation was made in his own home since, sadly, he had lost his sight as a result of an explosion.

One of Kippen's most useful and perhaps surprising contributions to the war effort was made by the tiny joinery firm of J. & N. Miller which in these years specialised in manufacturing lifeboats for installation in ships being built at Clydebank. The Miller brothers had come to Kippen from St Monans on the Fife coast where the skills of boat-building for in-shore fishermen had been handed on from an older generation. Because of the sudden increase in demand for ships, both to meet the requirements of the Royal Navy and to replace merchant vessels being lost to submarines, production in the shipyards of the Clyde shot up to record levels and small firms all over the west of Scotland were called into action to support the output of the big yards by making and supplying various essential fittings and equipment. Under the leadership of John and Niven (Mackie) Miller the Kippen joiners rose to the challenge and turned out a small but important stream of traditional clinker-built life boats.

From 1939 to 1945 all over the UK building materials and skilled workers were needed for emergency tasks which ranged from small operations such as Millers' boat work to large-scale activities – the construction of airfields and war production factories, repairing bomb-damage and so on. As a consequence there was very little domestic house-building at precisely the period when many dwellings were being permanently destroyed. At the same time and in the following years there was an abrupt increase both in the birth-rate and in the rate of household formation, and the inevitable result was that in the immediate post-war years there was a severe general shortage of houses. Moreover, some of the problems revealed by the condition of the evacuated urban children helped to convince the community as a whole that a major government initiative was required to address the housing problem once and for all. This was the context to the great council housing drive which dominated housing policy for the first two decades after the war. Licences and other controls were used to limit strictly private construction so that of the almost 410,000 houses built in Scotland from 1945 to 1960 only about 10 per cent were for private home owners. By contrast the overwhelming majority were erected by councils.

In Kippen the first sizeable estate was put up at Oakwood in 1950–1951. Some of the houses were of a conventional terraced form, but most were Blackburn 'sponsored' non-traditional houses, and were of a type used to ensure that the factories which had been engaged in military production for the previous five years or so still retained their labour forces after the war, thus helping to avoid serious unemployment while at the same time tackling the housing problem. In the event, the houses were typically good four-apartment dwellings, and the pleasantly laid-out area with its smart gardens gradually developed into an exceptionally pretty street. In 1952–1953 eight 'Weir' Swedish timber houses completed the estate.

Twelve of the Oakwood houses were specifically intended to be for agricultural workers, and similarly eight houses were constructed at Arnprior for the same purpose. These latter 'Atholl Steel' houses were located in a terrace at Kepp, and about 1987 they were comprehensively and attractively modernised so that their original structural form is no longer obvious.

The second major development at Kippen was completed in 1960–1961 at Burnside and consisted of 29 houses of traditional construction. To make space for these dwellings a number of older buildings were demolished, including Douglas Place (the first Free Church) and an old terrace of cottages known locally as 'The Pit', the site of a former distillery. Since the development lay close to the rear of the grounds of Dun Eaglais it was named Cameron Crescent in honour of D.Y. Cameron. Ten years later yet another similar sized council scheme was built, also at Burnside, but this time beyond the site of the old dairy, and it received the name Hay's Hill, since it was constructed in the field in which the dairyman/carter had grazed his horses.

During these post-war years and reflecting national policy, few houses for private purchase were built in Kippen, and not until the mid-1960s was a small development of modern bungalows commenced at Menteith Crescent. When these houses first came on the market the local people were fairly horrified at the apparent astronomical price range of £3000–£4000, which represented a more than doubling of prices since the war. What no one could have anticipated was that the country was still only in the very early days of the house price inflation that would dominate the following 25 years.

The next significant private developments were, of course, on the site of the old vine at Cauldhame, and on the other side of the Fintry Road on what had been the car park. Vinery and Denovan Crescents were the results and on this occasion the developer deliberately aimed at the more expensive end of the market, although there was great mirth in the community when the houses were advertised as 'Ranch Style Housing at Kippen', presumably in consequence of their relatively long low appearance.

From the 1960s another phenomenon which had an important effect was the trend towards the modernisation of older properties. Some of this was assisted by official policies deliberately intended to protect and improve old buildings and, for example, local authority improvement grants helped to meet some of the costs of essential tasks such as replacing lead piping, rewiring or renewing roof slates. However, much of the work was entirely a matter of private domestic investment, for, given the general shortage of suitable properties for private purchase, rising prices ensured that most people who restored an old house or cottage could expect a significant capital gain when the property was eventually sold. This activity resulted in the preservation and restoration of most of the older houses in the area.

During this period council planning policy was broadly to prevent ribbon or isolated developments, and instead to favour consolidated estates of the kind mentioned above. However, when, in the late 1970s, the huge post-war programmes of direct provision of local authority housing finally came to an end many councils had to adopt a more lenient view in order to give the building industry a more sympathetic planning environment. Increasingly, therefore, in-fill and one-off developments became much more common in and around Kippen. Through the 1980s and '90s houses of this kind were built on Burnside, at Music Hall, above the Crown Hotel and at Cauldhame. One generally welcome initiative which slightly complicated this situation occurred when the central part of the village was designated as a conservation area, which meant that subsequent buildings there had to conform where possible to traditional styles and materials.

An extremely interesting development at this time took place at Castlehill where the lead developer chose simply to sell off much of the land as serviced plots to allow individuals to construct their own houses. This resulted in a wide range of house types of mixed cost and produced a pleasant extension leading more or less from the bottom of Oakwood back round to the main street. Included in this project was a small community of sheltered houses owned and managed by Hanover Housing Association and a brand new surgery and health centre. Both of these were welcome additions to the village facilities. Generally, therefore, Castlehill Loan was a satisfactory venture. However, from an environmental perspective the planning decision to insist on the same choice of roof tiles, rough-cast and colour finish for all the buildings was absurd and simply imported the feel of a conventional estate into a street which had much more varied and interesting possibilities. Groups of houses which develop organically and over time (such as in the Main Street or Fore Road) tend to have many different types and styles of building, and this adds to their interest. The thirst which some planners have for uniformity (as distinct from a desire for a measure of broad sympathy between buildings) is depressing, and perhaps on this occasion detracted from what might have been achieved with a little more tolerance of individual choices.

As a consequence of the various initiatives discussed above the housing stock of Kippen village virtually doubled from 167 houses in 1949 to about 330 by 1989. The population, of course, did not increase in proportion, because of the trend towards smaller households, and in particular the increasing number of elderly villagers.

Of all the developments of the post-war period, by far the most controversial was the one undertaken in the late 1990s by J.B. Bennett of Kilsyth in a field at the rear of the school that subsequently became known as Scott Brae. This land, which was not part of Shirgarton farm, had been sold about 1950 by Colonel Leckie Ewing of Arngomery to a farmer, Mr Risk of Culmore, with the specific injunction that it be maintained as agricultural land, the purpose being to ensure that it remained an asset to the general amenity of the village. Usually thereafter the field was kept as grazing pasture, and indeed, when the snow was on the ground it was the place traditionally favoured by the village children for sledging. Eventually, however, on Mr Risk's death it was acquired by Bennett as part of the developer's land bank.

There were two reasons behind much of the opposition to the plans. First, the main street of the village runs up the crest of a ridge running east–west and virtually all the developments since the war had taken place to the south of this spine or were, to a greater or lesser degree, in-fill in nature. As a result, the essential shape of the village was not altered by any of the additions and nothing interfered with the magnificent unbroken views to the hills of the north available from the main road from the children's swing park up to Point End and thereafter on the Back Road to Arnmoulin. In the inter-war period three villas, Shoreland, Lynwood and St Michael's, were certainly built on the north side of the road, but from then on building in that area had been abandoned because of a general objection to any interference with the quality of the outlook. The second

reason for opposition to Scott Brae was that the builder at first proposed to create a high-density estate, packing in as many houses as
possible. This would have made an almost 30 per cent increase in the
size of the village and there were fears that it would start a process
that might eventually turn Kippen into a small town.

Aware of the strength of local hostility, the firm did not rush into
the project and delayed operations for several years. However, when
its proposals were finally published there were fierce objections from
some of the villagers and the plans were also rejected by the local
authority. The company therefore appealed to the Secretary of State
who initiated a public inquiry which was held in the village hall and
lasted for about a week. The inquirer's finding was that the project
could go ahead, but with a dramatically reduced number of houses,
and this, of course, induced the company to recast its plans and to
build the 36 upmarket villas that were completed between 1997 and
1999. In the event, if there was disruption to the village amenity it
was fairly minimal in the sense that because of the steepness of the
sloping land there was really very little loss of general outlook.
Moreover many of the incoming residents were soon contributing
positively to the community. To the extent that there was genuine
'loss', it was sustained almost exclusively by the parish minister and
his family, since the builder somewhat churlishly placed one house
and garage so close to the adjacent manse that its fine view to the
hills was almost completely forfeited. It was an unnecessary act of
meanness that could easily have been avoided by a little consideration and good manners.

A more welcome change loosely associated with the development
was the modernisation of the village school, partly to provide
additional accommodation for the increasing child population, but
also to bring the facilities up to a first-class modern standard.

In addition to the building activities in the villages (Buchlyvie also
experienced similar growth), scattered residential housing was
erected in the countryside. In the post-war period, and particularly
from the 1960s, farming became very highly mechanised and went
through some years of considerable prosperity assisted initially by
UK government support and subsequently by European funding.
During that time harvesting methods in particular were radically
improved so that the labour force and land management became
concentrated into a smaller number of hands. In many cases farmers
and their families came to operate two or more farms together. As a
result, some of the housing development involved altering older
farmhouses purely for residential purposes, or upgrading old

cottages. Elsewhere a number of new houses were built.

One major initiative that gave general pleasure took place in the early 1960s when the remaining elements of the Boquhan estate were obtained by a wealthy industrialist, J. Ross Anderson, who set about restoring the home farm and the adjacent mansion house. The old Boquhan mansion had fallen into decay through little more than neglect, and it seems to have been a victim of the hostile tax régime which made the possession of such properties in the early post-war period a real liability. By the time Anderson came on the scene the old house was, sadly, beyond redemption. It had been partially burned, had become little more than a shell, and many of its fine fittings had been pillaged. Anderson therefore decided to start from scratch by replacing the ruin with a brand new residence of Auchenlea stone. It was possibly the first new mansion-size house produced in Scotland after the war and, if it was fairly conventional in design, it nevertheless turned out to be a handsome building. In a decade notorious for utilitarian and ugly structures, the new Boquhan House gave its creators the opportunity to show what they could do when asked some sensible questions. A fine eight-acre garden was laid out south of the house.

The home farm was also transformed, being provided with state-of-the-art dairying facilities and, initially, a pedigree Friesian herd capable of producing a daily yield of 400 gallons of milk. Additional capacity to store hay and silage was constructed, together with modern stock houses, while nine new cottages were built, originally for the staff, and two lodges were modernised. The net result was a first-class dairy farm, as good as anything to be found anywhere in Scotland. Sadly, Anderson did not enjoy the outcome for long, for his son, who was intended to run the estate, was killed in a car accident. However, his successors at Boquhan have built on and developed his legacy, and today a magnificent herd of Jersey cattle occupies the farm.

The real driving forces behind the various housing developments in and around Kippen (as elsewhere in Scotland) were general levels of rising prosperity and the widening ownership of motor cars which enabled an ever-growing proportion of the population to live at an increasing distance from their places of work. From the early 1960s Glasgow's population went into steep decline and central Scotland experienced a strong 'counter urban' shift as people moved towards the suburbs and beyond into country communities. Kippen parish was at the fringe of this trend and only really began to experience its rippling effects from about 1980 when the M9, M80 motorway linkages were completed at Stirling. In the following years traffic flows along the Vale of Menteith grew strongly and brought the valley to the attention of increasing numbers of people.

Growth and development obviously produced many changes in the community and in lifestyle, although rarely so abruptly as to be uncomfortable. What was undoubtedly lost, as the traditional way of life gently drifted into the past, was the strange 'Oot o' the world' sense of being slightly isolated, but not remote, which was still a real feeling among residents as recently as the 1950s. Perhaps the point is best conveyed by a few examples of the experience of life in the district just three or four decades ago.

In the 1950s when the snow fell in winter Jimmy Dunlop would use his horse and a little wooden snow plough to clear all the pavements. Similarly, in the late autumn Geordie Hay and his friends would burn the scrub on Dasher Common and the Black Brae to clean things up and make way for new growth. These things were done voluntarily, spontaneously, and were simply traditional contributions to the commonweal which had nothing whatsoever to do with the council or any official body. Doors in the village were rarely locked and neighbours typically came and went as they wished. At Hogmanay the party in Oakwood seemed to involve every household and everyone was welcome. The weekly Saturday dance in the village hall was packed with all generations and invariably the proceedings were compèred by a real character, Willie Low (formerly gardener at Arngomery, but who latterly operated a thriving market garden at Castlehill). He could not bear to see anyone seated for any length of time and maintained a tremendous running commentary from the stage to get everyone up onto the dance floor. As often as not the band was 'Dick McQueen's' – a fiddle, two accordions, a saxophone or trumpet, piano and drums. The routine was one 'modern' dance followed by a Scottish country dance, and the quality of some of the dancing was often first-class without being in the least formal or restrictive. Boy's Brigade and Girl Guide companies were well organised, and almost without exception involved every boy and girl in the community. On communion Sundays the church was full, and on some occasions extra seats had to be brought in and placed down the side aisles; and when one young man, Willie Rankine, very sadly died almost the whole village turned up to fill every scrap of space in the church, the vestibule and church house. The village football team disgraced itself after one match by continuing the contest with increased vigour behind the team hut and so got itself suspended for a few years from the Forth and Endrick

League. However, when it was accepted back into the fold it soon managed once more to complete a cup and league double, and this took place in 1965. Two years later the Cancer Whist was commenced, largely under the leadership of Winnie and Jackie Dunlop, and created an annual event mainly to raise funds for cancer research, but also which came to form a landmark in the village calendar and which, perhaps as well as anything, perpetuates a little of the earlier spirit of the place.

It will be seen from the foregoing that there was a special ambience to the way of life in Kippen in the earlier post-war years. It was, no doubt, relatively unsophisticated, but from a youngster's point of view it was a wonderful place and time in which to grow up, particularly because of the strong sense of belonging to a genuine community. The increasing inclination to park passively in front of a television set and again, the greater personal mobility which resulted in social and economic circles extending inexorably beyond the immediate locality, were perhaps two of the factors that blunted people's willingness to participate and thus gradually blurred Kippen's particular sense of identity. This is not to suggest, of course, that the village is not still a lovely place in which to live.

One loss of recent years was the winding up in April 1992 of the family trucking company, Robert Davidson and Sons. This firm was perhaps a classic example of a rural transport business, with an economic history that extended for almost 150 years.

Theoretically the enterprise was founded in 1868 by Robert Davidson, but the probability is that some carting was begun several years earlier. To begin with it operated by carrying produce for the villagers and farmers and it grew with the arrival of the railway, using hansom-cabs and horse-drawn waggonettes to ferry passengers as well as goods. The company remained firmly in the hands of generations of the Davidson family, and in the early 20th century moved readily into motorised vehicles. In addition to serving the farms and local estates it used flat lorries to carry whisky barrels from the Highlands and the North-East to Lowland distilleries. In 1927, at the time of a rail strike, it carried out deliveries from dairy farms to Alloa for the Scottish Milk Marketing Board and six years later it received an important long-term contract from the Board. From then on its work was pre-eminently in transporting milk around many parts of west central Scotland, at first with flat lorries carrying steel urns, but later with a fleet of up to seven bulk tankers. Its work in this area was boosted in the early 1980s when it acquired the Balfron firm of Strathendrick Farmers.

For most of the modern period the company was run as a partnership by three brothers, Bertie, Billy and Geordie, and their sister Jean, who kept the firm going during the war years when the men were in the forces. To support the fleet of vehicles a garage and depot were maintained at Cauldhame and for much of the time the firm gave employment to as many as 12 men, either driving or working in the garage.

Ill health and a desire to retire seems to have been ultimately responsible for the winding up of the concern, and in 1992 the milk trucking activities were transferred to the Marketing Board's Paisley depot, with the Cauldhame garage and land being sold off for housing development. It was a quiet end not just to a fine family business, but to an era, for Davidsons individually and as a company had made an exceptional and enduring contribution to the economy of the district.

Another change of this time that should be mentioned was the closure of Arnprior Primary School and its ultimate resurrection as a nursery school.

In the post-war period the school had at first flourished with typically 30–40 pupils and two permanent teachers as well as a number of visiting specialists to provide music, art and PE instruction. Indeed, in the late 1950s the building had been fully upgraded with the addition of a new extension. For most of the next 30 years it had continued as an excellent little school, but by the mid-1980s falling pupil numbers were beginning to threaten its continued existence. A root cause of the problem was in fact increasing parental mobility. Whereas in the 1940s the headteacher, Mrs O'May, had marvelled at her pupils' resilience in walking two or more miles to school in all weathers, modern country mums were much more likely to use motor vehicles to ferry children backwards and forwards. However, once in a car it was just as easy to drive three or four miles as one or two, particularly if that suited the circumstances of the increasing numbers of families in which both parents were in employment. Moreover, the development of playgroups in Kippen and Buchlyvie meant that mothers and children were establishing relationships in the larger villages that they sometimes wished to continue through primary school.

By 1986 the Arnprior school roll was down to just 12 pupils and the local authority could no longer avoid addressing the situation. Closure plans were announced, but parents, friends, pupils and former pupils all rallied round and the reward for a magnificent campaign was a reprieve, albeit with the loss of the full-time assistant teacher.

For another decade the school functioned successfully on a single-teacher basis with visiting assistants, but finally, as a response to a national audit that showed that many small schools were now operating at unreasonably high costs per pupil, a reorganised Stirling Council took the decision to close Arnprior. Once again the community battled for retention, but this time there was to be no reprieve and the end finally came on Friday 29th June, 1996.

The blow to the Arnprior district was severe since the school had also acted as a community centre for the WRI branch, for the annual Spring Bulb Show and for various other social ventures. However, in retrospect, the school had survived just long enough. Instead of being sold off (as would have been probable a few years earlier), the excellent little building was retained by the local authority and in 1998 it was comprehensively refurbished and prepared for a new role as a nursery school serving the whole surrounding area. In effect it was the motor vehicle that produced such a happy outcome, since cars and mini-buses enabled parents to bring young children from Kippen, Buchlyvie, Port of Menteith and elsewhere, so that when it opened in 1999 the new staff could look forward with confidence to the future.[28]

Over the 20th century Kippen parish produced many interesting characters, and many more pages could easily be filled in telling something of their lives. However, it is quite impossible to do justice to more than a tiny selection of individuals who, in themselves, represented something of particular general interest. Included among the latter must be the brothers Gilbert and Andrew Rennie.

The brothers were descended from a long line of village blacksmiths and both distinguished themselves in the village school and were fine soccer players for the village team. But while Andrew was required by his father to enter the family business at the age of 13, Gilbert, younger by 5 years, embarked on a glittering career. He was a graduate of the University of Glasgow and served with distinction from 1915–1919 as a captain in the King's Own Scottish Borderers, being decorated with the Military Cross. He was one of the last great generation of colonial civil servants and from 1920–1937 he served in Ceylon (Sri Lanka), before transferring to Africa. He was financial secretary in the Gold Coast from 1937–1939 and throughout the Second War he was chief secretary to the government of Kenya. From 1948 to 1954 he was governor and commander-in-chief of Northern Rhodesia, and he was high commissioner for the Federation of Rhodesia and Nyasaland from 1954 to 1961. He was knighted in 1946 and was appointed Knight

Commander of the Order of St Michael and St George in 1949. Even in retirement his work was outstanding. For example, he chaired a number of Commonwealth economic committees which tried to address the problems of poverty and hunger in Africa and elsewhere and he was joint treasurer of the Royal Society of Arts from 1965 to 1970. He was awarded an LLD from his old university and for his efforts to tackle poverty he was appointed as a Knight of St John.

Andrew watched the progress of his brother's career with pride, but also, understandably, with a little envy. At school he had been every inch as capable and he too, might have done anything, had he been allowed the opportunity, but he was needed in the smiddy. In build he did not perhaps conform to the popular image of a blacksmith, being physically short and wiry, but he was strong and skilful. During his working lifetime, of course, the great day of horse-drawn farming passed into history and running a successful blacksmithing business became progressively more difficult. However, in the 1930s he was encouraged by D.Y. Cameron to turn his hand to wrought-iron work, making decorative railings and a range of other ornaments and fittings which he sold successfully at the Royal Highland Show and at various other venues. He also contributed fine work to the Church and no Kippen bride of his day was married without receiving something for her house which had been fashioned on his anvil. He therefore managed to maintain a decent living, and even after he retired, from time to time he would light his furnace and demonstrate his fine skills. As he grew older he became a notable prankster, and to the delight of the community, he was no respecter of persons in selecting his victims. He may not have been famous, but he was admired and liked by everyone and there was a genuine sense of loss when he died in 1985 at the age of 95. Remarkably he was the last of a line of no fewer than seven generations of blacksmiths who had worked in the smiddy at the village cross, and it was very appropriate that when the surrounding area was renovated in the 1980s by the National Trust the lane was given the name Rennie's Loan.

Another interesting Kippenite was Betty Harvie Anderson, Tory MP for East Renfrew from 1959 until 1979 and the first woman to occupy the speaker's chair in the House of Commons. Miss Harvie Anderson, later Baroness Skrimshire of Quarter, was descended from many generations of the Harvies of Kippen, and her family had owned part of the old barony of Shirgarton, including the farm of Strewiebank. She shared her childhood between Kippen and the Quarter estate near Denny which eventually became her main home. However, she never lost touch with Kippen and maintained her interest in the community, notably as one of the trustees of the Helensfield Trust.

In 1938 she enlisted in the Auxiliary Territorial Service in Glasgow, and from 1943 until the end of the war she was commander-in-chief of the Mixed Heavy Anti-Aircraft Brigade. Following a period of service on the old Stirling County Council she was elected to Parliament by East Renfrew in 1959 and was the first female deputy speaker from 1970 until 1973. In her obituary in the *Glasgow Herald* it was noted that she was appointed to the speaker's chair not in any sense as a 'gesture to the emergent forces of women's liberation', but purely on her merits as an outstanding parliamentarian, and as a first-class committee manager:

> Brisk, but stimulating in conversation, she combined an allegiance to traditional Conservative values with a thoroughly practical and up-to-date approach to her job as an MP, and if she was often and rightly referred to as redoubtable, it was always with affection and admiration ... [In her dress as Speaker] there were no frills, no furbelows – just clean, classic lines. She was a lady who meant business.

If not a great speaker, nor one who ever had the opportunity to serve as a minister, Betty Harvie Anderson was a real political operator who knew how to engage the levers of power in the interests of her constituents and of the people of Scotland as a whole, and she, in fact, achieved far more than most of the public ever realised. For example, when a Glasgow shipyard needed a contract it had no more skilful or assiduous advocate in the Commons. A later secretary of state, George Younger, commented on her death that 'she was a great lady in every respect who gained the admiration of both sides of the House. She made a tremendous impact on all aspects of Scottish life.'[29]

When she died in November 1979 she was laid to rest in Kippen cemetery, and it was pleasing to note that village friends of her childhood were among those called forward to assist her family in lowering her coffin into the grave.

But, of course, Kippen is not really about the fame and fortune achieved by individuals. Rather, if its history has a single connecting theme it has to be the sense of a genuine rural community with roots which run deep into the past of a district close to the very heart of Scotland. Moreover these roots are easily discernible from a gentle stroll among the gravestones in the old churchyard or the contemporary cemetery. Again and again the stones tell of members of families easily traceable far into the past. Indeed, the last word can be left to the inscription on one headstone, since the lines capture something of that sense of a continuum which is the hallmark of an enduring community.

As it happens, it is the headstone of a famous man, since it marks the last resting place of (John) Duncan Macrae (1905–1967), described by his colleagues as 'the outstanding Scottish actor of his generation'. Macrae's mother was Catherine Graham, daughter of a Kippen joiner, and although his childhood was largely spent in Glasgow, when his parents retired they resumed residence in the village at a cottage on the Burnside. It was to there that Macrae came frequently with his friends and there is no doubt that he regarded the place as his real home. Perhaps he is now best remembered for his performances in films such as *Whisky Galore* (1950), *The Kidnappers* (1954) and *Tunes of Glory* (1960), or in episodes of the television series *Para Handy* or the original *Dr Finlay's Casebook*; or most of all for his regular appearances on the BBC Hogmanay Party where he convulsed the nation with his rendition of 'The Wee Cock Sparra'. But it was as a stage actor that he really reached pre-eminence, particularly through his work with the Citizens' Theatre Company in Glasgow, which strove to promote the Scottish theatre as a whole. He excelled in plays such as Bridie's *Gog and Magog*, and *Dr Angelus* and Robert McLellan's *Jamie the Saxt* as well as in many classical productions.[30] In his *In Memoriam Duncan Macrae*, the great poet Hugh MacDiarmid perfectly captured the essence of the actor's performance:

> Every movement of the lanky lean
> Don Quixote-like figure
> Was a revelation that made one smile
> But never inclined to snigger.
>
> For there was keen intellect in the fun,
> A great comedian but no fool,
> Measuring everything precisely
> With movements like opening a joiner's rule.

Duncan Macrae departed too soon, the victim of a cruel brain tumour, but he had time to plan for his end and it was among his Kippen roots that he chose to lie down. On his stone are carved the lines from the 15th-century poet, William Dunbar:

> I se that Makaris amang the laif
> Playis heir ther pageant syne gois to graif.*

---

* I see that poets, among the rest, play here their pageants, then go to grave.

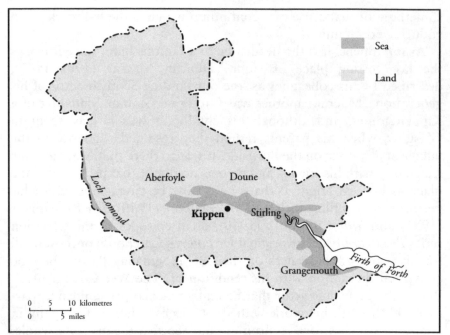

The shoreline of central Scotland about 6,500 years ago

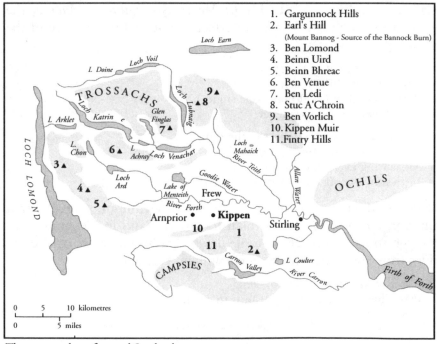

1. Gargunnock Hills
2. Earl's Hill
   (Mount Bannog - Source of the Bannock Burn)
3. Ben Lomond
4. Beinn Uird
5. Beinn Bhreac
6. Ben Venue
7. Ben Ledi
8. Stuc A'Chroin
9. Ben Vorlich
10. Kippen Muir
11. Fintry Hills

The topographry of central Scotland

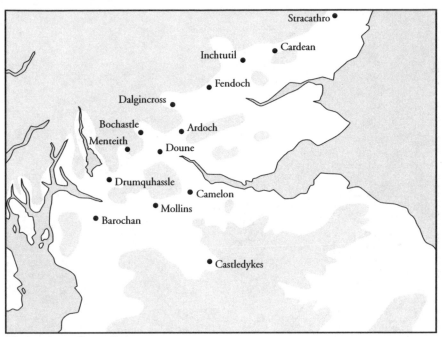

The locations of some Roman encampments

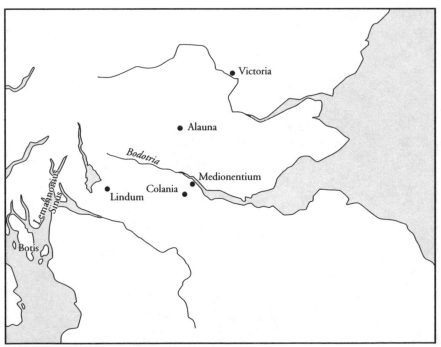

Central Scotland following the Roman geographers

The Kingdom of Strathclyde in the 11th century

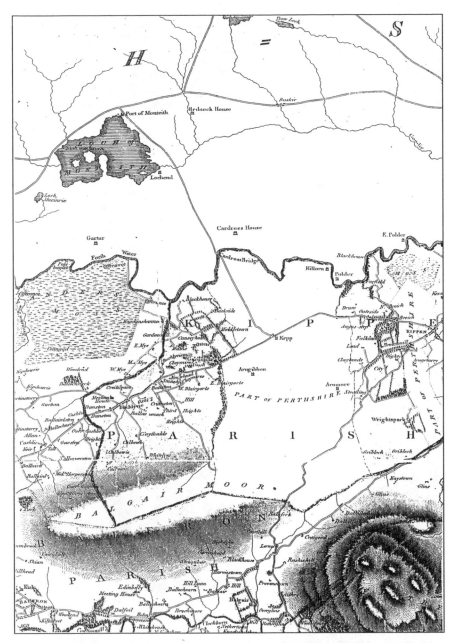

Grassum's map of Stirlingshire (1819). It shows the eccentric boundaries between the counties of Stirling and Perth and provides few details of the lands of the old baronies of Shirgarton, Arnbeg, Arnmore, Arnfinlay and Arnprior because they were all in Perthshire.

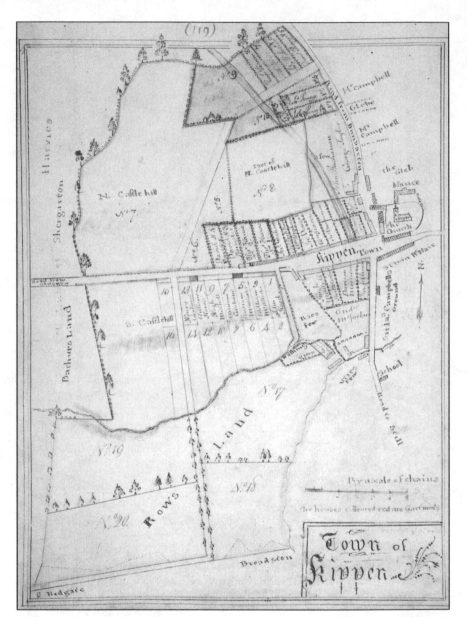

This 'feu map' of Kippen village was made *c.* 1790 with the purpose of marking out the properties of Robert Graham of Gartmore. At some stage about 1800 someone has drawn in the proposed route of the Fore Road.

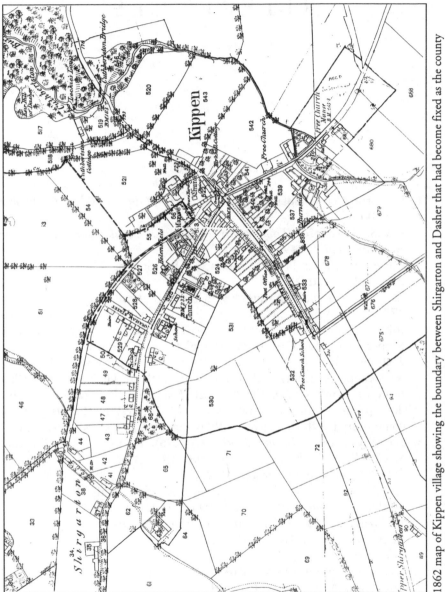

1862 map of Kippen village showing the boundary between Shirgarton and Dasher that had become fixed as the county boundary. The map also shows the locations of the three village schools at the time.

REFERENCES

CHAPTER 1

1. L. Corbett et al (eds), *Central Scotland – Land – Wildlife – People* (1993) pp. 12–15.
2. O.G.S. Crawford, *Topography of Roman Scotland North of the Antonine Wall* (1949) p. 20.
3. Carse of Stirling Project, conducted for Stirling Council by AOC Archaeology Ltd (1998).
4. Essay by the Rev. John Campbell in *The Statistical Account of Scotland 1791–1799*, Vol. ix, pp. 515–516. It would be very unwise to dismiss John Campbell as a scholar. He was the highly respected minister of Kippen from 1783 to 1806, at which point he was called to the Tolbooth Church in Edinburgh. Subsequently he became Moderator of the General Assembly of the Church of Scotland. He was very much a front rank minister of the 'Scottish Enlightenment' period and his description of Kippen combines a lively interest in the district and community in which he lived with evidence of first-class scholarship.
5. David J. Breeze, *Roman Scotland* (1996), p. 56. A.A.M. Duncan, *Scotland: The Making of the Kingdom* (1975) Ch. 2.
6. O.G.S. Crawford, op. cit. pp. 21–22.
7. Royal Commission on the Ancient and Historical Monuments of Scotland, *Inventory of Stirlingshire* (1963) p. 106.
8. W. Wilson, *The History and Traditions of the Parish of Kippen* (Lecture given in 1878 and published by the *Stirling Journal and Advertiser* 1884) pp. 18–19.
9. Carse of Stirling Project: Parks of Garden; conducted for Stirling Council by AOC Archaeology Ltd (1998).
10. David J. Breeze, op. cit., p. 20.
11. *Xiphilin ex Dione, lib. 39*, cited by John Campbell. (I am grateful to the Rev. William Turner for help in making this translation.)
12. P. Salway, *Roman Britain: Oxford History of England* (1998 edn), p. 144: and D.J. Breeze, op. cit., p. 35. See also his interesting comments on frontier control systems, pp. 60–63.

13. P. Salway, p. 226.
14. Ibid., p. 227. See also the comments in D.J. Breeze, op. cit., p. 106.
15. P. Salway, p. 229.
16. Ibid.
17. Ibid., pp. 230–231.
18. Ibid., p. 242; D.J. Breeze, op. cit., p. 106.
19. P. Salway, p. 319.
20. C. Lewis and C. Short, *A Latin Dictionary: Freund's Latin Dictionary*. A.L.F. Rivet and C.C. Smith, *The Place Names of Roman Britain* (1970) pp. 269–271 includes a long discussion of various interpretations of 'bodotria', but succeeds only in making clear that there is no agreement as to its meaning. The problem is probably a lack of understanding of the context in which it was used. The author's suggestion is that 'bodotria' derives from 'bod', 'botte' or 'buttis', a 'butt'. Normally this word is taken to mean a barrel; however, the English word butt means both a barrel and 'the trunk of a tree – especially the part just above the root'. In Danish or Low German 'but' also means a tree stump, as does the Dutch and Old French word 'bot' and the Old Norse, 'butt-r'. In Latin an area or field is 'often rendered by a particular subset', (e.g. 'historia', means the area or field of history, and no doubt passed down to us the notion of a subject of study as a 'field'). 'Bodotria', therefore, might be translated as 'the area or field of butts' or tree stumps. Intriguingly, however, and just to complicate the situation, the English word 'butt' has the additional meaning of a 'boundary or terminal point' which would, of course, also be appropriate in this case.
21. P. Salway, op. cit., pp. 553–562 for a discussion of this topic.
22. Ibid., pp. 559–560.
23. Glasgow Archaeological Society, *The Roman Occupation of South Western Scotland* (1952). Note by G.N. Millar, pp. 235–239, indicates the probability of Severus waging a short intensive campaign, mainly in central Scotland. He appears to have brought his troops by sea to the Firth of Forth and to have briefly reactivated some of the Antonine forts while he commenced his operations.
24. W. Wilson, op. cit., p. 13.
25. *Inventory of Stirlingshire*, introduction by Prof. K.H. Jackson, p. 5.
26. Ibid., See also J. MacQueen, *St Nynia* (1990), pp. 76–78 for an interesting discussion of the identification of the location of Mount Bannog.
27. M. Lynch, *Scotland: A New History* (1991), p. 44.
28. Ibid., p. 43.
29. O.G.S. Crawford, op. cit., p. 21.
30. Ibid., p. 20.
31. W.F.H. Nicolaisen, *Scottish Place Names* (1976), p. 162.
32. Ibid. Also P. McNeill and R. Nicholson, *An Historical Atlas of Scotland c. 400–c. 1600* (1975), essay by Nicolaisen on Pictish and British Place Names, pp. 3–4.
33. *Statistical Account 1791–1799*, op. cit., Vol. ix, p. 513.

34. W. Wilson, op. cit., p. 4.
35. M. Darton, *The Dictionary of Scottish Place Names* (1990).
36. *Inventory of Stirlingshire*, op. cit., p. 435 (No. 545).
37. A. McKerracher, *The Street and Place Names of Dunblane and District* (1992), p. 36.
38. M. Lynch, op. cit., p. 27.
39. See for example G. & A. Ritchie, *Scotland: Archaeology and Early History* (1981), p. 146.
40. J. MacQueen, op. cit., p. 2.
41. Ibid., p. 86.
42. C. Thomas, *Whithorn's Christian Beginnings: First Whithorn Lecture* (1992), pp. 13–20. See also E.A. Thompson, 'The Origin of Christianity in Scotland', *Scottish Historical Review*, xxxvii, (1958), pp. 17–22.
43. C. Thomas, op. cit., pp. 7–9.
44. E.A. Thompson, op. cit., pp. 20–21.
45. *Inventory of Stirlingshire*, op. cit., p. 418 (No. 485) for a description of the site. N.B. No significant archaeological investigation of the location has taken place.
46. See C. Thomas, *Christianity in Roman Britain to AD 500* (1981), for a full discussion of the nature of early British churches, and particularly Chapter 8 for an account of baptism and baptisteries.
47. Ibid., Ch. 9.
48. A.B. Barty, *The History of Dunblane* (1994 edn), p. 21.
49. W. Wilson, op. cit., p. 24.
50. Ibid., p. 23.
51. *The Cartulary of Cambuskenneth AD 1147–1535* (Edinburgh, 1872), p. cxxix; W. Fraser, *The Red Book of Menteith*, Vol. i (1880), pp. 33, 75.
52. W. Wilson, op. cit., p. 24, gives his translation of the original Latin including the relevant passage.
53. *The Cartulary*, op. cit., p. lxxi–lxxii.
54. *Inventory of Stirlingshire*, op. cit., pp. 176–178 (No. 187), includes an extensive report of the trial examination of the keir knowe of Drum which took place in 1957.
55. P.H. Brown, *History of Scotland* (1900), Vol. i, p. 40.
56. J. MacQueen, op. cit., pp. 1–2.
57. W. Wilson, op. cit., p. 32, quoting the *Register of the Diocesan Synod of Dunblane*, 11 April, 1665.
58. Ibid., p. 9.
59. W.F.H. Nicolaisen, op. cit., pp. 128–129.
60. J. Kirk (ed), *Stirling Presbytery Records 1581–1587*, (1981), pp. xxxiv–xxxvi.
61. *Third Statistical Account of Scotland* (1966), Vol xviii, essay by Rev. D. Dick on the Parish of St Ninians, p. 198.
62. J. Kirk, op. cit., pp. 134–136, pp. 149–151, pp. 115–116, and in various other places.

63. Ibid., pp. 292–293.
64. C. Thomas, *Christianity in Roman Britain to* AD *500*, op. cit., pp. 284–285.
65. Ibid., p. 291.
66. J. MacQueen, op. cit., p. 2.
67. D. Brooke, *The Search for Nynia* (1990), p. 3. See also C. Thomas, (1992) op. cit., pp. 17–18.

CHAPTER 2

1. *Statistical Account, 1791–1799*, op. cit., Vol. ix, pp. 551–553.
2. T.C. Smout, *A History of the Scottish People 1560–1830*, (1969), pp. 104–105.
3. W. Wilson, op. cit., p. 28.
4. J. D. Mackie, *A History of Scotland*, p. 85.
5. It was common for the stones and timbers of old buildings to be salvaged and re-used for other buildings. For example, the lintel and crest above the door of Mr MacDiarmid's cottage at the builder's yard in the main street of Kippen appears to have come from an older building. *The Inventory of Stirlingshire*, p. 325 (No. 284) notes that this is one of the oldest cottages in the village and it has 'a doorway-lintel representing a flat arch with a large monumental keystone; this lintel is so much too large for the cottage in question as to suggest that it is in secondary use, and a comparison with some of the lintels of neighbouring churches suggest further that it may have come from the old parish church, having perhaps been placed there during the reconstruction of 1737 – a date which would suit its style.'
6. W. Chrystal, *The Kingdom of Kippen: Its History and Traditions* (1903), p. 79.
7. J. Kirk (ed) op. cit., p. 150.
8. W. Wilson, op. cit., p. 6.
9. W. Chrystal, op. cit., p. 18.
10. Ibid., pp. 171–172.
11. Thomas McCrie, *Memoirs of William Veitch and George Bryson etc.* (1825), pp. 435–436.
12. W. Chrystal, op. cit., p. 171.
13. Ibid., p. 80.
14. *Inventory of Stirlingshire*, op. cit., pp. 176–178 (No. 187).
15. W. Wilson, op. cit., pp. 6–7.
16. Ibid., *Inventory of Stirlingshire*, op. cit., p. 417 (No. 482) for a brief description.
17. W. Wilson, op. cit., pp. 7–8.
18. J.R. Bureau, *Buchlyvie: A Village in Stirlingshire* (1996), pp. 10–13. Although Buchlyvie was one of the baronies of Kippen it is now, of

course, a distinct village with its own history. Interested readers are, therefore, warmly referred to Mr Bureau's book.

19. Ibid., p. 39.
20. W. Chrystal, op. cit., pp. 97–100.
21. W. Wilson, op. cit., p. 14.
22. W. Nimmo, *The History of Stirlingshire* (2nd edn, 1817), p. 499.
23. W. Chrystal, op. cit., p. 20; J.B. Johnston, *The Place Names of Stirlingshire* (1904).
24. W. Chrystal, p. 132.
25. W. Nimmo, op. cit., pp. 499–501.
26. T.C. Smout, op. cit., p. 42, p. 106, p. 117–134.

CHAPTER 3

1. P.H. Brown (ed), *Scotland before 1700 from Contemporary Documents* (1893), p. 11–12.
2. J. Kirk (ed), op. cit., p. xxxvi.
3. There are very many books on various aspects of the subject, particularly dating from the 19th century when the 'Disruption' of the Kirk in 1843 revived interest in the religious disputes of an earlier period. Such older publications tend to take a relatively narrow ecclesiastical focus which somewhat obscures the powerful social and economic political forces which were at work. Of the more modern accounts G. Donaldson, *Scotland: James V to James VII* (1965) provides a broad view of the events of the period. I.B. Cowan, *The Scottish Covenanters, 1660–1688* (1976), David Stevenson, *The Covenanters* (1988) and *Highland Warrior: Alasdair MacColla and the Civil Wars* (1980) are very useful on various facets of the period. John Morrill (ed), *The Scottish National Covenant in its British Context 1638–1651* (1990) is an interesting collection of essays, and R.C. Paterson, *A Land Afflicted: Scotland and the Covenanter Wars 1638–1690* (1998) gives a narrative of the various conflicts. However, none of these books gives much information on the Covenanters of the Vale of Menteith. Stevenson's *King or Covenant? Voices from Civil War* (1996) provides an interesting selection of portraits of the lives of people of various persuasions. On the later stages of the period and its aftermath perhaps the two most important recent works are Paul Hopkins, *Glencoe and the End of the Highland War* (1998) and B. Lenman, *The Jacobite Risings in Britain, 1688–1746* (1980).
4. See Hopkins, op. cit., for the best account of the state of the Highlands at the time.
5. M. Lynch, op. cit., p. 274.
6. See D. Stevenson, *Highland Warrior* (1980), Chapter 6, for an account of the ravaging of Argyll.
7. W. Nimmo, op. cit., p. 532.

8. M. Lynch, op. cit., p. 284.
9. Ibid., p. 286.
10. Quoted I. B. Cowan, *The Scottish Covenanters, 1660–1688* (1976), p. 45.
11. Ibid.
12. Ibid., p. 56.
13. Rev. T.P. Muirhead, *James Ure and his Times*, (a lecture delivered in the Gillespie Hall, Kippen and published 1886), pp. 9–10.
14. Ibid., p12.
15. James Taylor, *The Great Historic Families of Scotland*, Vol. 2 (1889), pp. 121–122; *Dictionary of National Biography* (1967–68 edn), Vol. vi.
16. *Register of the Diocesan Synod of Dunblane*, 10th October 1676, quoted in W. Wilson, op. cit., p. 33.
17. I.B. Cowan, op. cit., p. 84.
18. T. McCrie, *Memoirs of William Veitch & George Bryson etc* including *Narrative of the Rising Suppressed at Bothwell Bridge; Written by James Ure of Shirgarton with Notices of the Writer* (1825), p. 437.
19. Ibid., pp. 437–438.
20. T.P. Muirhead, op. cit., pp. 19–22; I.B. Cowan, op. cit., p. 94; James Dodds, *The Fifty Years' Struggle of the Scottish Covenanters 1638–1688* (1868), pp. 220–232.
21. *Register of the Privy Council of Scotland* (hereafter *RPCS*) (3rd Series) Vol. xii (1686), p. 112, p. 173, p. 405; *Presbytery of Dunblane Minutes* (18th October, 1710), p. 49. Thomas McCrie in his *Notices* and those who followed him, such as Patrick Muirhead, mistakenly suggested that Ure's wife was Elizabeth Montgomery, daughter of William Montgomery, laird of Macbethhill near Stewarton. In fact it was an easy error to make since Elizabeth was married to the Covenanter's son, also named James Ure. The latter was a lawyer and Writer to the Signet.
22. T. McCrie, op. cit., p. 445.
23. Ibid., pp. 457–458.
24. Ibid., p. 475.
25. Ibid., pp. 458–459.
26. Ibid., pp. 470–472.
27. Ibid., pp. 475–481 for Ure's account of the actual battle.
28. *Geschichte der Reformation in Schottland*, Karl Gustav von Rudloff, General Major (Berlin, 1849), Vol. ii, p. 320, cited in P.T. Muirhead, op. cit., p. 31.
29. T. McCrie, op. cit., pp. 478–479.
30. Ibid., p. 480.
31. P. Hopkins, op. cit., p. 26, p. 31, p. 60.
32. Robert Wodrow, *The History of the Sufferings of the Church of Scotland*, Vol. 3 (1721–22), pp. 408–409.
33. T. McCrie, op. cit., p. 447.
34. Ibid, pp. 445–446.

35. W. Wilson, op. cit., p. 35.
36. T. McCrie, op. cit., pp. 446–447.
37. *RPCS*, (3rd Series), Vol. x, p. 37.
38. T. McCrie, op. cit., p. 448.
39. Ibid., pp. 448–449.
40. Ibid., p. 448; *RPCS*, (3rd Series), Vol. xii (1686), p. 112, p. 173, p. 112.
41. T. McCrie, p. 450.
42. R. Wodrow, Vol. ii, pp. cxxviii.
43. *RPCS*, (3rd Series), vol xiii (1687), pp. 156–158.
44. Ibid.,Vol. xviii.
45. T. McCrie, op. cit., p. 449.

CHAPTER 4

1. W. Wilson, op. cit., p. 10.
2. Ibid., pp. 9–10.
3. J.R. Bureau, op. cit., p. 14.
4. Lecture delivered to Arnprior WRI by Mrs Marjorie Stirling and Mrs Jean Mailer, 20th February 1973, provided information on Arnprior. A.R.B. Haldane, *The Drove Roads of Scotland* (1952) p. 83, notes the significance of the trail by the Frews and the Falkirk Tryst. Strangely, however, he makes no comment about the important Balgair markets.
5. B. Lenman, op. cit., pp. 28–29.
6. P. Hopkins, op. cit., p. 126.
7. R. Wodrow, op. cit., pp. 408–409; T. McCrie, op. cit., p. 449.
8. *Acts of the Parliament of Scotland* (hereafter *APS*), Vol. ix, p. 165.
9. R. Wodrow, op. cit., p. 409; T. McCrie, op. cit., p. 449.
10. *APS*, Vol. ix, pp. 26–27.
11. P. Hopkins, op. cit., p. 125.
12. *APS*, Vol. ix, p. 50, pp. 58–59; S.H.F. Johnston, *The History of the Cameronians* (Scottish Rifles) Vol. i (1689–1910) (1957), Ch 2.
13. SRO, E100/11/1–7.
14. J. Prebble, *Glencoe* (1961), p. 132.
15. R. Wodrow, op. cit., p. 409.
16. For example, SRO PC 1/48, pp. 159–160, 9/4/1692 and, *RPCS*, Vol. xvi, (1691), p. 42, p. 541.
17. Ibid.
18. For example, P. Hopkins, op. cit., p. 241.
19. SRO, E110/14/18–28.
20. P. Hopkins, p. 153.
21. Stephen Wood, *The Scottish Soldier* (1987), pp. 24–25.
22. P. Hopkins, op. cit., p. 160, quoting a letter from Dundee's brother to Cannon asking for the return of his possessions.
23. Ibid., p. 180.

24. SRO GD 26/9/225, letter of 27th July, 1689.
25. Psalm 124.
26. P. Hopkins, op. cit., Ch. 5 for a good account of the battle. Also S.H.F. Johnston, op. cit., pp. 34–38.
27. P. Hopkins, op. cit., p. 190.
28. SRO GD 26/8/38, Declaration by Lord Cardross' tenants.
29. P. Hopkins, p. 199.
30. *RPCS* (3rd Series), Vol. xiv (1689), p. 299.
31. Ibid., p. 372.
32. P. Hopkins, op. cit., pp. 200–201.
33. *RPCS*, (3rd Series) Vol. xv (1690), p. 332.
34. *Est. Procs: An Account of the Proceedings of the Estates in Scotland, 1689–1690*, E.W.M. Balfour-Maitland (ed.) (SHS, 1954), Vol. ii, pp. 262–263, Lt. Col. Fullerton's Report.
35. W. Wodrow, op. cit., p. 409.
36. *Est. Procs*, Vol. ii, p. 270, p. 273, p. 277; *RPCS*, (3rd Series) Vol. xv (1690), p. 428.
37. J. Hog etc., Mackay's *Memoirs* (1833), p. 342, p. 356.
38. *RPCS*, (3rd Series), Vol. xvi, (1691), p. 70, p. 148.
39. W.H. Murray, *Rob Roy MacGregor* (1982), p. 100.
40. A.G.M. MacGregor, *History of the Clan Gregor* (1901).
41. W.H. Murray, op. cit., p. 102.
42. This account follows A.G.M. MacGregor, but see also H. Howlett, *Highland Constable: The Life and Times of Rob Roy MacGregor* (1950).
43. W.H. Murray, op. cit., p. 103.
44. H. Howlett, op. cit., p. 22, p. 26.
45. P. Hopkins, op. cit., p. 267.
46. For example, *RPCS* (3rd Series) Vol. xvi (1691), p. 43, pp. 19–199, p. 239.
47. Ibid., p. 15.
48. Ibid., pp. 296–297.
49. Ibid., p. 385.
50. Ibid., p. 247.
51. Ibid., p. 255.
52. P. Hopkins, op. cit., p. 312.
53. W.C. Dickenson & G. Donaldson, *A Source Book of Scottish History* (1961), Vol. iii, p. 212.
54. P. Hopkins, op. cit., Ch. 9.
55. W.H. Murray, op. cit., p. 101, gets the name Alexander right, but the estate wrong. The Laird of Bedlormie and Westquarter at the time was Sir James Livingstone.
56. *RPCS* (3rd Series), Vol. xvi (1691), pp. 592–593.
57. R. Wodrow, op. cit., p. 409; T. McCrie, op. cit., p. 450.
58. P. Hopkins, op. cit., p. 293.
59. Ibid., p. 288.

60. *RPCS* (3rd Series), Vol. xvi (1691), p. 451.
61. Ibid., pp. 537–538, pp. 615–616.
62. P. Hopkins, op. cit., p. 293. It is no real criticism of Hopkins that he did not dig into the background of the 'Hership of Kippen'. His monumental study covers a huge canvas in which this incident was no more than a rather obscure detail.
63. W.H. Murray, op. cit., pp. 125–126; Sir Walter Scott, *Rob Roy*, Appendix A, Author's Introduction (1817), (1995 Everyman edn), pp. 406–407.
64. SRO GD 26/9/232 – Cardross to . . . (Melville?) 31st August, 1689.
65. J. Prebble, op. cit., pp. 130–136 for a more detailed description of the regiment.
66. *RPCS*, (3rd Series), Vol. xvi (1691), p. 541.
67. Ibid., p. 42.
68. SRO, PC 1/48, pp. 159–160.
69. P. Hopkins, op. cit., p. 358, p. 384, note 52.
70. Lt. Col. R.M. Holden, *The First Highland Regiment: The Argyllshire Highlanders*, SHR, Vol. iii (1906).
71. SRO PC 1/48, pp. 159–160. Unfortunately unravelling this part of Ure's life was made more difficult and the narrative here may be incomplete because the author was unable to obtain access to the Argyll archive at Iveraray Castle where, according to John Prebble (p. 243), some of the relevant correspondence still exists. This highlights the problem of access created for historians when important archives remain in private hands, and it is very much to be hoped that before long appropriate modern arrangements can be made for inspection of the Argyll records.
72. Records of Presbytery of Dunblane, Minutes of 18th October and 28th November, 1710.
73. *Fountainhall's Decisions*, Vol. ii, p. 602.
74. For example, T.M. Devine, *The Scottish Nation, 1700–2000* (1999), Ch. 11, on Highlandism and Scottish Identity, for an interesting discussion of this subject.
75. R.B. Cunninghame Graham, *Notes on the District of Menteith for Tourists and Others* (1895), pp. 7–8.

CHAPTER 5

1. *Memoirs of the Insurrection in Scotland in 1715, by John, Master of Sinclair*, (1857 edn), p. 201.
2. P. Dickson, *Red John of the Battles: John Second Duke of Argyll and First Duke of Greenwich, 1680–1743* (1973), p. 186.
3. Sir Walter Scott, op. cit., pp. 412–413.
4. P.H. Brown, op. cit., Vol. iii, p. 291, pp. 316–317.
5. A.M. Mackenzie, *Scotland in Modern Times* (1941), p. 23.

6. J. Butt, *Industrial Archaeology of Scotland* (1967), p. 311.
7. Annette M. Smith, *Jacobite Estates of the '45* (1982), p. 197.
8. This story is recounted in various places including J.R. Bureau, op. cit., p. 23.
9. P. Hopkins, op. cit., pp. 452–456.
10. The narrative has been culled mainly from A.G.M. MacGregor, op. cit., Vol. ii, Chapter xxxiii, and is based on *The Trials of James, Duncan and Robert McGregor, three sons of the celebrated Rob Roy, before the High Court of Justiciary, 1752, 1753 and 1754* (Edinburgh, 1818).
11. Lecture by Mrs Marjorie Stirling and Mrs Jean Mailer, op. cit., quoting a lecture of 1945 given by Mrs Stirling's late husband.
12. *Statistical Account 1791–1799*, op. cit., p. 541.
13. This account has been culled from various sources including Tom Weir, 'From Swords to Ploughshares', article in *Scottish Field*, July 1965.
    A McKerrracher, *Perthshire in History and Legend* (2000) provides an interesting description of the project by a descendant of one of the original 'moss lairds'.
14. Lecture by R.W.A. Begg, 1965.
15. *Statistical Account*, op. cit., p. 518.
16. Quoted C. McKean, *Stirling and the Trossachs* (1985), p. 128.
17. W. Anderson, *Revised Statistical Account of Scotland* (1841), Vol. 8, pp. 268–269.
18. *Statistical Account*, op. cit., p. 538.
19. *Revised Statistical Account*, op. cit., p. 269.
20. *Statistical Account*, op. cit., p. 539.
21. Ibid., p. 525.
22. T.M. Devine & R. Mitchison (eds), *People & Society in Scotland*, Vol. i (1760–1830), (1988), p. 20.
23. *Statistical Account*, op. cit., pp. 529–530.
24. Ibid., pp. 527–528.
25. Ibid., pp. 535–537.
26. Ibid., p. 537; A. Scoular, 'Kippen, Past and Present', *Stirling Journal and Advertiser*, 6th July, 1900.
27. W. Chrystal, op. cit., pp. 150–151.
28. *Revised Statistical Account*, op. cit., p. 270.
29. Stirling Council Archives, Ch. 2/396, Minutes of Kippen Kirk Session (KKS), 20th September, 1778.
30. R.W.A. Begg, *The Renovation of Kippen Parish Church 1924–1986*, (5th edn, 1986), p. 5.
31. SCA, Ch 2/396, Minutes of KKS, February 1845.
32. The information contained in the narrative on the parish affairs has been extracted from Ch 2/396, Accounts and Financial Matters 1746–1811, KKS Account Book 1801–1848 and KKS Minutes 1778–1829 and 1829–1900.
33. *Revised Statistical Account*, op. cit., p. 534.

34. A. Scoular, op. cit., pp. 4–7; Lecture by R.W.A. Begg, 1965; *Revised Statistical Account*, op. cit., p. 270.
35. Ibid.
36. Lecture by R.W.A. Begg, 1965.
37. *Tourist Guide to Kippen, Buchlyvie and Port of Menteith* (1920?), p. 27.
38. J.R. Bureau, op. cit., pp. 39–41.
39. Kippen School Log Book, Vol. 1, pp. 178–179.
40. *3rd Annual Report (1893) to the County Council of Stirling by John McVail, Medical Officer of Health*, pp. 10–18.
41. *Third Statistical Account of Scotland*, Vol. xviii, essay on Kippen by J.C. Mitchell, p. 126, p. 130.
42. Alan A.B. Edwards, *The Kippen Big Vine* (1991), p. 6.

CHAPTER 6

1. A. Bain, *Education in Stirlingshire from the Reformation to the Act of 1872* (1965), p. 24.
2. Ibid., p. 34, quoting Act of 1567, *The Second Book of Discipline*.
3. Ibid., quoting Minutes of Presbytery of Stirling, 1696.
4. *Statistical Account*, op. cit., p. 531.
5. A. Bain, op. cit., p. 256 and p. 194.
6. Notes on Mr Auld's diary are included in the lecture by R.W.A. Begg, 1965 op. cit.
7. *Revised Statistical Account*, op. cit., p. 274.
8. Ibid.
9. *Stirling Observer*, 23rd August, 1850.
10. For an account of the Argyll Report see R.D. Anderson, *Education and the Scottish People, 1750–1918* (1995).
11. W. Chrystal, op. cit., p. 33.
12. Kippen School Log Book (KSLB), Vol. 1, p. 5.
13. Minutes of the School Board of Kippen Parish, Vol. 1, Return of Attendances, 3rd November, 1877.
14. *Stirling Observer*, 19th October, 1876.
15. KSLB, Vol. 1, p. 23.
16. Arnprior School Log Book (ASLB), Vol. 1, p. 190, p. 196.
17. Minutes of the School Board, 1891; ASLB, Vol. 1, p. 294.
18. KSLB, Vol. 1, p. 278, p. 305.
19. Ibid., p. 282.
20. See James Scotland, *The History of Scottish Education*, vol. 2 (1969), pp. 48–49 for an explanation of the Standards.
21. KSLB, Vol. 1, p. 146.
22. ASLB, Vol. 1, p. 303.
23. See Tom Begg, *The Excellent Women* (1994), for an account of this campaign.

24. KSLB, Vol. 1, p. 174.
25. Ibid., p. 141.
26. Ibid., p. 157.
27. Ibid., p. 314.
28. KSLB, Vol. 1, pp. 144–145.
29. ASLB, Vol. 1, p. 112.
30. KSLB, Vol. 1, p. 117.
31. Ibid., p. 240.
32. Ibid., p. 482.
33. Ibid., Vol. 2, pp. 63–64.
34. Ibid., p. 166.
35. Minutes of the School Board, Vol. 1, 1893 meetings.
36. KSLB, Vol. 1, p. 220.
37. Ibid., p. 284.
38. Reminiscences of William Hay in conversation with the author, 1995.
39. Ibid.; also reminiscences of Margaret Fickling, 1999.
40. KSLB, Vol. 1, p. 324.
41. *See Report of the Royal Commission on Physical Training* (Scotland), Cmnd 1507 (1903), and *Report of the Inter-Departmental Committee on Physical Deterioration*, Vol. 1 Cmnd 2175 (1904).
42. Tom Begg, op. cit., pp. 78–82 for a discussion of this subject.
43. KSLB, Vols 1 & 2, HMI reports (1900–1912).
44. Ibid., Vol. 1, p. 483.
45. Ibid., Vol. 2, pp. 34–35.
46. Ibid., p. 14, p. 27.
47. ASLB, Vol. 1, pp. 449–458, Vol. 2, p. 90, pp. 93–94, p. 100, p. 108, pp. 119–122. Minutes of the School Board, vol. 3, 1910.
48. Ibid., November 1914.
49. ASLB, Vol. 2, pp. 235–236, p. 115, p. 125, p. 127.
50. KSLB, Vol. 2, p. 139.
51. Ibid., Vol. 1, p. 478.
52. Ibid., Vol. 2, p. 3, p. 135; ASLB, Vol. 2, p. 149.
53. Reminiscences of Margaret Fickling (1999).
54. *Stirling Observer*, 28th August, 1941.
55. Reminiscences of William Hay.
56. ASLB, Vol. 3, p. 128.
57. KSLB, Vol. 2, pp. 301–301. (Also personal reminiscences. Between them the author and his wife attended three rural Scottish primary schools – including Kippen – in the 1940s and '50s and in all three the belt was used not only as a response to poor behaviour, but also as a punishment for inadequately prepared homework or minor errors such as spelling mistakes. The infliction of corporal punishment was a normal daily event. Occasional examples of the gross misuse of the strap were witnessed – in particular one instance in a Highland school when a head teacher subjected his son to a savage assault of no fewer than sixteen lashes.)

CHAPTER 7

1. *Stirling Journal and Advertiser*, 7th September, 1911.
2. KSLB, Vol. 2, p. 99.
3. Details on the war were culled from the roll of honour, the war memorial, and reports in the *Stirling Journal and Advertiser*, 2nd January 1919, 24th April 1919, 24th July 1919, 4th December 1919.
4. For a full account of the development of Scottish housing through the 20th century see Tom Begg, *Housing Policy in Scotland* (1996).
5. Charles McKean, *Stirling and the Trossachs* (1985), p. 130.
6. *Country Life*, 12th February, 1998, p. 57, article on Gribloch by Michael Hall.
7. For a full study of Gribloch, see Caroline MacGregor's paper in *Architectural Heritage*, Vol. 5, 1995.
8. Alan A.B. Edwards, op. cit., p. 7
9. Ibid., p. 9. (Also recollections of the author's wife, for, as a teenager, this was one of her jobs.)
10. Ibid., p. 10.
11. Ibid., pp. 12–15.
12. *The Times*, 19th October, 1968, article by Bevis Hillier.
13. A full account of the church and its contents is contained in the booklet, R.W.A. Begg, *The Renovation of Kippen Parish Church*, first published in 1962 and periodically updated to 1990. For an account of Cameron's life and work see B. Smith, *DY Cameron: The Vision of the Hills* (1992)
14. ASLB, Vol. 3, p. 147; KSLB, Vol. 2, pp. 242–244, p. 270.
15. Quoted, Ian Nimmo, *Scotland at War* (1989), unpaged.
16. KSLB, Vol. 2, p. 253.
17. ASLB, Vol. 3, p. 169.
18. Ibid., p. 295.
19. KSLB, Vol. 2, p. 251.
20. *Stirling Journal and Advertiser*, 20th March, 1941.
21. *Stirling Observer*, 19th October, 1939; *Stirling Journal and Advertiser*, 16th March, 1944.
22. Ian C. Cameron, *History of the Argyll & Sutherland Highlanders, 7th Battalion* (1946).
23. Most of the general information on individuals has been culled from various editions of the *Stirling Journal and Advertiser and Stirling Observer* 1939–1946.
24. *Stirling Journal and Advertiser*, 2nd August, 1945.
25. E. Brookes, *Destroyer*, (1973), pp. 129–134.
26. S.W. Roskill, *The War at Sea*, vol. 1 (1954), p. 535; *Stirling Journal*, 8th January, 1942.
27. *Stirling Observer*, 17th October, 1946; *Stirling Journal and Advertiser*, 7th March, 1946.
28. Mary and Tom Begg, 'Ane Old Sang', The Story of Arnprior Primary

School 1876–1996, (1996).
29. *Glasgow Herald*, 9th November, 1979.
30. Priscilla Barlow, *Wise Enough to Play the Fool: A Biography of Duncan Macrae* (1995).

INDEX